Articles on Aristotle

Plato and Aristotle in dialectical debate, by Luca della Robbia, from the
Campanile del Duomo, Florence (photo Mansell Alinari)

Articles on Aristotle

4. Psychology and Aesthetics

edited by
Jonathan Barnes
Malcolm Schofield
Richard Sorabji

St. Martin's Press
New York

CONTENTS

PREFACE

The modern student of philosophical psychology will be brought up with a start if he turns to Aristotle's psychological writings. For Aristotle does not think of philosophy of mind as a distinct and unitary subject: sometimes he treats psychology from the standpoint of a biologist interested in all living beings and their functions; sometimes – in the *Ethics* and *Politics*, the *Poetics* and *Rhetoric* – he confines himself to man and draws an entirely different set of distinctions related to the practical purposes of those works; sometimes he treats psychology as an adjunct of his metaphysics. Such a variety of approaches to what we regard as a single subject makes Aristotle's psychology hard for us to understand; but it also means that from time to time Aristotle rewards us with fresh viewpoints and with insights that a contemporary discussion may overlook. Such is the case in his treatment of the relation between body and soul, of the distinction between the five senses, and of the nature and rôle of the emotions.

Our first four papers deal with the relationship between body and soul. Kahn asks how Aristotle's concept of *aisthêsis* (which includes sense perception and more) is related to the Cartesian conception of consciousness. He concludes that it is more similar to that conception than any other Aristotelian notion is, but that it is by no means identical with it. (Kahn's exposition contains a major attack on certain uses of the genetic method, which interprets Aristotle's writings as a patchwork of fragments belonging to different periods of his life; compare Owen's paper in our Volume I.)

Barnes contends that Aristotle was neither a Cartesian nor a materialist; but while emphasising that Aristotle does not join Descartes in making the soul a non-physical *substance*, he argues that Aristotle does postulate non-physical *properties*. Thus the emotions and sense perception include a non-physical component; and there is a hesitant leaning toward the view that desire and one sort of intellect are wholly non-physical.

Sorabji offers a rival account. He agrees that Aristotle was no Cartesian; and he also rejects various proposals to assimilate Aristotle's theory to materialism, to behaviourism, and to intentionalism. Although Aristotle's view of the soul is never completely stated, we may, if we make judicious use of the materials Aristotle provides, arrived at a psychological theory which is free from some of the main problems which have perplexed the subject in recent centuries.

Sorabji speaks for, Barnes against, Aristotle's application to body and soul of his metaphysical distinction between matter and form. Ackrill examines some of the weaknesses of this application; and he shows why

Aristotle might have been unable to escape from the difficulties involved.

The next four papers consider some of the chief faculties of the soul. Sorabji argues that there is much to be said for Aristotle's distinguishing four of the senses by reference to their objects – colour, odour, sound, flavour; but that when he comes to the sense of touch he goes wrong in defining it as the contact sense, and should have stuck to Plato's characterisation of it as the sense which has no localised organ.

Norman takes up Aristotle's account of thinking, and considers the claim that 'God thinks himself': this does not mean that God thinks *about* himself, which would be a strange ideal to set before men as an activity they should aspire to; it is rather to be connected with the difficult doctrine that thought is identical with its object.

The imagination has a place between thinking and perceiving: Schofield examines Aristotle's attempts to distinguish it from those two neighbours. He denies that Aristotle supposes the imagination to be always active in perception (its sphere of operation is confined to unusual sensory experiences); and he dissociates Aristotle from the common view that imagination always involves a mental image.

Fortenbaugh argues that the definitions of the emotions in the *Rhetoric* are not mere commonplaces but constitute an analytical advance: Plato saw that the emotions (contrary to the view of some modern philosophers) involve cognition in some way or other; and Aristotle attempted to specify that way and to state it precisely. Thus anger, for example, is a disturbance *due to* certain beliefs. This is a contribution not only to philosophy of mind but also to philosophy of science; for definitions of the emotions may now be set alongside those causal definitions which Aristotle seeks in other branches of science. And it is a contribution to rhetoric, which, in influencing emotions, may now claim to be making a rational appeal to beliefs. The rational character of moral virtue also becomes clearer: virtue, being a disposition to have the right emotions on the right occasions, is something that can be guided by reason.

Emotions are a central theme in the *Poetics*: Plato had condemned poetry for playing on the emotions; and Aristotle took up his challenge to show what good that could do. He answered that tragedy leads to *katharsis*. Bernays' article, the main part of which is here translated into English for the first time, is one of the classics of Aristotelian scholarship; and its conclusions have won an almost universal assent. Bernays substitutes for more romantic or ethereal accounts of *katharsis* the suggestion that *katharsis* is a medical analogy, implying relief: it is the spectators who are relieved by having pity and fear aroused in them; and what they are relieved of is their excessive disposition to pity and fear. Aristotle's seminal idea has been interpreted in countless ways: this close inspection of what he actually meant is likely to be more rewarding philosophically than most of them.

The need to produce *katharsis* by arousing pity and fear dictates much else in Aristotle's account of tragedy: if our emotions are to be stirred, the tragic hero must be right, and his downfall must be due to *hamartia* or error. Moreover, as Gulley points out, what is portrayed must be the sort of thing that might happen, so that our emotions may be engaged. Hence the tragic poet's aim is not to state what is true – that is the business of history and of science. Poetry educates a different side of man: it regulates the emotions,

and hence it portrays what is plausible rather than what is true. Gulley is
not only concerned with the emotions: he also discusses Aristotle's general
conception of poetry as an imitation, not necessarily in verse, concerned
with the moral aspects of human behaviour, expressing what is universal,
and representing the plausible rather than the true.

We wish to thank authors and publishers who have generously allowed us to
incorporate copyright material. Acknowledgments are made as follows:

Chapter 1 and 8:   Walter de Gruyter Verlag, Berlin.
Chapter 2 and 4:   The Editor of the Aristotelian Society.
Chapter 3:   The Royal Institute of Philosophy.
Chapter 5:   *The Philosophical Review.*
Chapter 6:   *Phronesis.*
Chapter 7:   Faculty of Classics, University of Cambridge.
Chapter 10:   University of Wales Press.

The essays were originally published as follows:

Chapter 1   Charles H. Kahn   *Sensation   and   Consciousness   in   Aristotle's
    Psychology*
Archiv für Geschichte der Philosophie 48 (1966), pp.43-81.
Chapter 2   Jonathan Barnes   *Aristotle's Concept of Mind*
Proceedings of the Aristotelian Society 72 (1971-2), pp.101-14.
Chapter 3   Richard Sorabji   *Body and Soul in Aristotle*
Philosophy 49 (1974), pp.63-89.
Chapter 4   J. L. Ackrill   *Aristotle's Definitions of psuchê*
Proceedings of the Aristotelian Society 73 (1972-3), pp.119-33.
Chapter 5   Richard Sorabji   *Aristotle on Demarcating the Five Senses*
The Philosophical Review 80 (1971), pp.55-79.
Chapter 6   Richard Norman   *Aristotle's Philosopher-God*
Phronesis 14 (1969), pp.63-74.
Chapter 7   Malcolm Schofield   *Aristotle on the Imagination*
Aristotle on Mind and the Senses, ed. G.E.R. Lloyd and G.E.L. Owen
    (Cambridge, 1978).
Chapter 8   William W. Fortenbaugh   *Aristotle's Rhetoric on Emotions*
Archiv für Geschichte der Philosophie 52 (1970), pp.40-70.
Chapter 9   Jacob Bernays   *Aristotle on the Effect of Tragedy*
Translated by Jonathan and Jennifer Barnes from Bernays' *Zwei
    Abhandlungen über die aristotelische Theorie des Drama* (Berlin, 1880; first
    published Braslau, 1857).
Chapter 10   Norman Gulley   *Aristotle on the Purposes of Literature*
Inaugural lecture at St. David's College, Lampeter (Cardiff, 1971).
Chapters 1, 2 and 3 have undergone minor revisions; Chapter 8 has been
slightly abridged.

We should like again to thank the many friends and colleagues who have
helped us with advice and suggestions about the preparation of this volume.

Our particular gratitude goes to Elizabeth Schofield, who has prepared
the Index Locorum in this, as in our first three volumes.

J.B., M.S., R.S.

ABBREVIATIONS

A.Pr.	Analytica Priora
A.Pst.	Analytica Posteriora
Ath. Resp.	Atheniensium Respublica
Cael.	De Caelo
Cat.	Categoriae
Col.	De Coloribus
De An.	De Anima
Div.	De Divinatione per Somnum
EE	Ethica Eudemia
EN	Ethica Nicomachea
Eud.	Eudemus
fr.	Fragmenta
GA	De Generatione Animalium
GC	De Generatione et Corruptione
HA	Historia Animalium
IA	De Incessu Animalium
Id.	De Ideis
Insom.	De Insomniis
Int.	De Interpretatione
Iuv.	De Iuventute et Senectute, De Vita et Morte
Lin. Insec.	De Lineis Insecabilibus
Long.	De Longitudine et Brevitate Vitae
MA	De Motu Animalium
Mech.	Mechanica
Mem.	De Memoria et Reminiscentia
Meta.	Metaphysica
Meteor.	Meteorologica
Mir	De Mirabilibus Auscultationibus
MM	Magna Moralia
MXG	De Melisso, Xenophane et Gorgia
Oec.	Oeconomica
PA	De Partibus Animalium
PN	Parva Naturalia
Phys.	Physica
Plant.	De Plantis
Poet.	Poetica
Pol.	Politica
Probl.	Problemata

Protr.	*Protrepticus*
Resp.	*De Respiratione*
Rhet.	*Rhetorica*
Rhet.ad	*Rhetorica ad Alexandrum*
Alex.	
S.El. (or	*De Sophisticis Elenchis*
Top. IX)	
Sens.	*De Sensu*
Som.	*De Somno et Vigilia*
Spir.	*De Spiritu*
Top.	*Topica*
Virt.	*De Virtutibus et Vitiis*

We follow the book and chapter numbers used in the Oxford translation of Aristotle. Page, column and line numbers are based on Bekker's edition of 1831.

1

Charles H. Kahn

Sensation and Consciousness in Aristotle's Psychology

This study is conceived as a first step towards answering the question: is 　**43**
Aristotle a dualist in his theory of sensation?[1] Is there anything in his
account which corresponds to the traditional Cartesian distinction between
mind and mechanism, between the mental and the physical? If so, how are
the two terms related to one another? The question is easy to formulate, but
surprisingly difficult to answer, and the difficulties are due as much to the
general obscurity of the problem of dualism, as they are to the specific
perplexities of the Aristotelian view. The following pages are presented,
then, as a preliminary attempt to determine just where Aristotle stands with
regard to one of the most controversial issues of modern philosophy of mind.

The need for some clarification of Aristotle's position is suggested by a
strange disagreement among his recent interpreters. In an article published
in 1961, one writer maintains that (in the *De Anima*, at any rate) 'Aristotle
tries to explain perception simply as an event in the sense organ', that is, as
a localised bodily event, with no dualistic or 'psychic' complications.[2] On 　**44**
the other hand, another study published in the same year holds that
Aristotle's view of perception as an act of the soul has so reduced the body's
share in the process that 'it is doubtful whether the movement or the
actualisation occurring when the eye sees or the ear hears has any physical
or physiological aspect'.[3] The possibility of such contradictory
interpretations arises from the fact that Aristotle does not speak the
language of traditional dualism. He does not contrast the mental with the
physical, the human consciousness with the body to which it is attached.
When he describes vision, for example, as the reception of visible forms
without their matter, he does not tell us whether he is referring to the arrival
of light rays in the eye or the conscious perception of shapes and colours in
the 'mind'.

It is true that Aristotle does distinguish two factors in sensation, the body
(*sôma*) and the soul (*psuchê*), which might at first sight be taken for the

1. An earlier version of this paper was included among essays presented to John
Hermann Randall, Jr., on his 65th Birthday, 14 February 1964.

I would like to express my gratitude to the American Council of Learned Societies
for a research grant in 1963-4, which provided me with the leisure to prepare this
study.

2. Thomas J. Slakey [68].

3. Solmsen [103], p.170. For earlier disagreements on this point, see Paul Siwek
[71] pp.96 and 104.

Cartesian couple, body and mind. Thus Aristotle describes sensation as an activity 'common to both body and soul',[4] 'a movement of the soul <which is produced> through the body',[5] or, more precisely, a movement which passes through the body and reaches 'to the soul'.[6] Familiar as these statements may sound, nothing could be more misleading than to equate Aristotle's notion of the *psuchê* with the Cartesian view of the soul or mind as a distinct substance, whose essence consists in conscious 'thought', and which is mysteriously adjoined to a bodily mechanism with which it should in principle have nothing to do. In the first place Aristotle insists upon the substantial unity of body and soul: the *psuchê* is by definition the form and realisation of a living body (*De An.* II 1-2). In the second place, the *psuchê* which operates in sensation is not necessarily that of men, but of animals in general. And, in a wider sense, *psuchê* for Aristotle is something which even plants possess.

It is impossible, then, simply to equate Aristotle's distinction between body and *psuchê* with the terms of the modern dichotomy. Yet some relationship between the two sets of terms must be established if Aristotle's psychology is to be intelligible at all. For the distinction between the mental and the physical has been so influential, and remains so familiar, that even those contemporary thinkers who entirely reject the principle of Cartesian dualism are obliged to make use of this dichotomy as a negative point of reference for the definition of their own view. It is precisely the lack of any such reference in the case of Aristotle which makes his psychology so difficult to interpret. It is essentially a reference of this kind which the present study seeks to provide.

In order to make the relationship clear, the terms of the comparison must be limited at both ends. We cannot compare all of Aristotle's psychology with all of the modern discussions of the problem of dualism. For the purpose in hand we may ignore the individual variations in the tradition which stretches from the Cartesian *Meditations* to William James' *Principles of Psychology*, and regard this modern view *en bloc* as accepting the fundamental character of the distinction between mind and matter: between thought or consciousness, on the one hand, and the physical reality of extended bodies on the other. It is the acceptance of this distinction as fundamental which will here be described as the traditional view. And we shall also refer to it as the 'modern' view, since, however antiquated it may appear to some contemporary eyes, it remains distinctively modern by reference to Aristotle.

Our task, then, is to relate the Aristotelian terms body and *psuchê* to the modern distinction between body and mind or consciousness. In the interest of simplicity, we may treat the concept of body as relatively constant, and focus our attention on the differences between the two psychological terms – between *psuchê* and consciousness. Specifically, we shall use the concept of consciousness as a point of reference by which to define what Aristotle calls the 'sensory soul', the part or power of the *psuchê* which operates in sense

4. *Sens.* 436a8.
5. *Som.* 454a9.
6. *De An.* 408b16-17; cf. *Sens.* 436b6: *dia sômatos gignetai têi psuchêi*.

perception.[7] But before relating it to the modern concept with any hope of accuracy, we must first expound Aristotle's doctrine from his own point of view.

Since our exposition is given in language which may suggest other, more modern theories, some discrepancies in terminology should be borne in **46** mind. In the first place, I shall throughout use 'sensation', 'perception', and 'sense perception' as equivalent renderings of the Greek *aisthêsis*. We are not here concerned with what James calls the perception of 'things', something more complex and intellectual than mere sensation. This would involve Aristotle's doctrine of incidental sensation or sensation *per accidens* (*aisthêsis kata sumbebêkos*), which is not an act of the sense faculty as such and therefore lies outside the present study. On the other hand, Aristotle's *aisthêsis* is not quite the modern notion of sensation. The problem as Aristotle poses it concerns neither the immediate data of consciousness (e.g. what are called 'sense data' or 'raw feels') nor the perceptions we have of our own body, but, properly speaking, any capacity possessed by living animals for obtaining information concerning the outside world – for entering into contact with, and hence responding to, their food, their enemies, their mates, their offspring. The more distinctively human capacity for a subjective or reflexive awareness of such sensation is also called *aisthêsis*, but it constitutes a special problem, to be discussed in what follows. In general, Aristotle thinks of sensation as external and 'intentional', as directed towards an object outside the sentient body itself.[8]

It is characteristic of Aristotle that his account of sensation should take its starting-point not from an analysis of the human mind but from the study of living things generally – of animals, and even of plants. Yet this biological background is also indicated by the normal associations of the Greek term *psuchê*, whose etymological value is that of a life-breath, the vital power which one 'expires' at the moment of death, or in a deep faint.[9] This old meaning is preserved in the derivative adjective *empsuchos*, 'having a *psuchê*', i.e. 'living, animate'; whereas *apsuchos*, 'with no *psuchê*', designates what is **47** lifeless and inert. Thus classical authors may speak of the *psuchê* of a horse or other animal; Aristotle himself applies the term to plants. The philosophical associations of the term are often materialistic rather than 'spiritual'; most

7. In concentrating here on the analysis of the sensory *psuchê* I am obliged to leave aside the problem of the sense object, and hence to ignore the much debated definition of sensation as 'the reception of sensible forms without their matter'. I hope to return to these problems in a later study, since they must obviously be considered in any comprehensive answer to the question, 'is Aristotle a dualist?'

8. As a result, pleasure and pain are not recognised by Aristotle as sensations in the strict sense. See below, pp.23-4 with nn. 66-7.

9. See, for example, *Iliad* V 696-8, where the connexions between *psuchê*, vitality, breathing, and wind are clearly indicated:

The *psuchê* left him, and the mist mantled over his eyes,

but he got his breath back again, and the blast of the north wind

blowing brought back to life the spirit (*thumos*) gasped out in agony.

(Lattimore's transl., slightly adapted.)

Although the Greek term develops many special meanings of its own, it never entirely loses contact with the underlying sense of life-breath, which is roughly that of Latin *anima*, or of the 'breath of life' which the Lord breathes into Adam's nostrils.

4 *Charles H. Kahn*

early theorists identified the *psuchê* with some power in the air, some substance breathed in by the body, or with the vital heat of the body itself.[10] Plato had of course underlined the contrast between the body and the *psuchê* or soul, but his precedent was not immediately decisive. In ordinary parlance, the antithetical term to *psuchê* was likely to be not 'body' but 'death'.[11]

It is within this biological, rather than strictly psychological context that Aristotle places his own doctrine of the *psuchê*. The context is clear from the methodical arrangement of the treatises, where the *De Anima* stands, within natural philosophy, as introduction to the short essays in psycho-biology (*Parva Naturalia*) and to the great systematic works in zoology: the *Parts* and the *Generation of Animals*.[12] This orientation is clear from the very definition of the soul as the form and realisation of an organic body. The same biological perspective is further indicated by the fact that the list of parts or faculties of *psuchê* begins with the 'nutritive soul', the principle of biological life as such, said to be 'the primary and most general power of *psuchê*' (*De An.* 415a24), the principle without which the higher powers of sense and intellect cannot exist, although it may exist without them, as it does in plants. Even in the case of animals, which are by definition sentient and must therefore possess a sensory *psuchê*, this faculty is not concretely separable from their sheer capacity to live.[13]

Now this conception of a nutritive soul possessed by plants, and of a sensory soul shared by the lowest forms of animal life, clearly does not square with the traditional dualistic antithesis between body and soul. Post-Cartesian authors who use the term 'soul' would not normally be prepared to assign one to trees and insects, much less to bacteria and amoebae. On the other hand, there are passages in which Aristotle analyses the phenomena of sensation, of memory, and of dreams, on the basis of a kind of introspective reflection which seems characteristically modern. We shall have occasion to return to his special interest in the question: 'With what

48

10. See *De An.* I, *passim*. This old, half-physical conception of the 'soul' was still familiar in Descartes' time, as it was throughout antiquity. When, in the second *Meditation*, Descartes examines 'the thoughts which previously arose of themselves' concerning his own identity, he claims that he had heretofore imagined the soul as 'something extremely rare, and subtle, like a wind, a flame, or a very fine air entering into and spreading throughout my grosser parts'. It is a measure of Descartes' own influence that this semi-corporeal view of the soul has been entirely replaced by the identification of the soul with the mind or 'thinking substance'.
11. Thus *philopsucheô*, 'to love one's *psuchê*', means in fact to fear death.
12. The intended order is clear from the cross-references in the *De Anima* and in most of the other treatises. See, for instance, the passages listed in Ross' edition of the *De An.*, pp.7-8. A typical example (not included in Ross' list) is *GA* 779b22: 'as was said earlier in the treatise on sensations (*PN*), and earlier still in the discussion of the soul (*De An.*)'. I assume that this order is Aristotle's own, not that of some ancient editor, and that its significance is primarily systematic or expository, not chronological.
13. See *De An.* 411b28-30 and *passim*; in particular 414b28ff., the comparison of the psychic faculties to the elementary figures in geometry: 'both in figures and in animate creatures, the prior element is always present potentially in what follows, as the triangle is present in the square, the nutritive faculty in the sensory'.

faculty do we perceive that we are seeing and hearing?' In general it is clear that Aristotle associates sensation with some faculty of awareness: it differs from inanimate change in that the sentient subject 'notices what is going on'.[14] Some passages have a truly Cartesian ring, as when Aristotle asserts that the perception of our own existence is necessarily implied by our perception that we are sensing or thinking, 'for our life and being <sc. as men> is properly to sense or to think'.[15]

Thus if we are to comprehend Aristotle's conception of the sensory soul in its full complexity, we must be prepared to follow it from its roots in the vital physiology of the organism to this flowering in a faculty of critical awareness, including the specifically human awareness of ourselves and of our own existence as thinking, sentient beings. We must, in short, see sense perception within the context of Aristotle's psychology as a whole.

Consider for a moment the place occupied by the theory of sensation in Aristotle's treatise on the soul. The *De Anima* opens with a double introduction. The first (occupying the whole of Book I) contains a preliminary discussion of certain fundamental problems in the definition of the *psuchē*, presented in the form of a review of earlier theories. The second introduction (consisting of the first three chapters of Book II) presents Aristotle's own definition of the soul, together with some very severe remarks on the limited usefulness of a general definition. To present a definition of the soul in general, says Aristotle, without specifying it in regard to individual faculties, would be like presenting a definition of geometric figure in general, without specifying what is a triangle, a square, and the like. Accordingly, the soul must be understood by reference to its specific powers of nutrition, sensation, desire, locomotion, and rational thought.

The exposition proper then consists of a discussion of these five faculties: the nutritive in II 4; the sensory in II 5-12 and III 1-2; the intellect in III 4-8; the motive and desiderative in III 9-11. Three chapters fall outside this simplified scheme.[16] Omitting them from our reckoning, we see that there are 10 chapters of the *De Anima* devoted to sensation, whereas the other three or four faculties together account for only 9. In terms of fullness of treatment there can be no doubt: Aristotle's work on the Soul is primarily a treatise on Sensation.[17] This fact underlines the close relationship between this work and the zoological studies; the sense faculty is for Aristotle the essential principle of the animal as such. And the discussion of this faculty is by no means completed in the *De Anima*. Of the short treatises which form a sequel to this work, the first, *On Sense and Sensibilia*, constitutes a direct continuation of *De Anima* II 5-12, on the special senses. And the next three essays (*On Memory, On Sleep,* and *On Dreams*), although they do not treat of

14. *Phys.* 245a1: *ou lanthanei paschon.*
15. *EN* 1170a16-b1, to be discussed below.
16. One chapter (III 3) deals with the imagination, which appears here as transitional between sense and intellect although it belongs more properly to sense. The last two chapters of the work (III 12-13) form a kind of appendix on the inter-relationship of the faculties, though again sensation is the chief subject discussed.
17. In terms of Bekker pages, the figures are still more striking: 10 pages for sense, 3 for intellect, 4 for the other faculties combined.

external sense perception, deal with the 'inner sense', with phenomena
assigned by Aristotle to the sense faculty in its broadest extension, including
the faculty of imagination.[18] This means that the 11 chapters of the *De
Anima* which deal with sense and imagination are directly supplemented by
the 15 chapters of these four treatises in the *Parva Naturalia*. And since the
supplement is half as long again as the original exposition, it is clear that no
analysis of the latter can be satisfactory unless it takes some account of the
former as well.

50 Reserving for the moment the chronological question as to which treatise
was composed first, I propose to regard the entire discussion of the sense
faculty or *aisthêtikon* in the *De Anima* and *Parva Naturalia* as one continuous
exposition, whose sequence may be summarised as follows. After a chapter
dealing with the general characteristics of sensation, as a distinct form of
passivity or qualitative change (*De An.* II 5), Aristotle distinguishes the
several types of sense object – special, common, and incidental (II 6), and
proceeds to treat of the five special senses, in five successive chapters (II 7-
11). The bulk of the entire discussion of sensation is constituted by these
chapters on the special senses. The twelfth chapter of *De Anima* II then
formulates a general definition of the sense faculty and the sense organ, with
direct reference to the special senses discussed in the five preceding
chapters. The traditional division between Books II and III which
intervenes at this point has often been regarded as arbitrary, since it severs
two further chapters on sensation from the preceding discussion, and
groups them instead in Book III with the other faculties, including the
intellect.[19] Without wishing to defend the post-Aristotelian division into
books, I would point out that this break accurately reflects an important
difference in character between the two parts of the discussion of sense:
chapters 5-12 of Book II form a unified, largely self-contained exposition
focused on the account of the special senses, whereas chapters 1-2 of Book
III are of a much looser literary texture, dealing with a variety of
miscellaneous questions, some of which are too complex for full treatment in
the *De Anima*. These two final chapters on sensation thus illustrate the same
type of incomplete, partially incoherent, exposition which is found in a more
extreme form in the following chapters on *nous*.[20] The traditional book
division serves to underline this similarity. But whereas for *nous* we are
unfortunately provided with no sequel, some of the problems raised in *De
Anima* III 1-3 are discussed further, and in detail, in the *Parva Naturalia*.

A recent study by Irving Block has called attention to the very incomplete
and inconclusive account of the 'common sense' in the *De Anima*, in contrast
51 with the much fuller doctrine on the same subject in the first four treatises of

18. *Insom.* 459a15: 'While imagination is the same as perception, the being of each differs'.
19. Most editors remark that *De An.* III 1-2 (or even 1-3) might more properly have been included in Book II; see Rodier [42], II 341, Hicks [43], p.422, Theiler [45], p.130, Ross [8], p.268.
20. Cf. Theiler [45], p.130: 'Chapters 1-7 (of Book III) are the hardest in the treatise; not everything is completely intelligible.'

the *Parva Naturalia*.[21] Now the title 'common sense' refers to that part of Aristotle's theory which is of central importance for our own problem of the rôle of the soul in sensation, and the analysis of this theory will largely occupy our attention throughout the remainder of this paper. Our analysis will begin on the working hypothesis – whose justification must come later – that Aristotle's different statements on the subject *do* constitute a single theory, rather than discrepant phases in a variegated development. The developmental approach to Aristotle has become so fashionable that this use of an older, pre-Jaegerian methodology may appear anachronistic, not to say' retrograde. In its general defence I must say that the developmental hypothesis seems to me more often to mask than to reveal the true train of Aristotle's thought as reflected in the text. In the specific case of the theory before us, I shall undertake to *prove* that this is so, and that the *De Anima* and *Parva Naturalia* are in essential agreement – in doctrine, of course, if not always in phraseology.

From the fact that the doctrine of the *Parva Naturalia* on the subject of the *sensus communis* is much fuller than that of the *De Anima*, Block infers that the *Parva Naturalia* was composed later. Now in an externally continuous exposition concerned with a single subject, it is plausible – though certainly not necessary – to suppose that the later sections were in fact written last. This of course tells us nothing about the date of *discovery* of the ideas expressed at different moments in the exposition. And in any case, much more significant than this (inevitably speculative) question of the order of composition is the unmistakable fact that a problem raised and tentatively discussed in the *De Anima* is renewed and finally resolved in successive treatises of the *Parva Naturalia*. For this means that the exposition is truly progressive, and that the treatises which occur later in the traditional, systematic order of the *De Anima-Parva Naturalia* do (at least in this case) represent a definite advance over the preceding discussion – precisely in the same way as statements at the end of any treatise will normally represent an advance over discussions which appear at the beginning. This progressive character of the exposition is very clearly marked in the case of the *sensus communis*, that is, in the theory of all aspects of perception which go beyond the separate operation of the special senses. Since this theory holds the key to our problem of the rôle played by consciousness in Aristotle's view, we must consider it now in detail.

52

Strictly speaking, the *De Anima* expounds no doctrine of a 'common sense', although the phrase itself does appear once or twice. As we have noted, chapters 5-12 of Book II are focused on the functioning of the special senses, and so exclusively focused on them that some interpreters have believed that Aristotle regards these senses as autonomous, self-dependent faculties, which by themselves 'accomplish all the phenomena of elementary perception and self-awareness'.[22] This is, I think, a considerable overstatement of the case, but it does truly reflect the extent to which Aristotle here refrains from introducing any sense faculty beyond that of the

21. Block [60], pp.62ff. I am much indebted to Block's study, despite my disagreement with some of his conclusions.
22. *Ibid.*, pp.63-4. A more moderate statement of this view is to be found in Beare [55], pp.326-7.

individual senses. He does of course distinguish between *idia* and *koina aisthêta* (in *De An.* II 6), that is, between special and common *objects* of sense; and much of the obscurity surrounding the doctrine of the *sensus communis* derives from the fact that this traditional (and largely post-Aristotelian) term for the *faculty* makes use of the adjective which Aristotle first introduces in reference not to a faculty but to a class of objects. The systematic use of the same term 'common' for both object and faculty tends inevitably to suggest a one-to-one relationship between the two, whereas in fact nothing could be more misleading. If the common sensibles are perceived by the common sense, that is because (as we shall see) *all* sense objects without exception are perceived by this sense, which is neither more nor less than the sense faculty conceived as a single whole. But when the common sensibles are introduced in *De Anima* II 6, they are presented as *objects of the special senses*. When the term 'common' is used in this context, it means simply that a quality like shape or motion may be perceived by *at least two senses*, sight and touch, whereas a 'special sensible' like colour is perceived by sight alone. There is no suggestion, at this point in the exposition, that the several senses which perceive shape must therefore be related to some **53**   common faculty.[23] Such an inference would probably be legitimate. For how could we recognise shape-as-seen and shape-as-touched as the *same* property if the sensations of sight and touch were wholly separate from one another? But Aristotle carefully refrains from drawing any such conclusion in *De An.* II 5-12, because he is there concerned with the operation of the special senses as such, and does not wish to obscure their analysis by introducing complications from without. The individual objects of the special senses provide the clearest and strictest case of sense perception (418a24). It is characteristic of Aristotle's method that he accordingly treats them *as if* they functioned independently of one another and of any common faculty, although the mere mention of common sensibles shows that in fact the matter cannot be so simple.

Aristotle is prepared to return to these complications as soon as his primary analysis is complete, i.e. in the first chapter of Book III. Looking back on the account of the special senses, he now undertakes to show that his account is exhaustive, and that there is no sixth sense. It is in this context that he reverts to the problem of the common sensibles. There is no special sense organ for the perception of such qualities as motion, shape, and number, says Aristotle. If there were, these qualities would be special objects of their own sense and we would perceive them by sight and touch

23. The confusion between common sensibilia and common sense has misled even such good Aristotelians as Theiler, Siwek, and Ross, all of whom would add 'time' to Aristotle's list of the common sensibles in *De An.* II 6, on the strength of his statement in *Mem.* 450a10-12 and 451a17. (See Ross [8], p.33; Theiler [45], pp.119 and 131; Siwek [47], p.153, n. 24.) But what the *De Memoria* says in fact is that time is perceived by the common *faculty*, the *prôton aisthêtikon.* Now if a property is to be a common sensible as defined in *De An.* II 6, it must first be the object of at least two special senses. (So also *De An.* III 1, 425b4ff.; *Sens.* 437a8.) Time, however, is not directly perceived by any external sense, much less by more than one. (Since time is the 'number of the motion' for Aristotle, it is of course directly related to the common sensible, motion. But the *sense* of time is not identical with the sense of motion; if it were, it would be common to all animals.)

only incidentally, as by sight we may recognise that something is hot or sweet. But in fact there is no such special organ or sense for motion, shape, size, and number. Although they are true sense objects, perceived *per se* and not incidentally, they are objects of a *common sense (aisthêsis koinê)*, that is of a faculty shared by more than one special sense.[24]

With this first mention of a common sense, Aristotle begins his inference **54** from the fact of common sensibilia to the existence of a single faculty; but he begins still with reference to the special senses, and with no assumption of a power distinct from their own. The common sense described in this passage is nothing but the *coincidence* of the special senses. Similarly in what follows. 'The special senses perceive one another's objects incidentally, not as special but *as one sense*, when their sensation occurs together in reference to a single object; for example, in the sensation of bile as bitter and as yellow. For it certainly does not require some additional sense to declare that the two <separate qualities> are one single thing'.[25] This unity of the special senses is not, as such, the 'common sense' of the previous section, since it is here concerned with *idia* rather than *koina*, with the special objects of two senses rather than with the common objects of them all. Aristotle is in fact now taking the second step in his ingressive exploration of the notion of a common faculty. Just as the special senses share the same type of object in their perception of the *koina*, so they unite in the perception of a single object which presents their *idia* together. In the first case they overlap *qua* faculties; in the second case they coincide in a single, momentary act. Both points provide implicit arguments for the convergence of these faculties in a common root or agency, but Aristotle does not here make the argument explicit. He has thus far asserted the existence of no faculty beyond that of the special senses and their combination.

The aporias of *De Anima* III 2 bring us one step closer to such an assertion. Here for the first time we are confronted with activities of sense which are not simply identical with the operation by which external objects

24. *De An.* 425a14-29. Some interpreters (including Beare and Ross) have failed to see that 'which we perceive incidentally by each sense' in line a15 is part of the hypothesis which Aristotle is rejecting, and have erroneously concluded that he believed the common sensibles to be perceived *incidentally* by the special senses, although that is explicitly denied at a24-8, and had already been excluded at 418a8ff., both of which passages recognise the common sensibles as sense objects *per se (aisthêta kath' hauta)*.

The passage is rightly construed by Theiler ([45], p.131), who remarks that the thought would be clearer if Aristotle had written *aisthanoimeth' an* in line 15. Theiler's interpretation is that of Rodier and of all the Greek commentators (cited by Rodier [42], II 353f.). The alternative, but much less natural view is to distinguish two senses of *aisthêton kata sumbebêkos*, only one of which applies to the common sensibles (so Zeller and others, cited by Rodier, *loc. cit.*; also Hicks [43], pp.426f., and De Corte [94], pp.189-91, who quotes St Thomas to this effect).

25. 425a30-b3. The words which are here translated 'For it certainly does not require some additional source to declare that the two <separate qualities> are one single thing' are ambiguous; I follow Theiler (so also Rodier and Hicks). Ross and the Oxford translator (J.A. Smith) understand *heteras* to refer to *either* vision or taste: 'the assertion of the identity of both (bitter and yellow) cannot be the act of either of the senses'.

are perceived. For Aristotle now considers two aspects of the reflexive act by which the sense faculty takes its own operations as object. The first aspect is **55** the awareness of perception as such: 'since we perceive that we are seeing and hearing, it must either be by sight that we perceive we are seeing, or by another sense' (425b12). The second aspect of the reflexive act is the differentiation of the *content* of perception, that is, the discrimination of the special sense objects from one another.

> Since each sense ... which is present in the sense organ as sense organ, discriminates <or judges, *krinei*> the differences which belong to its sensible object, as vision discriminates white and black, taste judges sweet and bitter ..., and since we also discriminate white from sweet, and each of the sense qualities from one another; by what faculty do we perceive *that they differ*?[26] It must be by sensation; for these are sensible qualities. ... Nor is is possible to judge by <two> separate faculties <sc. by taste and sight> that sweet is different from white, but *both of these qualities must be evident to some single faculty*. <For the supposition that two separate faculties could discriminate them> would be as if I were to perceive one of the qualities and you the other, and it would then be evident that they are different from one another! Rather, there must be *one* principle which says that they are different. (426b8-21)

With these two aporias, Aristotle has entered the area of psychological enquiry in which modern introspective philosophy normally begins, but which he has methodically avoided until his account of external perception is provisionally complete. It is probably impossible to overestimate the importance of this difference in methodology for an understanding of the radical contrast in conceptual framework between the Aristotelian and the post-Cartesian views. For the moment we simply remark that both of the questions raised here really *do* involve an introspective, anthropocentric view of sensation, as distinguished from the objective, zoological approach which generally prevails in his account of the special senses. This is as true of the second aporia as it is of the first, despite the fact that the question is formulated as if it referred to direct and not to reflective perception. Aristotle asks, not, 'how do we discriminate vision from taste?' but, 'how do we differentiate white from sweet?' This is, however, merely his objective mode of framing the same question. For although it is essential for animals **56** to discriminate between different colours or between different flavours, only men – and really, only philosophers – are interested in discriminating colours from flavours.

There is clearly one solution to both aporias: the special senses must be regarded not as ultimately independent faculties but rather as converging lines, joined at the centre in a single, generalised faculty of sense. Thus when one directs one's attention outward, the several senses appear entirely distinct from one another, operating through different bodily channels and focused upon entirely different kinds of objects; yet when the gaze is turned

---

26. In reading this as a question, I again follow Theiler. The traditional punctuation implies a weak assertion: 'by some faculty we perceive that they differ.'

inward, one sees that they actually converge – in concrete experience, as we would say – in the unifying and discriminating activity of a single centre. And it is, of course, in virtue of this union at the centre – in 'consciousness', let us say – that the special senses are able to share in the 'common perception' of the same common sensibles, as well as to perceive one another's objects incidentally in a single simultaneous act. It is, in short, not only the two aporias of *De Anima* III 1, but also the two statements concerning the unity of the senses in the preceding chapter, which find their full elucidation in the doctrine of a unified sense faculty, as expounded in the *Parva Naturalia*.

We can only speculate as to Aristotle's reasons for leaving the exposition of this doctrine incomplete in the *De Anima*, while he went on to discuss intellect and locomotion. Apparently he wished to link the broader treatment of sense to the discussion of the related faculties of memory and imagination which is found in the later treatises. He may have preferred to leave the more difficult theories only partially stated in the *De Anima* in order to complete his survey of the other psychic faculties discussed in that treatise. Whatever the explanation, we may be certain that, in Aristotle's view, the aporias of *De Anima* III 2 are in fact resolved by the doctrine of the *Parva Naturalia* concerning the unitary sense faculty, and are not resolved until this doctrine has been stated.

In regard to the first problem – the faculty by which we perceive that we are seeing or hearing – the inconclusive nature of the discussion in *De Anima* III 2 has not always been noted, and Aristotle has accordingly been understood to say that the faculty of sight located in the eye is immediately aware of itself, and stands in need of no higher or more general mode of perception.[27] Such a doctrine would imply that the perception or **57** 'awareness' that we are hearing is of an entirely different nature, and exercised by an entirely different faculty, from the perception or awareness that we are seeing. This may or may not be a *possible* view, but it is certainly the very reverse of the view which Aristotle expounds elsewhere, as we shall see. His inconclusive discussion of the problem here can only be understood as a preparation for the full solution to come.

The connection between the second aporia in *De Anima* III 2 – with what faculty do we distinguish colours from flavours? – and the final solution in the *Parva Naturalia* is much more definitely marked, for the solution is adumbrated here in some detail, and the same two examples (sweet and white) reappear both when the problem is discussed further in *De Anima* III 7 and when it is finally resolved in *De Sensu* 7. The original statement of the aporia, in the passage quoted above (p. 10), asserts that the objects of different senses must in fact be perceived by some single faculty, but it does not define the nature of this faculty, nor its relationship to the special senses. Aristotle does here suggest the formula that the faculty is concretely 'one and indivisible, but separate in its being' (i.e. as considered in relation to its

---

27. So Block [60], p.63. On this as on many other points, the most accurate analysis is that given long ago by Rodier [42], II, p.266: 'It is not in fact as a special and distinct sense that vision gives us consciousness of itself; rather, it does so insofar as it partakes of characteristics common to all perception.'

object, as formulated in the definition of special sense).[28] But when it comes to explaining this simultaneous unity and plurality, Aristotle leaves us with a mathematical analogy: it is one and indivisible like the geometric point which separates two line segments, but which is taken twice, as end-point of each line. When Aristotle returns to this problem in the fragmentary set of notes which constitutes chapter 7 of *De Anima* III,[29] he again makes use of the language of geometry: the air affects the pupil of the eye, this affects something else; something similar occurs in the case of hearing; but the final term (in each sequence) is *one*; and 'there is one mean <for all sensation>, although its mode of being is plural' (431a17 ff.). It is in the same context that Aristotle returns to the problem of discriminating objects of different senses, and offers another geometrical analogy, this time to the mean proportional (rather than to the midpoint) between two lines. Like the mean proportional, the central faculty 'is related to each <extreme> as they are related to one another' (431a23). Both text and interpretation of this passage offer considerable difficulties, which need not concern us here. What is clear, in any case, is that Aristotle explicitly reverts[30] to the second aporia of III 2 and essays a new formula for the single faculty which unites the special senses.

Both aporias are finally resolved in two important sections of the *Parva Naturalia*.

1. In the last chapter of the *De Sensu*, Aristotle returns once more to the problem of discriminating objects of different senses, and gives his solution in these terms:[31]

> If the soul perceives sweet and white with different parts (of itself), either some unity is formed from these parts or there is no unity. But there must be a unity; for the part capable of sensation is one. ... There is then necessarily *one (faculty) of the soul by which it perceives all things*, as has been said earlier,[32] but different kinds (of objects)

28. *De An.* 427a2 (similarly in 427a5).

29. I assume that the incoherence of *De An.* III 7 is due to the fact that Aristotle jotted down these remarks as they occurred to him, more or less in their present form. It is also possible that they represent mere fragments of a more polished exposition which has been lost. In that case the present arrangement would be that of some ancient editor (as Torstrik and others have believed). But the first alternative seems much the more likely, since the chain of association linking one item to the next has precisely the implicit and elliptical character of Aristotle's own thought (as Rodier and Theiler appear to have seen).

30. 'We have said earlier what is the faculty which distinguishes sweet and hot; but we must also formulate the matter as follows' (431a20).

31. *Sens.* 449a5-20. I add in parenthesis words which are elliptically omitted in the Greek, but implied by the context.

32. Where has this been said 'earlier'? Ross suggests the immediately preceding passage in *De Sensu* 7, but I can find nothing there to justify the reference. Beare (in his note to the Oxford translation) refers more plausibly to *De An.* III 2 (see esp. 427a5); similarly Siwek [47], p.125, n. 337, and also Alexander, *In De Sensu* (ed. Thurot, 1875), p.344. Perhaps the most exact antecedent is *De An.* III 7, 431a19 and 28-9. The backward reference here is one sign, among many, of the continuity of exposition between *De An.* and *P.N.* For another mark of continuity, note the

through different means (i.e. through different organs). ... As in the case of (corporeal) things ... something numerically one and the same may be both white and sweet, ... so in the case of the soul one must assume that *the faculty of perception for all* (objects or qualities) *is numerically one and the same*, although its being is different (as considered in relation to its objects), and sometimes different in genus or kind (between the different senses), sometimes different in species or form (within a given sense). So that a man perceives (different qualities) simultaneously with one and the same faculty, though in its definition it is not the same.   **59**

2. In the treatise *On Sleep and Waking*, Aristotle notes as the essential characteristic of sleep the incapacitation of all the senses together. This leads him to the classical statement of the doctrine of *sensus communis*.

Each sense possesses something which is special and something which is common. Special to vision, for example, is seeing, special to the auditory sense is hearing, and similarly for each of the others; but there is also *a common power which accompanies them all, in virtue of which one perceives that one is seeing and hearing.* For it is not by vision, after all, that one sees one is seeing; nor is it by taste or by sight or by both that one judges, and is capable of judging, that sweet things are different from white ones; but it is by *some part which is common to all the sense organs.* For there is *one faculty of sense, and one master sense organ,* although the being of sense is different for each genus, e.g. for sound and colour. (455a12-22)

Here the twin aporias of *De Anima* III 2 are jointly recalled and resolved in the definitive assertion of the unity of the entire sense faculty, which is now for the first time linked to the physiological doctrine of the unity of the sense apparatus in the common sensorium, the heart (or, as we would say, the brain), 'the common sense organ for the special organs of sense, in which actual sensations must present themselves'.[33] It is here, in fact, in the explanation of sleep, that Aristotle's psychology meets his physiology; and (despite his errors of fact) the theoretical joint is perfect.

Now this 'common power which accompanies all the senses, in virtue of which one perceives that one is seeing and hearing', would not seem to be so very different from the modern notion of consciousness as defined by Locke, 'the perception of what passes in a man's own mind'.[34] But before following up the comparison and contrasts with the modern view, we must first summarise the functions which Aristotle assigns to this central faculty of perception in the *Parva Naturalia*, and decide whether or not this theory is compatible with the account of sensation given in the *De Anima*.

---

recurrence of 'sweet' and 'white', already offered as examples in *De An.* III 2 (426b13 ff.) and III 7 (431b1).

33. *Iuv.* 467b28; cf. 469a12.

34. *Essay concerning Human Understanding,* Bk. II, Ch. 1, sect. 19.

To begin with some remarks on terminology. In the first place, this
'common power' (*koinê dunamis*) accompanying all of the special senses
cannot simply be identified with the 'common sense' (*koinê aisthêsis*)
mentioned in the *De Anima* as perceiving the common sensibles.[35] For as we
have seen, the latter is defined objectively, by reference to certain qualities it
perceives, but the former is defined subjectively, by reference to the
awareness of any sensation as such. This subjective power is clearly the
more general, and in no way more closely connected with the perception of
the common sensibles (such as motion and shape) than with the perception
of colours, sounds, and flavours. What is characteristic of both these notions
of 'common sense' is that they refer to a faculty located in the central
sensorium, rather than in any special sense organ as such. There is one
passage in the *Parva Naturalia* and one in the *Parts of Animals* which seem to
use the term 'common sense' with just this connotation: the general faculty
of sensibility located in the heart;[36] and it is this usage which has prevailed
in the later designation of the *sensus communis*. The more frequent
Aristotelian expression for this idea is, however, *to (prôton) aisthêtikon*, 'the
(primary) capacity of sense',[37] where for brevity the adjective 'primary' is
often omitted. Similar in meaning is the term 'sensation proper'.[38] Since the
faculty is defined by reference to the heart, the organ itself is even more
frequently designated by the corresponding terms: the 'primary sense
organ', the 'source or principle of sensation' (*archê tês aisthêseôs*), the
'common sense organ', or the 'sense organ proper'.[39] All of these expressions
refer to a single doctrine, most fully formulated in the passage quoted from
the *De Somno*, where the heart is referred to precisely as the *kurion aisthêtêrion*,
the master sense organ or sensorium proper.

Although this doctrine is not explicitly formulated until the third treatise
of the *Parva Naturalia*, it is very definitely implied by the first two, since the
De Sensu speaks of 'the single capacity of the soul by which it perceives all
things', and the *De Memoria* refers to the 'primary capacity of sense' which is
responsible for perceiving time as well as the common sensibles, and which
is also the seat of imagination.[40] Whether or not the treatises of the *Parva
Naturalia* were all planned and composed at one time, they clearly form an
integrated exposition of a single doctrine, with a definite relationship to the

---

35. *De An.* 425a27, with 431b5 where *têi koinêi* (*aisthêsei*) is mentioned for the
perception of motion.

36. *Mem.* 450a10 (where imagination is said to affect the *koinê aisthêsis* and *PA*
686a31, where the context makes clear that this faculty is located in the heart. (The
reference is to animals generally, and not only to men.) The textual position of the
passage in the *De Memoria* causes some trouble. It may well represent a marginal
gloss which has become incorporated into the text. In that case it would reflect the
later, more generalised use of 'common sense', found in the Greek commentators.

37. After *hen to aisthêtikon pantôn* of *Sens.* 449a17, the term *prôton aisthêtikon* is
introduced in *Mem.* 450a11, a14 and 451a16; so also *Som.* 454a23. Elsewhere *to
aisthêtikon* has the same sense (e.g. in *Insom.* 459a12).

38. *Som.* 456a6.

39. *Prôton aisthêtêrion*, *Som.* 455b10, 456a21, etc., *kurion aisthêtêrion*, *ibid.* 455a21, a33;
cf. *to kurion tôn aisthêseôn*, *tês aisthêseôs*, 8 examples in Bonitz, *Index Arist.* 20b18-24;
koinon aisthêtêrion, *Iuv.* 467b28, 469a12; *archê tês aisthêseôs*, *Insom.* 461a6, etc.

40. *Sens.* 449a7-9; *Mem.* 450a9-14 (cf. 451a16).

De Anima as far as the theory of sensation is concerned. For the first treatise of the group deals with the sense faculty in precisely the same way as the *De Anima*. It is focused upon what we may call the external function of sense: the operation of the special senses in providing information concerning the outside world. This is the properly cognitive aspect of sensation, and if Aristotle has so largely limited himself to this aspect in the *De Anima*, that is no doubt due to his desire to emphasise the parallel between sense and intellect. For his analysis of sensation (and above all of vision, the cognitive sense par excellence) is to serve as the model for his analysis of the intellect.

Considered in reference to this external cognitive function, the central faculty appears above all as the point of convergence – of recognition and discrimination – between the special channels of external sensation. It is this concentric system of contact with the outside world which constitutes sensation proper, which is common (in principle) to all animals, and which ceases to operate in sleep.[41] The treatise *On Memory* goes beyond this primary system of sensation to deal with a number of secondary functions that may be loosely described as the activity of internal sense – where 'internal' refers simply to the fact that these activities are exercised by the central faculty directly, without the need for simultaneous contact with the **62** outside world through an external organ. The three functions mentioned in this treatise are: (1) the sense of time, (2) the faculty of imagination or image-formation (*phantastikon*), and (3) memory, which presupposes the first two. To these three functions of the internal sense is later added another: (4) the power of dreaming, which also belongs to 'the sense faculty considered as a capacity to form images'.[42] These secondary faculties all depend not upon the momentary activity of the external senses but upon a certain persistence of the motion or stimulus received from them in the form of 'decaying sense', which is precisely Aristotle's definition of the imagination.[43] These powers of internal sense are not so widely distributed among the animals, and are much more characteristic of human beings, in whose case they merge almost imperceptibly into the rational faculty.[44] If Aristotle refrains from introducing these broader functions of the sense

41. Aristotle never considers 'proprioception' or muscle sense, but would no doubt have included it under touch (which also comprises what is now distinguished as the temperature sense). As has been noted, his treatment of pleasure and pain is ambiguous: he sometimes describes it as a sensation, elsewhere (and more strictly) as an accompaniment of sensation. One may compare the ambiguity which Kant notices in the use of the term 'sensation' (*Empfindung*) to refer to pleasure and pain, in the *Critique of Judgment* § 3. Aristotle would have been quite satisfied with Kant's distinction between sensation and 'feeling'.

42. *Insom.* 459a21.

43. *De An.* 428b10 ff., closely followed by Hobbes in *Leviathan*, Ch. 2.

44. Whether or not all animals possess imagination is a question which Aristotle hesitates to answer categorically (see *De An.* 431b22, 414b15, 415a10, 428a8-11, 434a1 ff.). He definitely believes that they do not all have a sense of time and the power of memory (*Mem.* 450a15-19; cf. 449b28-30, *Meta.* 980a29), and sometimes speaks as if the sense of time was inseparable from the faculty of reason (*Phys.* 223a25; cf. *De An.* 433b7). The close link between intellect and imagination is often stressed (e.g. *De An.* 403a8, 427b16, 431a17, b2, *Mem.* 449b31 ff.), and in one case he actually refers to a rational imagination (*De An.* 433b29).

faculty in the *De Anima* (where the imagination is not even definitely assigned to the *aisthêtikon*, but treated as somehow intermediate between sense and intellect), he had good reasons for such restraint.[45] The broader conception of the sense faculty, including memory and imagination, would have obscured the sharp features of parallelism and contrast between sense and intellect which are so important for the argument of that treatise. Hence it is only in the *Parva Naturalia*, where sense perception is considered less as a form of cognition than as a part of the total psycho-physiology of the organism, that the notion of the sense faculty is definitely broadened to include these activities of decaying sense. This extension is not required by the subject of the *De Sensu*, and it makes no appearance in that work. The broader view is naturally provoked by the discussion of memory, but the *De Memoria* still expounds the doctrine of the internal sense with no mention of its physiological base. Only in the third treatise, *On Sleep*, does the reference to the bodily apparatus become indispensable; and it is at this point (as we have seen) that the doctrine of *sensus communis* receives its full and definitive statement.[46]

63

As traditionally presented, the concept of the *sensus communis* is merely a truncated form of this Aristotelian doctrine of the unified faculty of perception. There are few modern expositions which do justice to the comprehensive unity of Aristotle's notion of the 'sensory soul', and which emphasise the extent to which he goes beyond his own methodological fiction of treating the special senses as independent of one another. This distortion is due to the fact that most, if not all commentators have failed to see that the *De Anima* and the *Parva Naturalia* form a continuous and progressive exposition. Even Sir David Ross gives a misleading account of the *sensus communis*, although he recognises that sense for Aristotle is 'a single faculty which for certain purposes is specified into the five senses, but

---

45. The chronologically minded reader might infer that Aristotle had not yet 'discovered' that imagination belongs to the *aisthêtikon*, as he is to tell us in the *De Memoria* (450a10-12; cf. *Insom.* 459a15). But in fact this is an obvious conclusion from the definition of imagination in *De An.* III 3: a motion due to active perceiving (429a 1; cf. 425b24: perceptions and imaginings are present in the organs). Aristotle had no new discoveries to make in the matter. But the relationship of these persistent phantasy images to actual sensation cannot be cleared up until the faculty of sense is defined in its full generality; and this Aristotle is not prepared to do in the *De Anima*.

46. Assuming, as we must, that Aristotle knew (or thought he knew) all along that the heart was the actual sensorium, and did not make this discovery in the course of composing his treatise *On Sleep*, why did he reserve the announcement until this point, when the mention of the common organ might have simplified the earlier discussions of the common faculty? The question involves the whole problem of Aristotelian methodology and style of exposition, and we must be satisfied here with a few suggestions: (1) the aporetic technique aims at making things *difficult* before they are simplified – at tying the knot properly before it is untied, so that the scope and importance of the solution may be seen; (2) the aporias concerning the self-awareness of sense are posed in purely psychological, even introspective terms, and could not validly be resolved by physiological considerations; the latter are introduced only when the psychological solution is essentially complete, since (3) the soul, in Aristotle's way of thinking, is a causal principle which explains the action of the body, and not *vice versa*.

discharges certain functions in virtue of its generic nature'. Ross lists five such functions of common sensibility:

1. the perception of the common sensibles;
2. the perception of the incidental sensibles;
3. the perception that we perceive;
4. the discrimination between objects of two senses;
5. the common inactivity of all the senses in sleep.[47]

Items 3, 4, and 5 of Ross' list accurately describe the functions of the central **64** faculty in regard to the primary activity of external sense perception. Item 1 also refers to this activity, though not quite so accurately.[48] (Since item 2 belongs to the sense faculty only *incidentally*, it has perhaps no proper place on the list.) On the other hand, this summary takes no account of the secondary or internal operations of the same faculty, all of which involve the prolongation of direct perception in the processes of 'decaying sense': the sense of time, the capacity for imagination, for memory, and for dreaming.[49]

The more recent and detailed study of the 'common sense' by Irving Block rightly emphasises the extent to which the *Parva Naturalia* takes us beyond the doctrine of the *De Anima*. Block's article has, to my mind, definitely refuted the view of Nuyens and Ross that the *Parva Naturalia* represents an earlier stage in the development of Aristotle's psychology. On this point, the present study simply provides a confirmation of Block's results. On the other hand, I am not convinced by Block's own chronological view, which conceives the doctrines of the two works as 'divergent if not incompatible', and which implies that when Aristotle composed the *Parva Naturalia* he had learned much physiology and psychology of which he was totally ignorant when he composed the *De Anima*. Most of the arguments for this intellectual advance on Aristotle's part are drawn only from silence — for example, from Aristotle's failure in the *De Anima* to specify the rôle of the heart as central sensorium.[50] Once

.

47. Ross [8], pp.33-6, reprinted with slight changes from the same author's [16] 5th ed. 1953, pp.140ff.

48. Ross fails to point out that the common faculty does not apprehend the common sensibles directly, but via the special senses (see above, n. 23). Furthermore, in his detailed account of the common sensibles he confounds them with the incidental sensibles, following an error of Beare. (See Beare [55], pp.283 ff., and above n24). The true distinction is accurately formulated by De Corte [94], p.192: 'it is precisely because incidental sensibles do not, *qua* incidental, have any effect on the senses that they differ from common sensibles'; cf. *De An.* 418a23.

49. The sense of time is erroneously listed under the common sensibles (for the error, see above, n23). In fairness to Ross, it must be noted that the faculty of imagination and memory is elsewhere recognised by him as one of the 'outgrowths from the sensitive faculty', although these are misleadingly compared to the quite distinct faculty of movement ([16], 5th edition, p.130).

50. There are four explicit references to the heart in the *De An.*, three of which identify it as the seat of emotions such as anger and fear (403a31, 408b8, 432b31); the fourth tells us that 'the region of the heart' is in need of respiration, and states that the voice is produced by the soul 'in these parts' (420b25-9). In view of Aristotle's general silence on physiology in the *De Anima*, these passages are revealing enough. The

65 one has grasped the methodical and ingressive structure of Aristotle's exposition, both here and elsewhere, all such arguments from silence fall to the ground.[51]

There is one difference between the *De Anima* and the *Parva Naturalia* claimed by Block which, if it were actually to be found in these works, would imply that Aristotle had indeed changed his mind on a matter of real importance. This is the contention that, in the *De Anima*, the external senses are regarded as 'self-dependent faculties', which exercise not only sensation but also self-awareness independently 'of the function of any other organ of the body'.[52] Now if one considers for a moment the implications of such a view, it seems scarcely credible that Aristotle can ever have held it – or if he did, we are glad to know that he quickly repented before composing the *Parva Naturalia*. For what are we to make of an act of self-awareness limited to the eye or to the tongue? And can Aristotle really have believed that

66 'when the proper stimulating motions reach the eye *and no farther*, we see'?[53] We know, of course, that the visual stimulus must in fact pass through the optic nerve and reach the brain, or no vision occurs. Was Aristotle so much more ignorant of human anatomy and physiology? Certainly not when he wrote the *Parva Naturalia*, nor when he composed his biological works. Despite his ignorance of the nervous system in general, Aristotle was quite familiar with the optic nerve as a channel between eye and brain (it had

---

doctrine of the heart as seat of the emotions might perhaps be taken from Plato's *Timaeus* (but see *Resp.* 479b22; *Probl.* 869a5); the heart in need of breath and the rational or sensitive soul operating in the chest can hardly reflect anything but Aristotle's own biology. As Theiler remarks ([45], p.77), the mention of the heart in 420b25-9 shows precisely that it may have a 'biological future' – by which I understand a future of exposition, not of discovery. (The passage contains two forward references to the *De Respiratione* and the relevant sections of the *PA*: 420b22 and 421a6. I see no reason to suppose that both of these are 'later insertions'.)

There are also two implicit references to Aristotle's doctrine of the sensorium (i.e. the heart) in the mention of the *eschaton* (last) *aisthētērion* at 426b16, and *to eschaton* again at 431a18 (see Hicks [43] *ad loc.*). What is the *prôton* (first) *aisthētērion* elsewhere is the *eschaton* in the *De An.*, since in that treatise Aristotle begins his analysis from the external object, and hence regards the external organs as the 'first'.

51. Block suggests that the vagueness of the *De Anima* on many questions should be seen as a sign that Aristotle's 'views are at an incomplete stage ... and should not ... be taken as his final doctrine' (p.69). Granted, as long as the incompleteness is seen as a stage in the exposition, and not in the process of discovery, concerning which we know nothing.

After writing this, I find that exactly the same interpretation of Aristotle's silence or apparent hesitation has been given by Father Owens for the *Metaphysics*: the aporetic technique presupposes 'only that the question at issue is not yet decided *in the minds of the "hearers"* ' (*The Doctrine of Being in the Aristotelian 'Metaphysics'* (Toronto, 1957), pp.30f.).

For a clear example of such rhetorical or methodological hesitation on the question at issue, consider Aristotle's refusal to decide whether the essence of man (i.e. the soul) is located in the heart or in the brain, at *Meta.* VII, 1035b26.

52. Block [60], p.64. Block has restated his developmental hypothesis in [91].

53. *Op cit.*, p.63 (italics added). This is essentially the view which Plato dismisses as absurd in *Theaet.* 184D: 'It would be rather strange if there were many (unconnected) senses seated within us, like so many heroes in the Trojan horse.'

apparently been observed more than a century earlier, by Alcmaeon); and he is perfectly aware that a stimulus must pass through it towards the brain (and then onwards to the heart, as he believed), if vision was to occur.[54] 'For some men wounded in battle on the temple in such a way that the passages of the eye are cut off are known to have had the sensation of darkness as if a lamp had gone out.'[55] Are we to believe that such incidents were reported to Aristotle only after he completed the *De Anima*? But in fact the close connection of sight (and hearing) with the brain is not a new discovery on Aristotle's part, any more than the central rôle which he assigns to the heart. Both are his own adaptations of traditional views, utilised earlier in a different form by Plato in the *Timaeus*.[56] To suppose that this adaptation, which is as complete in the *Parva Naturalia* as it is in the biological works, and which obviously required years of careful investigation, had not even *begun* when Aristotle composed the *De Anima* – in other words, to suppose that the author of that treatise did not know as much physiology as he might have learned simply from reading the *Timaeus* – this is a very strange supposition indeed, and fortunately the evidence cited by Block does not oblige us to make it.[57]

67

The one point which Block makes that deserves very careful consideration is the assertion that the individual sense faculties are located *in* the organs of which they are the form and realisation (*entelecheia*), for this is truly Aristotle's doctrine in the *De Anima* (412b17-413a3; 424a24-8). But is this view contradicted by the role which Aristotle elsewhere assigns to the heart as the seat of the central faculty of sense? In *De Anima* II 1 where he describes vision as the form or realisation of the eye, he continues: 'One must apply what has been said of the part to the whole living body; for just as part is related to part <viz. partial faculty to partial organ>, so is the whole sense faculty proportionately related to the whole sensitive body, as such', i.e. to the whole body as capable of sensation (412b22-5). The

54. For Aristotle's knowledge of what 'were half a century later to be identified as the optic nerves', see Solmsen [103], p.173 (with n25); for Alcmaeon, *ibid.*, pp. 152 and 187, n10.

55. *Sens.* 438b12. The passage presents some difficulties but surely the *poroi* severed by a wound on the temples must be those which lead 'from the eyes to the veins around the brain' (*PA* 656b17; cf. *GA* 744a10), and which nearly all commentators have recognised as the optic nerves. In his note on *P.N* 438b13-14, Ross seems to doubt this obvious identification for the curious reason that '*poroi* must always means passages, not nerves'. Of course, but Aristotle did not *know* they were nerves; and Herophilus, the discoverer of the nervous system, still referred to these particular nerves as *poroi* (Solmsen [103], pp.186f.; cf. Bonitz, *Index Arist.* 623a47-b12).

56. See Solmsen [103], *passim*.

57. For example, from the alleged fact that the external organs are the only ones mentioned in the *De An.*, Block concluded that 'eyesight is a function solely of the eye and hearing of the ear'. Such an inference could be valid only if the *De An.* claimed to give a thorough account of the physiology of sensation, whereas in fact it does not deal with physiology at all – not even with the physiology of the external organs.

Even the *De An.*, however, contains at least two references to an 'ultimate sense organ' (see above, n. 50). It is difficult to see how Block's view could be reconciled with the second of these passages (431a17-19), where Aristotle recognises a single sensory centre (*mesotês*) for vision and hearing.

individual faculty of special sense is thus a part of the general faculty of sense, just as the individual sense organ is a part of the general sense apparatus of the whole body. This view of the sense faculty as a unified whole, of which the special senses are parts, is not limited to the sentence just quoted; it pervades the entire *De Anima*, which continuously refers to the sensory power of the soul as a single unit (*to aisthêtikon* or *hê aisthêtikê psuchê*), comparable to the faculties of intellect and nutrition. The conception of the individual senses as independent faculties would be just as alien to Aristotle as the conception of individual organs in abstraction from the body of which they form a part. The doctrine of a single, unified sense faculty, of which the individual senses are so many diverse modes or aspects – this doctrine which gradually emerges as the solution to the problems posed by the analysis of the special senses – faithfully reflects the point of view from which Aristotle originally began his discussion of the sensory soul.

68 Now this view of the sense faculty of the soul as a unified whole unmistakably implies that the individual organs also combine to form a unit, a physiological system, which can serve as instrument for the sense faculty as a whole. For the sensory soul is, by definition, the form and realisation of the sensory body; and the unity of one is unthinkable without the unity of the other. Far from contradicting the psychological doctrine of the *De Anima*, the physiology of the *Parva Naturalia* and of the biological works is *required* if the doctrine of sense perception as a single faculty of the soul is to be understood at all. The inference from unity of faculty to unity of physiological system is explicitly made by Aristotle himself in the *Parts of Animals* (667b21-31), where the fact that 'all animals possess a sensory soul which is actually one' is cited as a causal explanation for the unity of the vascular system in the heart. If with a touch of the magic wand we free Aristotle from his factual errors, we see that he is formulating (in his own language of teleological causation, where function explains mechanism) almost exactly the same point which a modern zoologist makes in describing the nerve net of a simple coelenterate: 'it enables an animal composed of many thousands of cells to react as one integrated individual.'[58]

Thus the physiology of the *Parts of Animals* and the psychology of the *De Anima* are fully compatible, and they are in fact united in the psycho-physiology of the *Parva Naturalia*. I do not pretend to know which of these three treatises was completed first,[59] nor do I see that the matter is of any philosophic importance. The *Parva Naturalia* and the biological works are

58. Ralph Buchsbaum, *Animals Without Backbones* (Pelican ed., 1951), I, p.95. Aristotle discusses this integrative action from the point of view of sensory reception, whereas the quotation refers to motor response; but in either case the functional unity of the organism is essential.

59. Perhaps the most plausible guess is that of Theiler ([45], p.76), who supposes that the treatises *De An., PN, PA, GA* were composed one after another in their present, systematic order. This is likely enough, if by 'composed' one means *put into final form*; for the occasion of composition will then have been Aristotle's last and most comprehensive series of lectures on psychology and zoology. But we can never know how much of Aristotle's material was prepared by him in advance, whether in his mind or on paper, long before the moment of final composition. For this and other

clearly in agreement on all essentials. The *De Anima* takes up a somewhat different point of view, since it abstracts from all considerations of physiological detail. But there is really no reason to suppose that the physiological model in Aristotle's mind, which he systematically refrains from introducing into the *De Anima*, is in any way different from that which is actually expounded by him in the other works.   **69**

Now this view of the physiological apparatus of sense is easy enough for us to understand, if whenever Aristotle says 'veins' or 'channels' we substitute 'nerves', and whenever he refers to the heart we think of the brain instead. Once these substitutions have been made there is nothing strange in his notion of a central organ serving as sensorium proper, the point at which all stimuli from the external organs converge and in which they must appear for any genuine sensation to occur. The central faculty lodged in this organ obviously exercises many of the functions which we now refer to 'consciousness', and which modern physiology connects with the cerebral cortex.

But if Aristotle's view of the physiological apparatus is parallel to our own, his location of the *faculty* is somewhat different. For although the central faculty, and the 'sensation proper' which it exercises, are definitely placed in the heart, that does not prevent Aristotle from locating the power of vision as such in the eye. For not only is the eye a necessary condition of sight – since without it we cannot see at all – but it contributes everything which is specifically *visual* in the final sensation. The definition of the soul as the realisation of the organic possibilities of the body implies that the psychic power of vision is the realisation of the specific possibilities offered by the eye, although the possibility of *sensation as such* is not offered by the eye alone, but only by the central organ with which it is connected.[60] Since the sensory soul of a normally functioning animal includes not only the general power of sensation but also the special faculties of external sense, it must be thought of as *informing the entire sense apparatus*, although it does so *from its source or foundation (archê) in the heart*. Thus there is a derivative psychic power resident in the eye, a power which departs when the organ can no longer function, either because of local injury – when the eye 'goes dead' – or because the animal itself is no longer alive. In the case of death, the   **70** sensory soul is wholly destroyed. But in the case of local injury, for example to an eye, the psychic power remains intact in the central organ, and may continue to exercise its visual function through the other eye.

Thus the psychic faculty of vision is indeed located in the eye, in so far as

reasons, attempts to reconstruct a philosophic development by analysis of the preserved texts are largely doomed to arbitrary methods and uncertain results.

60. See the quotation from Rodier in n27 above. It is true that the passages connecting the sense faculty with a special organ, or with the body as a whole, are found above all in the *De An.*, whereas the *PN* tends to speak only of the central faculty in the heart. This, however, does not reflect a change of opinion on Aristotle's part, but only a change of subject. The *De An.* deals with the general definition of psychic faculties and with the theory of the special senses; the *PN* (except for the *De Sensu*) is concerned almost exclusively with the 'internal sense' – with memory, imagination, and generalised sensory awareness.

the latter is a functioning organ of a sentient animal.[61] But it is certainly not located in the eye in the sense that one could see with the eye alone, in independence from the sensory apparatus of which it is a part. Such a view can never have been held by Aristotle, nor, I suspect, by anyone else.

Having concluded this survey of Aristotle's conception of the sensory soul, we may now attempt to correlate it more closely with the modern notion of consciousness. There is of course no direct correspondence between the use of the term 'consciousness' in the modern tradition and the use of *psuchê* or 'soul' by Aristotle. The modern predilection for 'consciousness' is perhaps due precisely to the fact that it does not necessarily suggest anything so substantial as a soul. And although the soul is not for Aristotle, as it is for Descartes, a *separate* substance in its own right, it is nevertheless an active causal principle with enough substantial character to be responsible for the unity of the living compound which it forms together with the body. On the other hand, there are passages in Greek where the philosophic usage of *psuchê* would seem to correspond more closely to that of the modern term 'mind', for example, in the epistemological sections of the *Theaetetus*, where most translators, from Jowett to Cornford, do actually make use of 'mind' as the English equivalent. But in view of the importance of the distinction between *psuchê* and *nous* in Greek, this rendering of *psuchê* by 'mind' can only lead to confusion. We are therefore obliged to remain with the old-fashioned term 'soul', as we have done here throughout.

71   On the other hand, the Greek of Aristotle's day has no term which really corresponds to the modern usage of 'consciousness', for the process or condition of awareness as such. Neither the word *suneidêsis*, on which Latin *conscientia* was modelled (and which serves today to translate many of the derivatives of *conscientia* into modern Greek), nor the parallel formation *sunaisthêsis* was in use in this sense in Aristotle's time. A fifth-century medical author describing the loss and return of consciousness in epilepsy resorts to a number of different terms, all of which have for Aristotle too

---

61. Would it be possible to give a concrete physiological sense to this notion of a psychic power present in the eye, and capable of local damage? In the 1966 version of this study I wrote: 'Apparently not, if it is true that severing the optic nerve produces no physiological change in the eye itself. In that case the sensory "power" which is lost by the eye is simply the capacity to transmit impulses to the brain (for Aristotle, to the heart).' Since then I have learned from discussions with a neurophysiologist that the matter is not so simple, and that it should be possible to construct a much more sophisticated physiological interpretation of the sensitive *psuchê* than I have suggested here. For one thing, it is not true that severing the optic nerve produces no change in the eye. In mammals, for example, the ganglion cells in the retina (i.e. the neurons whose axons go to the brain) will slowly atrophy and die if their connection with the brain is cut. Even more significant, perhaps, is the extent to which the processing of visual stimuli begins with the external receptors. What is transmitted to the brain is of course not a little picture, but a diversified set of discriminations, the result of a many-levelled process of transformation and synthesis of stimuli, the first levels of which take place in the retina itself. It seems that the complexity of this process is just beginning to be understood. (Note added in 1973.)

special, and too specifically intellectual, a sense to convey the same idea.[62] Curiously enough, it is the term for sense perception – *aisthêsis* – which comes closest to providing a parallel to the modern notion of consciousness in Aristotle's language. Our survey of his theory of the sense faculty has thus been, in part, an account of the Aristotelian concept of consciousness. But we must note some major discrepancies between the ancient and the modern notions.

1. In the first place, the modern usage of 'consciousness' is dominated by the need for a term to specify the peculiar quality of mental, as opposed to bodily or physical existence, in the spirit of the Cartesian distinction. Thus Descartes himself, in restating his view against Hobbes' objections, emphasised the differences between corporeal and 'cogitative' activities: the latter include 'understanding, willing, imagining, feeling (or sensing, *sentire*), etc., which agree in falling under the common principle of thought, perception, or consciousness (*conscientia*)'.[63] For Descartes, the term 'thought' served as the most general expression for the common property of all mental acts as such; other authors, like Mill, preferred 'feeling'. In contemporary usage, however, 'consciousness' or 'states of consciousness' has prevailed as the most common response to the need which William James expressed for 'a term to cover sensation and thought indifferently', to refer to 'mental states at large, irrespective of their kind'.[64]

72

Now it is a fact that *aisthêsis* (with its verb *aisthanesthai*) can indeed cover the whole range of meaning of thought, feeling, and perception, including the affective feelings of pleasure, pain, desire, and the like.[65] Aristotle's usage tends to be more precise, but he never really breaks with this wider meaning of the term in non-technical Greek. Thus, although (and particularly in the *De Anima*) he tends to restrict *aisthêsis* to objective perception via the external senses, and avoids using the term for 'subjective'

62. See the treatise *On the Sacred Disease*, chapters 10-20 (I cite from the Loeb ed. of Hippocrates, Vol. 2, by W.H.S. Jones). The author's most common expression for 'consciousness' is *phronêsis, phronêma, phronein* (cf. *ephronêsan*, p.162, 54; *kataphronêsêi*, p.176, 30); Jones' rendering 'intelligence' is too narrow. But the author also uses *sunesis, gnômê,* and *diagnôsis* in closely related senses (chs. 19-20). It is characteristic, on the other hand, that he can use *aisthanetai* for the effects of a wind as felt by *inanimate* objects (p.172, 24 and 29). It would seem that the Ionic writers of the fifth century had developed no fixed psychological vocabulary. It is hard to estimate the role of Democritus, but on the whole it seems that the terminology of Plato and Aristotle is an Attic invention – perhaps very largely the work of Plato himself.

63. *Third Objections*, reply to objection two; translation adapted from Haldane and Ross. Descartes actually wrote: '(actus cogitativi) qui omnes sub ratione communi cogitationis, sive perceptionis, sive conscientiae, conveniunt.' The French of Clerselier has 'tours lesquels conviennent entr'eux en ce qu'ils ne peuvent estre sans pensée, ou perception, ou conscience et connoissance'.

64. William James, *The Principles of Psychology* (Dover paperback, 1950), I, p.185 ff.

65. See, e.g., Plato, *Theaetetus* 156B where *aisthêsis* is used to include pleasure and pain, desire and fear. For an example of the term in the *most* general sense, as equivalent to 'consciousness' or 'awareness', see *Apology* 40C: death may be the total absence of *aisthêsis*, like a sleep in which one has no dreams. In Modern Greek to lose consciousness is literally 'to lose one's senses', *chanô tas aisthêseis*.

experience such as pleasure and pain,[66] he everywhere insists upon the close and necessary link between *aisthêsis* on the one hand, and pleasure, pain and desire on the other.[67] Furthermore, by introducing the aporias on reflective awareness in *De Anima* III 2 and by finally including phantasy and memory within the sphere of the sense faculty, Aristotle has in effect re-established contact between his concept of *aisthêsis* and the general range of thought, feeling and emotion designated by the term in normal usage. The only absolute restriction lies in the Aristotelian (and Platonic) antithesis between the two faculties of discernment: sense and intellect.[68] But since, in its concrete operations, the human intellect for Aristotle requires at every step an internal image or phantasm provided by the faculty of sense, this restriction is not as sweeping in fact as it might appear in principle.

The use of the term *aisthêsis* or *aisthanesthai* does not permit one to distinguish in Greek between the cognitive or objective aspect of sensation, on the one hand – receiving information concerning the outside world – and the subjective or affective aspect of felt awareness, where sensation merges with other 'raw feels' such as pleasure, desire, impatience, and the like. In this ambiguity the Greek usage is parallel to that of our own verbs 'sensing' and 'perceiving'. Language seems to be spontaneously *objective*; to specify the subjective moment the philosopher must introduce a terminology of his own.[69] The most natural device is to 'objectify' the subjective aspect of awareness by casting the perception into reflexive form. Thus Aristotle speaks of our perceiving that we are seeing and hearing, just as Locke describes consciousness in reflexive terms as the perception of 'what passes in a man's own mind'. The importance of this reflexive stance in modern introspective philosophy can scarcely be exaggerated; and, as Ross has noted, Aristotle's treatment of the question contains 'one of the earliest

66. For an exception to this restriction, see *PA* 666a12: 'the motions of pleasure and pain, and in general of all *aisthêsis*, begin and end in the heart.' So *De An.* 431a10 refers pleasure and pain to the activity of the *aisthêtikê mesotês*.

67. *De An.* 413b23, 414b4-6, 434a1-3; *PN* 454b29-31, etc.

68. In contrast, Thucydides could use the verb *aisthanomai* for *intellectual* discernment: *aisthanomenos te têi hêlikiâi kai prosechôn tên gnômên.*

69. Thus in post-classical (as in Modern) Greek, the subjective element in *aisthêsis* is emphasised by the prefix *sun-*: *sunaisthêsis* (cf. *suneidêsis, conscientia*). It is *sunaisthêsis* which perhaps comes closest to meaning 'consciousness' in a late author like Plotinus. For the relevant ancient theories see H. Siebeck, 'Der Begriff des Bewusstseyns in der alten Philosophie', *Zeitschrift für Philosophie und philos. Kritik* 80 (1882), p.213. For the history of the terminology see G. Jung, '*Suneidêsis, conscientia*, Bewusstsein', *Archiv für die gesamte Psychologie* 89 (1933), p.528. Aristotle once makes use of the term *sunaisthêsis*, in *Eudemian Ethics* 1245b24, but certainly not in the later sense. The meaning is simply 'shared perception, perception together with others', as the use of *suzên* in the immediate context shows. Similarly for *sunaisthanesthai* in the same context. At *EN* 1170b4 and b10, however, the sense of the verb is 'to perceive at the same time', and it may be (as Gauthier and Jolif suggest in their commentary) that this use for 'simultaneous perception' prefigures the later sense of 'apperception, consciousness'.

For some links between Aristotelian *koinê aisthêsis* and doctrines of consciousness in later antiquity, see A.C. Lloyd, 'Nosce Teipsum and Conscientia', *Archiv für Geschichte der Philosophie* 46 (1964), pp.188-200.

discussions, in any author, of the difficulties involved in self-consciousness'.[70] But it is characteristic of Aristotle that he should raise the question of *self*-awareness (in the aporia, 'by what faculty do we perceive that we are having sensations?') simply in order to focus attention upon the primary fact of awareness as such, and that this notion of direct awareness is given a firm conceptual basis by its connection with the overt zoological phenomenon of sleep. It is clearly this notion of a 'subjective', but not necessarily reflexive awareness which Aristotle has in mind when he speaks of 'the common power accompanying all the senses, in virtue of which we perceive that we are seeing and hearing' (*Som.* 455a15). This common power is for Aristotle that of 'perception proper', *kuria aisthêsis* (*ibid.* 456a6), the one, central activity of sense without which the special senses cannot do their work. The empirical link which Aristotle establishes between this notion and the phenomena of Sleep and Waking provides us with a kind of operational definition for his concept of consciousness. 'Perception proper' is neither more nor less than the normal consciousness of waking life, the faculty which is somehow incapacitated when we fall 'unconscious' in sleep or syncope (455b2-8; 456b9ff.).   **74**

2. This general faculty of awareness is definitely located in the common sensorium, that is (for Aristotle) in the heart or, in lower animals, in the corresponding part.[71] It is interesting to speculate as to how far Aristotle would envisage 'consciousness' in very simple animals, which have no distinct organ corresponding to heart or brain. If he had known of one-celled animals, for example, and had been willing to grant them a share in 'perception proper' (as he would in principle have been obliged to do, since the possession of a sense faculty is included in his definition of an animal), he would presumably have situated this capacity in the only known control centre for cellular activity, in the nucleus. Of course we cannot properly commit Aristotle to a judgment on factual matters with which he was entirely unfamiliar. It is, after all, conceivable (though very unlikely) that an acquaintance with microscopic animals would have led him to revise his definition of animal, or to make some exception for the more primitive varieties. But if we assume that Aristotle would have accepted the amoeba as a true animal according to his own definition, he would then inevitably have assigned to it a 'sensory soul' operating from the nucleus (as from the heart – or rather brain – in higher animals), and would have recognised in its adaptive responses to external stimuli the operation of a faculty comparable in type to human consciousness, though obviously very different in degree of complexity.

There is, however, one other possibility which would not carry Aristotle quite so far along the road to 'panpsychism'. Waking consciousness is, for Aristotle, the opposite of sleep, and he maintains that 'any creature which is awake can go to sleep, for it is impossible <for the power of sense> to be always actualised'.[72] If it were demonstrated that the simpler forms of animal *never go to sleep*, Aristotle must consistently conclude that they are *not*   **75**

70. Ross [8], p.35.
71. *Iuv.* 469b6; *PA* 647a31.
72. *Som.* 454b8.

awake, that is, not 'conscious' in the sense he has defined. Their apparent sensory activities would then fall in – or near – the same category as the purely vegetative responses of plants to their environment. On this view perception proper, accompanied by consciousness, would occur only in the higher, not in the lower forms of animal life. This solution might claim to be Aristotelian in principle, although it goes against his express conviction as to the facts. For Aristotle definitely believes that all animals *do* go to sleep, although he admits that this has not been proved.[73]

3. As we have seen above, the sensory soul is thought of as informing the entire sense apparatus, or as Aristotle puts it, 'the entire body in so far as it is sensitive'; i.e. it does not inform hair or finger nails at all, and it informs the eye differently from the skin. At the same time, this psychic faculty is clearly centred in the heart (or, we would say, in the brain); and this fact of the *centring* of the soul is normally expressed by the characteristically Aristotelian term *archê* (*tês aisthêseôs, tês aisthêtikês psuchês*): it is the 'source' or 'principle' of sensation which is located in the heart.[74] Sensation proper occurs only when the stimulus reaches this centre; and unless it does so, the eye cannot see nor the ear hear.[75]

In one respect, Aristotle's localisation of the sensory soul is not very different from Descartes'. Both philosophers connect the soul with the body as a whole; and both recognise its special relationship to a central organ. Thus Descartes remarks that the soul is joined to the whole body in such a way that it cannot be said to be 'in one bodily part to the exclusion of the others'; yet it has its principal seat in the middle of the brain, which is the only 'part of the body in which the soul exercises its functions immediately'.[76] This agreement between Aristotle and Descartes is largely due to their common desire to explain the physiological facts. But their positions diverge sharply when it comes to *defining* the soul and its mode of interaction with the body. For Aristotle there can be nothing mysterious about the soul's capacity to perceive through the eyes, since the soul, as a sensory faculty, is nothing more nor less than the natural realisation of this entire physiological apparatus. For Descartes, who has defined body and soul as entities which should in principle have nothing in common, the union of a conscious perception with a particular extended mechanism can only be conceived as a miracle of divine providence. The great difference in

76

---

73. *Som.* 454b14-27.

74. *PN* 456a5, 461a6, 469a5, etc. It is because of this that Aristotle can sometimes speak as if the soul as a whole were located in the heart (*MA* 703a3, a37), in the region of the heart and lungs (*De An.* 420b28), or, more vaguely, 'within' the body. So *Sens.* 438b10; recent editors notwithstanding, I believe Alexander was correct in referring this to the soul in the heart, not in the eye, since otherwise the following reference to a temple wound would be irrelevant. Similarly in *Mem.* 450a28-9: 'memory takes place in the soul and in the part of the body which possesses it' (the context shows this is the heart). And does Aristotle ever speak of the soul – as opposed to the faculty of vision – as resident in the eye? It must also be the location of the *archê* that he has in mind when he speaks of sensation as reaching *to the soul* through the body (*De An.* 408b16; *Sens.* 436b6).

75. *PN* 467b28-9; cf. 455a33, 455b11, 461a30 ff., 469a12.

76. Descartes, *Les Passions de l'âme*, art. 30-2.

Aristotle's view is the total lack of the Cartesian sense of a radical and necessary incompatibility between 'thought' or awareness, on the one hand, and physical extension, on the other. The soul is defined for Aristotle not by those properties in which no body can share, but precisely by those capacities which only a body can provide.[77] A philosopher who believes, as Descartes does, that the soul is of such a nature as to have 'no relationship to extension, nor to the dimensions or other properties of the matter of which the body is composed',[78] can scarcely feel at home with the Aristotelian view that the psychic faculty of sight is *in* the eye as the general sense faculty is in the body as a sensitive whole.

It is a more delicate question whether, for Aristotle, the specific activity of waking consciousness or 'perception proper' is as widely distributed throughout the body as is the sensitive soul itself. Aristotle's statements on this point are not unambiguous. They leave no doubt that the source and principle of such consciousness is located in the central organ, but they do not exclude the possibility that, at the moment of actual sensation, the felt awareness is thought of as stretching inwardly, as it were, from the heart to the part or organ directly concerned. In fact this seems to follow directly from Aristotle's conception of the life activities, including sensation, as the 'second entelechy' of the body, the final actualisation of the first entelechy or soul (*De An.* 412a19-28, b27-413a 1). Thus waking consciousness, as the full and proper activity of the sense capacity, will be located in the same **77** place as the power itself, that is, in the whole body in so far as it is sensitive. A conscious act of vision, for example, would thus be located simultaneously in the heart and in the eye, though it is *primarily* located in the heart. This view is not to be found in Aristotle in express terms, but it is pretty clearly implied by the principles he lays down.[79] It is, perhaps, essentially the view of common sense as instructed by a rudimentary knowledge of the anatomy of sensation. In any case, in so far as Aristotle's view implies a primary localisation of the act of awareness in the central organ, it presents a striking analogy to some contemporary theories of the identity between states of consciousness and neuro-physiological activity. But whereas most modern theories of identity tend to reduce the psychological aspect to the physiological, Aristotle would regard the bodily processes in sensation

77. This is, strictly speaking, true only for the nutritive and sensory soul. The intellect as such constitutes a special case, which Aristotle recognises as falling outside the general definition of the soul as *entelecheia* of the body. The intellect can certainly not be defined by reference to a condition from which it is separable without loss. See *De An.* 413a3-7, b24-7; cf. *PA* 641a17-b10.

78. *Les Passions de l'âme*, art. 30.

79. Thus *De An.* 426a9-11 says simply that 'actual sensation' is located 'in that which is capable of sensation' (*en tôi aisthêtikôi*). But the sense capacity itself is located in the body *qua* sensitive. The localisation must be thought of as functional: it does not of course imply that either the sensory *psuché* or perception itself is a physical entity or structure with a concrete position in the body. See n. 61 above.

Professor Randall suggests to me another solution: the sense activities should be located not in the organs but 'in the sensible world, i.e. in the whole situation'. This view is attractive in itself, but seems to conflict with Aristotle's general doctrine that processes of activity-passivity are localised *in the patient*, in this case in the sentient animal. (See Hicks' commentary on *De An.* 426a2.)

simply as the immediate instrument or 'matter', whose form and final completion (*entelecheia*) is provided by the act of perceptive awareness.

4. The final and perhaps the most fundamental contrast between Aristotle's view and the modern notion of consciousness is that, for Aristotle, the act of awareness or 'perception proper' is neither identical with thinking in the strict sense, nor does it include rational thought as one of its varieties. In the traditional usage, as represented by John Stuart Mill, 'feeling' and 'state of consciousness' are equivalent expressions for 'a genus, of which Sensation, Emotion, and Thought are subordinate species'.[80] The intellectual act for Aristotle, however, is the work of a distinct faculty of the soul, and the most distinct of all, since it is the only faculty which may ultimately be separated from the body. In its concrete operation within the human organism, this faculty is of course married to the rest of the soul by its intimate dependence upon the images provided by the faculty of sense and imagination: 'the rational faculty thinks the forms *in the images*' (*De Anima* 431b2). But if the gaze of the intellect is directed towards the images of sense and imagination, can the sense faculty in turn observe the discursive act of reasoning? More precisely, is the reflexive act by which we are aware of our own thinking an act of rational thought or an act of sense?

There is, as far as I can see, only one passage in Aristotle which bears directly on this point, and it seems to decide the matter in favour of sense.

> The man who is seeing perceives that he is seeing and the one who is hearing (perceives) that he is hearing, and the one who walks (perceives) that he walks, and similarly for other activities *there is something which perceives that we are acting*, so that if we are perceiving (it perceives) that we are perceiving, and *if we are thinking (it perceives) that we are thinking*. But (to perceive) that we are perceiving or thinking is (to perceive) that we exist – for our life and being (as men) has been defined as perceiving or thinking; and to perceive that one is alive is a thing which is intrinsically pleasant.[81]

This passage in the *Nicomachean Ethics* would be decisive, except for the fact that the second of the two statements italicised above reflects not the traditional text of Aristotle but an emendation proposed by Bywater in 1890. The older text is more ambiguous, and seems to hesitate between the first assertion, that there is a faculty which *perceives all our actions*, including our life and existence as thinking, sentient beings (and this can only be the central faculty of sense, the 'common power' defined in the *De Somno*), and a second statement that 'we perceive that we perceive, *and think that we think*'.[82]

---

80. J.S. Mill, *A System of Logic*, Bk. I, ch. iii, § 3. Compare Descartes' parallel grouping of 'understanding, willing, imagining, feeling, etc.' under the head of 'thought' (above, p.23).

81. *EN* 1170a29-b1. The words in parenthesis are elliptically omitted in the Greek.

82. *EN* 1170a31-2, Bekker: *hôste aisthanoimeth' an hoti aisthanometha kai nooimen hoti nooumen*; Bywater: *hôste an aisthanômeth', hoti aisthanometha, k'an noômen, hoti nooumen*. I believe Bywater's emendation to be certainly correct. It not only improves the logic of the passage but renders the expression more trenchant and more characteristically Aristotelian; the same clause in Bekker's text is almost absurdly redundant. The

Now there is a passage in the *Metaphysics* which seems also to assert that **79** 'knowledge and perception and opinion and thought (*dianoia*)' are all primarily directed to something else as their object, but may refer secondarily to themselves.[83] From this it has been inferred that 'Aristotle does not assign all self-consciousness to a single central faculty. Knowledge, perception, opinion, and reason, while primarily engaged with objects other than themselves, are described as each *en passant* apprehending itself'.[84] But this interpretation transforms into a fixed doctrine concerning human faculties what appears in its context only as a dialectical, aporetic discussion of the problem of self-intellection *in the case of the divine mind*. The only conclusion concerning the human soul which seems to be justified by the passage from the *Metaphysics* is that a man does not exercise self-cognisance in the same fashion as deity. It is obviously true that we can have knowledge about knowledge, and thought about thinking;[85] but this has nothing to do with the immediate act of self-awareness discussed in the passage quoted previously from the *Nicomachean Ethics*. Whenever such direct self-consciousness is described *in the case of a human being*, it seems to be assigned to the faculty which characterises man as an animal, i.e. as a **80** sentient being.[86] Only in the case of deity does Aristotle speak of *noêsis noêseôs*, an immediate reflex grasping of the intellect by itself. This is an uninterrupted exercise of pure activity. But the intermittent act of human

---

emendation was accepted by Stewart, by Ross, and by most modern editors and translators. As Gauthier and Jolif remark 'everywhere in the context the activity of consciousness is designated by the word *perceive*, and the connexion with the next line presupposes that it is the same here' (*l'Éthique à Nicomaque*, II 758). Bywater himself noted that, 'in default of a better word … throughout this section the word *aisthanesthai* has, in addition to its ordinary meaning, a more general sense corresponding to our modern term "consciousness" '; *Contributions to the Textual Criticism of Aristotle's Nicomachean Ethics* (Oxford 1892), p.65.

The text of Bekker has, however, made an unexpected reappearance in the German translation of Franz Dirlmeier (1960), who declares Bywater's emendation unnecessary without any discussion of the problems involved. (His reference to Joachim proves nothing to the point, since Joachim apparently accepted Bywater's text.)

83. *Meta.* 1074b35: 'Knowledge, perception, opinion, and thought seem always to have something other than themselves as object, and themselves only by the way.'

84. Ross [8], p.35 (=[16], 5th edition, p.141). Ross seems to be following Beare [55], p.290. But whereas Beare accepted the old text of *EN* 1170a32 ('we *think* we are thinking'), Ross renders Bywater's text in his own translation of the *Ethics* ('we *perceive* we are thinking'). His notion of the self-consciousness of reason is thus apparently based only on *Meta.* 1074b35. Note that in this passage Aristotle does not use the proper term for the rational faculty (*nous*) but the vaguer expression for 'thinking', *dianoia* (see text in preceding note).

85. Ross' example (in his commentary to *Metaphysics* 1074b36) is apt: 'The medical man knows primarily about health, and secondly that his knowledge is knowledge about health.'

86. Besides the passage from the *EN*, see *Sens.* 448a26-30: when one is perceiving oneself or anything else, it is impossible to be unaware of one's own existence at the same time. (The whole context shows that such self-awareness is thought of as the work of the sense faculty; and this point is made explicit in Alexander's commentary *ad loc.*, ed. Thurot, pp.309ff.)

self-awareness, regularly interrupted by sleep, appears to be the function of the sense faculty – as it is the same faculty which is responsible for the secondary activity of the 'subconscious' in dreaming.

If this interpretation is sound, there is for Aristotle an important distinction, which the traditional concept of consciousness tends to ignore, between the intellectual activity as such and our personal awareness of it.[87] In Aristotle's view, our personal consciousness as men belongs essentially to our sentient, animal nature; so that whereas sensation and the awareness of sensation are simultaneous (and really identical) acts of the same faculty, reasoning and the awareness of reasoning belong properly to different faculties, and the two acts coincide only in so far as the faculties of sense and intellect are concretely united in the *psuchê* of a particular man. This point is of relatively little importance for the theory of sensation, but of very great importance for the doctrine of the 'separate intellect'.

Postscript

Professor Roy Finch has called my attention to the fact that the distinction made above between the sensory self-awareness of man as an animal and the noetic self-awareness of the divine mind might suggest a parallel with Husserl's distinction between natural and transcendental reflections.[88] Although the phenomenological theory of consciousness falls outside the **81** limits of the 'traditional' view assumed here for purposes of reference, on this point the contrast between Husserl and Aristotle is so instructive that it may be worth dwelling for a moment on the apparent parallel. In the first place, Aristotle would probably have recognised in the transcendental ego of the phenomenological reduction (as in all modern theories of consciousness) an illegitimate fusion of what are for him two distinct powers of awareness: the sense faculty we share with animals and the intellectual apprehension we share with God or gods. If, for the sake of the comparison, we accept this distinction and understand Husserl's transcendental reflection to be an act of the intellect alone, the question remains whether Aristotle would have granted to human beings a share in what is the characteristic act of deity, the self-apprehension of *noêsis*. There is perhaps no explicit statement to this effect in the texts, but it might be argued that so much is implied by Aristotle's suggestion that as we are in our best moments, so is deity always.[89] Let us assume then that there is some self-

---

Compare Aristotle's remarks concerning the memory of intellectual objects (*ta noêta*): it belongs *per se* to the primary sense faculty, and only incidentally to the intellect (*Mem.* 450a13-14). The knowledge or apprehension of such objects belongs properly to *nous*; but the memory of this knowledge as realised in an earlier, momentary act, like the concomitant awareness of the act and like the mental image which provided its occasion – all this is a function of the sense faculty of the individual, mortal soul.

87. This distinction is made explicitly by Plotinus, and plays an important role in his psychology. See *Enneads*, I.1. 11; I. 4. 10.

88. See e.g., *Cartesianische Meditationen, Husserliana* I (The Hague, 1950), pp.72ff.

89. See *Meta.* XII 7, 1072b25, 1075a7-10; *EN* 1177b26ff.; *De An.* 430a2 with Hicks' note.

awareness which belongs to the purely intellectual principle of the human intellect (i.e. to the active intellect), and which may be compared to the realm of transcendental self-experience in Husserl. On this assumption, the phenomenological reduction might be described from Aristotle's point of view as a methodical technique for 'separating' the separate intellect and establishing it in a condition of pure self-knowledge comparable to that of the divine mind. But whereas for Husserl the transcendental experience of the ego so purified preserves all normal human experience (including memory and sense perception) as part of its objective content, the corresponding 'reduction' of the Aristotelian intellect would be best represented by the actual separation at death, and would entail a complete break with all human experience, including all memory thereof (*De An.* 430a22-5). Since the Aristotelian faculties are defined by reference to their objects, it is only the *sensory* faculty of the soul which can perceive sense objects and can preserve the memory of such perception. But it is precisely from this perishable faculty that the intellect may be separated.

This result may serve as a kind of *reductio ad absurdum* of our original comparison, and an indirect proof of incommensurability between the Aristotelian view and most, if not all, modern theories of consciousness. It is Aristotle's fundamental distinction between noetic and sensory awareness which here makes all the difference.

2

Jonathan Barnes

Aristotle's Concept of Mind

1.

101 What is the nature of Aristotle's mental philosophy? Did he, as some think, transcend Democritus to adumbrate a modern and sophisticated physicalism? Or did he rather remain in Plato's camp, elaborating a fresh and subtler dualism? The current orthodoxy relies on syncretism and psychogenetics: first, physicalism and dualism are both countenanced – for while most mental features are dissolved into body, the Aristotelian intellect (or perhaps only the 'creative' intellect) stands out anomalously as an independent immaterial substance. Then it is explained that the youthful Aristotle, drunk on Plato, saw ghostly doubles for all psychic things; and that as he grew older these hallucinations diminished in extent but never entirely disappeared.

Such a story is not wholly satisfying: its psychogenetic component, unconvincing in itself, ignores the fact that the *De Anima* and the *Parva Naturalia*, whatever their origins, are presented to us as a more or less continuous and connected course in psychology;[1] and the terms of its syncretism are vague, indeterminate, and inadequate.

2.

The physicalist interpretation of Aristotle's psychology is founded on the general account of *psuchê* at the beginning of *De Anima* II. Many scholars call
102 a halt here: for, they say, it is characteristic of Aristotle's psychology that souls form an ordered series (*ephexês*: 414b29) – vegetative, perceptive, intellectual (404b5-6; 410b15-411a2; 413a26-b10) – and it is a familiar feature of his logic that there can be no general account of terms falling into an ordered series (see *Meta.* 999a6-7; *EN* 1096a19-35; *EE* 1218a1-8; *Pol.* 1275a34-8). Thus Aristotle has no room for any general account of soul; and indeed in II 3 he roundly asserts that 'it is ridiculous to seek a common formula' for all types of soul (414b25: cf. 402b3-9).

This argument is common but erroneous. First, Aristotle does not condemn the search for a common formula for soul; rather, 'it is ridiculous to seek *the* common formula ... while neglecting the formula' *proper to each particular type of soul*. Secondly, soul is compared to *schêma* (shape; 414b20)

---

1. Jaeger's genetic hypotheses ([28], pp.332-4) were supplanted by the more elaborate proposals of Nuyens ([30]; cf. Ross [7], pp. 3-18); Nuyens has been refuted by Block [60] and by Hardie [61] (see also Owen, Vol.1, pp. 15-19). On the value of psychogenetics in this context see esp. Kahn, above, p.20, n.59, p.4, n.12 (cf. Block [60], pp. 76-7).

which is explicitly stated to be amenable to a general account (414b23). Thirdly, Aristotle's strictures on ordered series have an ontological and not a semantic sense: he denies that when A's form an ordered series $<a_1, a_2, \ldots, a_n>$ there exists an A over and above the a_i's; he does not deny that the term 'A' is susceptible to definition.[2] Thus the general account of soul in *De Anima* II 1-2 may be taken seriously.

The argument that justifies that account is, alas, obscure, jargon-ridden, and textually corrupt; and in any event it is almost certainly unsound (412a16-19: cf. 414a14-19). Its conclusion is this: 'if, then, we must say something common for every soul, it will be the first actuality of an organic natural body' (412b4-6). I take this to amount to:

(D1) x has a soul $= df\, x$ is a living organic natural body.

After some discussion, the next chapter opens with a caution that 'the definitory formula must not only show the fact … but the explanation too must inhere in it and shine through' (413a13-16). A second argument then leads to a second general account: 'the soul is a principle of the aforesaid things, i.e., it is defined by these – nutritive, perceptive, intellectual, motion' (413b11-13). I take this to amount to:

(D2) x has a soul $= df\, x$ can nourish itself OR x can perceive OR
x can think OR x can move itself.

103

Since the features disjoined on the right of this equation are precisely those in virtue of which a natural body is called living (413a22-5), (D2) in a sense provides an 'explanation' of the 'fact' laid down in (D1).

The crucial characteristic of both these definitions is that they construe the soul not as a substance (like, say, the heart or the brain) but as an attribute (like, say, life or health). Neither (D1) nor (D2) gives or implies any definition of the term 'soul' or the predicate ' … is a soul': the *definiendum* is ' … has a soul'; and, as each *definiens* makes clear, this one-place predicate is not analysable into a two-place predicate ' … has –' and a substance term 'soul', as ' … has a brain' might be analysed into ' … has –' and 'brain'. If 'an animal is made from soul and body' (*Pol.* 1277a6), it is not as a motor-car is made from engine and coachwork, but rather as a motor-car with its engine running is 'made from' the running and the works.

This feature of Aristotle's account of soul comes out in various ways in the *De Anima*: it is implicit in the close connexion which, in orthodox Greek fashion, Aristotle observes between soul and life (e.g. 402a6, 411a16, 413a21); it is reflected in Aristotle's frequent and unapologetic use of the terms *empsuchos* ('ensouled') and *apsuchos* ('soulless') (e.g. 403b25, 404b7, 413a21), and again in the terms – 'straight' (403a13), 'white' (405b18), 'sight' (412b19), 'art' (407b23: cf. *PA* 652b14) – which, in various contexts, Aristotle parallels to 'soul'; and it is prepared for in that celebrated Rylean

2. On all this see Cook Wilson, *Classical Review* 1904. The correct view of the 'common formula' for *psuchê* is clearly expressed by Philoponus (*In De An.* CIAG XV 257.7-12); see also Innes, *Classical Review* 1902.

passage where we are urged 'to say not that the soul pities or learns or thinks, but that the man does with his soul' (408b13-15).[3]

3.

The general account of soul is non-substantialist; this is often supposed to commit Aristotle to some sort of physicalism: in fact non-substantialism entails neither physicalism nor non-physicalism. The soul may be taken for (i) a physical substance, (ii) a non-physical substance, (iii) physical and non-substantial, or (iv) non-physical and non-substantial. *De Anima* II 1-2 commits Aristotle to the rejection of (i) and (ii); but he is still at liberty to choose between (iii) and (iv).

The language in which these issues are discussed is not always pellucid. Aristotle will sometimes approach physicalism by asking of some psychic function whether or not it is 'with body' or 'bodily' (*meta sômatos* or *sômatikon*) (e.g. 403a6,9,17, 407b4, 427a26, 433b19; *Mem.* 453a14; *MA* 702a3); more often he uses the language of separation, *chôrismos*. This term must be treated with care: '*X* is separate' is an incomplete expression, and its sense will depend upon the intended completion – 'separate *from Y*'. Talk about the separation of psychic elements is not always talk about the relation between soul and body.[4]

The expressions 'with body', 'bodily', 'inseparable from body' might, like the term 'physical', figure in more than one thesis. Let ψ be any mental, or psychological, predicate. (The term 'mental' has no contentious sense: all that matters is that mental predicates should include '... has a soul' and also any predicate contained in, or subsumable under those contained in, the right-hand side of (D2).) Let φ be any physical predicate. 'Physical' here is a technical term; a rough definition, sufficient for present purposes, is this: φ is physical if φ is definable in terms of the primitive predicates of physics (and, if necessary, of chemistry; and, if necessary, of biology).

We are familiar with two strong physicalisms, the characteristic schemata of which are:

(1) 'ψa' means 'φa'

and:

(2) $\psi = \varphi$.

Of these (1) covers Carnapian physicalism, and some varieties of behaviourism; (2) represents the 'Identity Theory' of Feigl, Smart, and others. To these schemata two others can be added:

---

3. 'with his soul' – *têi psuchêi* – i.e. 'by virtue of the fact that he has a soul'. cf. 402a10 (*di' ekeinên <tên psuchên>* – 'because of his soul'); 408b27 (*hêi ekeino* [sc. *tên psuchên*] *echei* – '*qua* having a soul').

4. The ends of II 1 (413a3-10) and of II 2 (413b14-414a3) are superficially parallel: both deal with the *chôrismos* of psychic parts. But in fact they discuss perfectly distinct topics: II 1, the separation of psychic parts *from body*; II 2, the separation of psychic parts *from one another*.

(3) 'ψa' means 'φa & P'

– where the content of P is left undetermined – and: **105**

(4) That ψa entails that φa.

These might, I suggest, be called schemata of weak physicalism. The difficult sentence at 403b17-19 probably means to distinguish (3) from (4).

At the end of II 1 Aristotle concludes: 'That the soul is not separable from the body ... is not unclear' (413a4-5). This states a type-(4) thesis with respect to '... has a soul'. It is plain that (D1) commits Aristotle to a type-(3) thesis, and hence to a type-(4) thesis.

4.

The sentence just quoted reads in full: 'That the soul is not separable from the body, or some parts of it (if it is partionable), is not unclear; (?) for they are the actuality of some of the parts <of the body> themselves (?). But nothing prevents *some* <psychic parts from being separable from the body>, though not being actualities of any body' (413a3-7). This has caused puzzlement: for how can the soul be inseparable from the body unless all its parts are? (The language of parts need not trouble us: *morion* ('part') is used interchangeably with *dunamis* ('faculty') and *archê* ('principle'), without any substantialist implications – cf. *Meta.* V 25; Bonitz, *Index* 864b60 ff.)

Aristotle appears to mean that:

(A) x has a soul $\rightarrow \varphi x$
is compatible with:
(B) $(\exists \psi) \sim (\psi x \rightarrow \varphi x)$.

But, on the assumption that all mental predicates are subsumable under those on the right-hand side of (D2), we have:

(C) $(\psi)(\psi x \rightarrow x$ has a soul).

And (A), (B) and (C) are incompatible.

The best solution to this difficulty is to emend (D2) to:

(D2') x has a soul $=_{df} x$ can nourish itself OR (x can nourish itself and x can perceive) OR (x can nourish itself and x can perceive and x can move itself) OR (x can nourish itself and x can perceive and x can move itself and x can think).

(D2') incorporates the hierarchical aspect of the psychic functions (see   **106** above, p.32), and it does not generate (C). Thus Aristotle may assert both (A) and (B).

To prosecute the physicalist question, then, we must consider the various psychic parts individually. This is no more than Aristotle announced at the beginning of the treatise: 'There is a problem about the affections of the soul, whether they are all common to what has a soul or there is one which is proper to soul itself; ... If there is one of the soul's functions or affections proper to it, it is possible for it to be separated; but if none is proper to it, it will not be separable' (403a3-11, omitting 5-10: cf. 408b25-9). To ask whether an affection is proper to the soul or common to soul and body (cf. 402a9, 433b20; *Sens.* 436a8, b2; *Som.* 453b12) has a misleadingly substantialist air to it; but Aristotle's point is clear enough: the issue of separability turns on the question whether any psychic part or faculty is separable from the body.

In the rest of this paper I shall look briefly at the question as it touches the emotions, perception, and intellect.

5.

'It seems likely that the affections of the soul are all with body – rage, tranquillity, fear, pity, boldness, again joy and both loving and hating ... And if this is so, it is clear that the affections are formulae in matter (*logoi en hulêi*;[5] 403a16-25, omitting 18-24). 'Affections', *pathê*, may be either properties or undergoings or emotions: I shall take the safest course and interpret them narrowly as emotions.

The reference to *logoi en hulêi* precipitates a question I have so far ducked. In the *De Anima* the terms 'matter' and 'form' regularly carry the contrast I am expressing by 'physical' and 'non-physical': the presence of *matter* in a psychic part is taken for the presence of a *physical* element in it.[6] This is not happy; for on the one hand it seems clear that a thing's form need not be non-physical; and on the other, its matter (as Aristotle's references to *hulê noêtê* – intelligible matter – show)[7] need not be physical. The truth is that the apparatus of matter and form was developed by Aristotle in order to solve certain puzzles about the nature of change; its success with those puzzles encouraged him to extend it to other fields and other puzzles, where as often as not it proves merely obfuscating. That, I think, is so in the *De Anima*.

However that may be, 403a16-25 requires that the definitions of the emotions include reference to (parts of) the body. The archetype of a *logos en hulêi* is the snub (e.g., *Meta.* 1025b30 ff., 1064a23; cf. 429b14): being snub is having a concave nose – and noses are of necessity physical. Similarly, raging, say, will be or contain some physical affection; 'so that the definitions are such as: being angry is a certain change in such-and-such a body or part or faculty by this for the sake of this' (403a25-7). How is the physical part of this schema to be filled in? We might think of some fairly neutral reference to 'anger-appropriate' states of the body; but Aristotle wishes to specify the state: part of the meaning of '*x* is angry', he implies, is 'the blood about *x*'s heart is boiling' (403a31; cf. *PA* 650b35 ff.; *Timaeus*

107

---

5. I read this rather than the OCT's *logoi enuloi*; the sense of Aristotle's remark is clear enough.

6. For a clear example see 403b11: 'The natural scientist is concerned with all the functions and affections of such and such a body (*sômatos*) and of such and such a matter (*hulês*)'. See also Kirwan *Aristotle's Metaphysics*, Books Gamma, Delta, Epsilon (Oxford, 1971), p.125.

7. See esp. *Meta.* 1036a9, 1045a34; cf. Bonitz, *Index* 787a12-22; Ross [4] I, pp. 199-200.

70B); and elsewhere '*x* is afraid' is taken to imply 'the blood about *x*'s heart is cold' (*PA* 692a20-4; *Rhet.* 1389b32).[8]

6.

The beginning of the *De Sensu* reduces the inseparability of a large number of psychic functions to the inseparability of perception; for these functions involve perception, and 'that perception comes about for the soul through body is clear both through argument and apart from argument' (436b6; cf. 429b5; *Som.* 454a9; *Phys.* 244b11).

The argument is in *De Anima* II 1: the statement of 413a7 that some psychic functions are actualities of bodily parts (above, p.35) is illustrated a few lines earlier: 'for if the eye were a living creature, sight would be its soul; for this is the essence ... of eye' (412b18-20). As having a soul is having a living body, so to have sight is to have an actual, i.e. functioning, eye. (It does not, of course, follow that *only* the eye is implicated in sight.) Similar accounts are available for the four other senses.

108

These remarks on the five senses do not yield a weakly physicalist account of perception as such, for they do not exclude the possibility of some non-physicalist mode of sensation apart from our five senses. The further step is presented in the *De Anima* as a sort of analogical generalisation: 'for as the part is related to the part <e.g. sight to eye> so perception as a whole is related to the perceptive body *qua* perceptive' (412b23-5). A different argument is suggested by the view that there is·a central organ of perception, the heart (e.g. *Som.* 455a20; *Iuv.* 467b28, 469a12): as sight is to the eye, so, it might seem, perception in general is to the heart. Finally, it is worth recalling that, according to *De Anima* III 1, the five senses exhaust the possibilities of perception: if that is so, and if each individual sense is physicalist, then perception as such will be weakly physicalist.

7.

Thus Aristotle offers weakly physicalist accounts both of the emotions and of perception: can we go further and ascribe a strong physicalism to him?

The emotions are certainly supposed to have irreducibly non-physical elements; for that is the sense of saying that they are compounded of matter and form (above p.36). If *ψ* is an emotional predicate, defined by '*φx* & *P*', then *P* is not identical with any *φy*. In the illustrative case of anger, *P* appears to be '*x* desires revenge' (403b30). The implication that desire, *orexis*, is non-physical, occurs in a different context at 433b19; but it is denied at *De Sensu*, 436a9 (cf. 433b29 ∼ 403a8-10).

Perception is more problematic. According to Aristotle, perceiving (or rather, coming to perceive) is an 'alteration', *alloiôsis* (e.g., 410a25, 415b24, 416b33-5); moreover, it is an alteration of the *sense-organs* (422a7, b15,

8. The emotions are treated at length at *Rhet.* II 2-11 (cf. Fortenbaugh, below, ch. 8); but there the accounts seem to be 'dialectical' (403a29) – they make no overt reference to physical goings-on. The 'dialectical' definition of anger takes pain (*lupê*) to be a constituent (*Rhet.* 1378a30; *Top.* 151a15); and pain, according to *Sens.* 436a10-b2, being 'with perception' is 'with body'. This suggests a rather more subtle physicalist analysis of anger than that indicated in the *De Anima*; it is readily generalised to cover the other emotions.

109   423b30, 435a22; *Insom.* 459b6). Aristotle explains the alteration in terms of
the sense organ's becoming like what it comes to perceive (418a4, 422a7,
423b31), or of its 'receiving the form without the matter' (424a18, 425b23,
434a29). The position appears to be this: when I gaze at a glass of green
Chartreuse, my eyes, or some parts of them, become green – the perceptible
form of the Chartreuse – even though none of the physical parts of the
liqueur actually enters my eyes. To see something green just is for my eyes
to become green by the action of the green object; and so for other sense
objects and other senses. Thus we have a purely physiological, and hence
strongly physicalist, analysis of perception.[9]
    I doubt if this analysis was Aristotle's.
    First, it is, I think, worth observing that the argument it contains is not
obviously sound. From the fact that perceiving is an *alloiôsis* of a sense
organ, it does not follow that perceiving is a purely physiological change; it
is a mere assumption that all properties of physical objects must themselves
be physical.
    Secondly, the physiological account of perception is open to devastatingly
obvious attack on both empirical and logical grounds: when I see something
square, there is simply no part of my eye which becomes square; I may hear
things loud even though it is absurd to suppose that my ears might become
loud.
    Thirdly, Aristotle's repeated assertions that perception is common to
body and soul (*Sens.* 436b7; *Mem.* 450a27; *Som.* 454a7-11) at least suggest
that perceiving is not merely physiological.
    Fourthly, Aristotle faces the objection that his account of perception will
allow plants and inanimate objects to perceive (424a32-b18; cf. *Sens.*
438a5ff.). His reply is difficult; but it issues in the clear conclusion that
'smelling <e.g.> is something over and above <physical> undergoing'
(424b17).
    Fifthly, the physiological analysis relies on perfectly standard cases of
alloiôsis; yet Aristotle explicitly says that to perceive is to 'alter' and to
'undergo' only in *special* senses of *alloiousthai* and *paschein* (417b2-9; cf.
429b29-430a1). The special senses remain obscure. Perhaps 'receiving the
form without the matter' amounts to receiving the form but not standing to
it as matter. Thus if you inject green Chartreuse (or some other green dye)
into my eyeball, my eye becomes like the Chartreuse inasmuch as its matter
supports the same form as the Chartreuse; if you show me a green
Chartreuse, my eye becomes like it in a sense – but it does not support the
same form. I doubt if anything more positive than this can be elicited from
110   Aristotle's text; but the negative point, that perceiving is not a purely
physiological change, seems established.[10]

9. This view has been presented lucidly and persuasively by Slakey [68].
10. On all this see Brentano [66], pp. 79-98: '... nicht insofern wir kalt werden,
empfinden wir das Kalte ..., sondern insofern das Kalt objectiv, d.h. als Erkanntes in
uns existirt, also insofern wir die Kälte aufnehmen, ohne selber das physische Subjekt
derselber zu sein' (p.80; cf. pp.86, 120, n.23). Compare Philoponus, *op. cit.* 303.3-6:
'In the case of the senses too, when we say that they become what the sensed object is,
one must think not that the sight becomes white or black but that the senses receive in

8.

I now turn to the case of intellect or *nous*; it is hardly necessary to say that my discussion will trip nonchalantly over ground wired and mined by platoons of past scholars.

Nous parades regularly as a potential exception to psychological generalisations, and in particular to the thesis that psychic functions are body-bound (e.g., 403a8, 407a3, b4, 408b19 etc.; *PA* 641a18; *GA* 736b24; *Meta.* 1026a5; *EN* 1178a22). Such passages reflect not an unreasoned intellectual inheritance, but an acute rational dilemma.

Two lines of thought seemed to lead to a weakly physicalist account of *nous*. First, Aristotle's empiricist principle that all knowledge and thought ultimately depend upon sense experience (cf. 432a7; *Sens.* 445b16; *A. Pst.* 81a38) entails that any thinker must be, or have been, embodied; for thought requires prior perception, and perception needs bodily organs.

Secondly, though 'thinking especially seems like something proper to the soul, ... if even this is a sort of phantasy, or not with phantasy, then not even this could exist without a body' (403a8-10); for phantasy, being 'a movement that comes about as a result of actual perception' (429a1; cf. *Insom.* 461a14-25, 462a8), is inseparable from body. The claim that 'thought is not without phantasy' is vexatiously indeterminate; but it is undeniably central to Aristotle's account of the intellect (cf. 427b16, 431a15, 432a8; *Mem.* 449b31; *Rhet.* 1378b9).

There are two main opposing arguments. First, thought seems indifferent **111** to the physical world in at least two ways: unlike the objects of perception, the objects of thought 'are in a sense in the soul itself – hence thinking is in a man's power whenever he likes' (417b23-4, 427b18); moreover, thought is not impaired by the excessively thinkable as hearing, say, is impaired by the excessively audible (429a31-b5).

Secondly, Aristotle inferred the separability of thought from the premiss that we 'think of everything' (429a18-26). His argument is adopted from Plato's *Timaeus* (50E); if x can think of something F, then x is capable of 'becoming' F in some sense (cf. 431a1, b17; *MA* 701b19-23), i.e., x is potentially F (e.g., 429a16, b30). Hence x is not actually F (cf. 422b1, 424a8); for if it were, 'the mind's Fness would impede and obscure the object's Fness' (429a20). Thus 'the mind is actually nothing before it thinks' (429a24); i.e. for no value of F does 'x can think' entail 'x is (actually) F' – and in particular the entailment fails for every φ-predicate (429a25). Thus whereas each of the senses, since it contains a physical component, must be blind to some quality or other (424a1-4), the intellect, since it is cognisant of all qualities, can have no physical component.

One of the functions of *De Anima* III 5 is to resolve this dilemma and reconcile the opposing arguments. This notorious chapter distinguishes two sorts of intellect: one is the 'matter' of thought (430a10) and 'becomes all

---

themselves, cognitively (*gnôstikôs* – als Erkanntes), the forms of the sense objects without their matter.'

It should be noted that *Phys.* 244b7-15 goes out of its way to assert that *aisthêsis* is an ordinary case of *alloiôsis*; but it also explicitly says that the *alloiôsis* is not physical.

things' (430a15); it is called the 'passive' intellect, *ho pathêtikos nous*,[11] and it is perishable (430a25), because it is inseparable from body. The other intellect was called *nous poiêtikos* by Aristotle's successors because it 'makes everything' (430a15): 'And this intellect is separable and unaffected and unmixed, being in essence activity' (430a18). Thus we have a characteristically Aristotelian solution to the question of the separability of intellect: one sort of intellect is separable, one is not.

The adequacy of Aristotle's solution depends on the nature of the distinction he is making; but that, despite two millennia of discussion, **112** remains quite obscure. Conceivably, the distinction in III 5 is tied to the distinction in III 4 between two stages in thinking (429b5-9; cf. 417a20-32); those stages are, roughly speaking, the acquisition of concepts and their use. Perhaps, then, the characteristic of 'passive' *nous* is to acquire and store concepts; it is passive inasmuch as its work depends upon the impressions of phantasy and sense. The use of concepts – thinking proper – is the province of creative *nous*; it 'makes' things in the etiolated sense that concepts, the 'matter' provided by passive *nous*, form the object of its activity. In us creative intellect is dependent upon passive intellect, and hence upon the body; but this dependence is not logical – '*x* thinks' entails '*x* has concepts' but it does not entail '*x* acquires concepts'. The immortal gods may exercise their minds without first having to stock them.

If III 5 is striving towards some such position as this, its efforts face two large obstacles: first, it offers no account of the nature of concept-use as opposed to concept-acquisition; secondly, it does not answer the argument from our 'thinking of everything', for that appears to show the separability of *passive nous*. But *no* account of III 5 can hope to avoid obstacles at least as large as these. The distinction between creative and passive intellect appears nowhere else in Aristotle; III 5 is a sketch – faint, careless, suggestive. Its suggestions were never worked out.

9.

III 5 intimates a type-(4) physicalism for passive *nous* and non-physicalism for 'creative' *nous*. This in no way commits Aristotle to a substantialist doctrine of intellect: he should maintain theory (iv) of p.34 above, and not theory (ii). I think that Aristotle appreciated this; linguistically speaking, the *De Anima* almost invariably treats *nous* like any other psychic faculty. In particular, *nous* is regularly denominated a power, *dunamis* (e.g. 404a30, 414a31, 428a3, 432a15, 433b2); and such language is resolutely non-substantialist.

Two passages tell in the opposite direction. First, at 408b18 Aristotle says that 'the intellect seems to come about in us as being a sort of substance **113** (*ousia tis ousa*), and seems not to be destroyed'. But what sort of substance is *nous*? The context is a difficult one; it is, I think, possible that the sort of substance in question is form (cf. 412a6-9). At least this both explains the imperishability of *nous* (for forms are not destroyed) and also escapes substantialism (for forms are substances only in a secondary sense).

---

11. Here I differ from Brentano and the Thomists who identify *nous pathêtikos* with *phantasia*; this seems to me inadmissible on linguistic grounds. But Brentano's discussion of III 5 remains the best.

Secondly, 430a22-3 says of 'creative' intellect that 'only when separated (*chôristheis*) is it just what it is; and it alone is deathless and eternal'. Some interpreters, emphasising the tense of the participle, *chôristheis*, gloss the sentence by 'when human intellect is separated from the human body', and add that eternity in any event requires substantiality. But it is as probable that we should think rather of the divine intellects of *Metaphysics* XII, and gloss by 'when the thinking substance is not physical' (for the tense see e.g. *EN* 1159a5). This reading leaves non-physical substances in the *De Anima*, but *Metaphysics* and *De Caelo* require these anyway; the essential point remains that *nous* is an attribute of substances and not a substance itself.

10.

Aristotle thus emerges as a fairly consistent upholder of an attribute theory of mind; and that, I suggest, is his greatest contribution to mental philosophy.

His voice in the physicalist debate is a subtle one: first, he is clear that one psychic part may have a different status from another; secondly, for most psychic parts he holds a weak physicalism of type (3), rejecting the stronger physicalisms of types (1) and (2); thirdly, in the case of at least two psychic functions, *orexis* and *nous*, he leans, hesitantly, toward non-physicalism. (His rejection of strong physicalism of course commits him to non-physicalism for at least some *components* of psychic parts.)

This survey of Aristotle's concept of mind has been broad in scope and deficient in the details of scholarship. My main excuse is the belief that if the *De Anima* retains any purely philosophical value, it does so on account of the very general features I have been discussing; for Aristotle's particular observations and hypotheses about the mind are by and large outgrown. I **114** do not maintain that Aristotle's concept of mind is correct; but it does seem to me at least as good a buy as anything else currently on the philosophical market. Philosophy of mind has for centuries been whirled between a Cartesian Charybdis and a scientific Scylla: Aristotle has the look of an Odysseus.[12]

12. A draft of this paper was kindly criticised by three friends, Robert Delahunty, Christopher Kirwan, and Howard Robinson. Of published works I have been most stimulated by Brentano's brilliant book; and I find myself in comfortably close agreement with the views of Hardie [61], and Chs. 5 and 16 of [62]).

3

Richard Sorabji

Body and Soul in Aristotle

1: Aristotle's view

(i) Interpretations of Aristotle's account of the relation between body and
soul have been widely divergent.[1] At one extreme, Thomas Slakey has said
that in the *De Anima* 'Aristotle tries to explain perception simply as an event
in the sense-organs'. Wallace Matson has generalised the point. Of the
Greeks in general he says, 'Mind-body identity was taken for granted ...
Indeed, in the whole classical corpus there exists no denial of the view that
sensing is a bodily process throughout'. At the opposite extreme, Friedrich
Solmsen has said of Aristotle's theory, 'it is doubtful whether the movement
or the actualization occurring when the eye sees or the ear hears has any
physical or physiological aspect.' Similarly, R.D. Hicks thinks that Aristotle
makes the faculty of desire wholly psychical as opposed to corporeal, and
Jonathan Barnes has described Aristotle as leaning hesitantly towards the
view that desire and thought are wholly non-physical. But on the emotions
and sense perception, Barnes takes an intermediate position. Aristotle treats
these, he says, as including physical and non-physical components. Other
writers too have sought a position somewhere in the middle. Thus G.R.T.
Ross concedes that we find in Aristotle 'what looks like the crudest
materialism'. It appears that objects produce changes in an organism, 'and
the reception of these changes in the sense organ *is* perception'. But, he
maintains, this gives us only half the picture. The complete theory 'may in a
way be designated as a doctrine of psychophysical parallelism'. W.D. Ross
also seeks a middle position. He thinks that Aristotle sometimes brings out
'the distinctively mental, non-corporeal nature of the act [of sensation]. ...
But Aristotle cannot be said to hold successfully to the notion of sensation as
a purely mental activity having nothing in common with anything physical.
He is still under the influence of earlier materialism'.

The most popular alternatives have been to regard Aristotle as some kind
of materialist, or as some kind of Cartesian. But, as we shall see, there have

63

64

---

1. Thomas Slakey [68], p.470. Wallace I. Matson, 'Why isn't the mind-body
problem ancient?', in *Mind, Matter and Method*, ed. Feyerabend and Maxwell
(University of Minnesota, 1966), p.93. Friedrich Solmsen [103], p.170, who claims,
'Nor does the "common sense" which receives, collects and synthesizes depend for its
functioning on any physiological process'. He does, however, find (and write
illuminatingly about) a physiological process that occurs at a different stage in
perception. R.D. Hicks [43], p.563. Jonathan Barnes, reprinted as Chapter 2 above.
G.R.T. Ross [49], Introduction, pp. 5-7. W.D. Ross [16], p.136.

been other assimilations. I believe that all these interpretations are mistaken, and that Aristotle's view is something *sui generis*. It is not to be identified with the positions of more recent philosophers. Moreover, when we see what his view is, we shall find that it has interesting implications of its own. But first, by way of background information, I must make two preliminary points about Aristotle's concept of the soul.

(ii) *Preliminaries: the soul as capacities.* Aristotle sometimes thinks of the soul as a set of capacities, such as the capacity for nutrition, the capacity of sense perception and the capacity for thought. These capacities are not a mere conglomeration, but are related to each other in intimate ways, so as to form a unity. The lowest capacity (nutrition) can exist without the higher ones, but not *vice versa*.

According to Aristotle's best-known definition, the soul is the form, or first actuality, of a natural body with organs (*De An.* II 1, 412a19, b5). But it is not always noticed that he regards this definition as insufficiently informative. He calls it an 'impression' or 'sketch', and a 'very general statement'. But it would be ridiculous, he says, to give a general definition of the soul, to the neglect of definitions that pick out the particular kinds of soul, the soul of a plant, a beast, or a man (*De An.* II 1-3, 412a7, b4, b10, 413a9-10, 414b25-8, b32-3). An account that does pick out the various capacities by which living things differ from each other will in fact be the most appropriate account of the soul (*De An.* II 3, 415a12-13). And with this statement at the end of *De An.* II 3, he provides the plan of the rest of the *De Anima*. For the rest of the work considers in turn the capacity for nutrition, the capacity of sense perception, the related capacity of imagination, the capacity for thought, and the capacity for voluntary movement.

Aristotle's statement, that the most appropriate account of the soul is the one which picks out these capacities, already suggests the thought that perhaps the soul just *is* these capacities. This thought is confirmed when we notice that Aristotle speaks of the capacities as *parts* of the soul (e.g. *De An.* 413b7, b27-32, 429a10-13, 432a19; *Mem.* 449b5, 450a17). It is confirmed again when, using one of his technical terms, Aristotle calls the soul a first actuality (*De An.* 412a22-8). For a first actuality is also describable as a second potentiality (*De An.* 417a21-b2), in other works as a capacity. The interpretation is also confirmed by Aristotle's claim that the relation of soul to body is parallel to that of sight to the eye.[2]

I shall follow Aristotle below, by thinking of the soul as a set of capacities. The conception does, incidentally, have one great advantage, namely that we undeniably have a soul of the kind Aristotle describes. At least, we have

65

2. *De An.* 412b17-413a3. Willie Charlton and Professor Wiggins have pointed out that Aristotle sometimes thinks of the soul as that which *has* capacities, i.e. the person (Charlton, *Aristotle's Physics Books I and II* (Oxford, 1970), pp. 70-3; Wiggins, *Identity and Spatio-Temporal Continuity* (Oxford, 1967), part 4, sec. 2). This observation is illuminating, especially for the study of *Metaphysics*, Book VII. But it must be insisted that sometimes, and in the *De Anima* often, Aristotle thinks of the soul as being the capacities themselves. He is not thinking of the soul as that which *has* capacities, when he says that a person is angry with his soul (408b1-15), or that the soul is the cause of living, and the efficient cause of perception and growth, and that only what partakes of soul perceives (415b8-28).

a soul, if this means that we have the capacity to grow, perceive and think. But it must be admitted that Aristotle sometimes adds the difficult idea that we have a capacity to perceive and grow which *explains* our perceiving and growing.[3]

(iii) *Preliminaries: the biological conception of the soul.* The word 'soul' may sound archaic to some modern ears, and people may be tempted to substitute the word 'mind'. But then they are likely to confine the functions of the soul to what we call mental acts, and this will take them away from Aristotle's conception of the soul. In all this, people have been influenced by Descartes. He explains that previously the word 'soul' (*anima*) had been applied to the principle of nutrition as well as to the principle of consciousness (*cogitatio*). But he will use the word only for the latter, and, to avoid confusion, will, whenever possible, substitute the word 'mind' (*mens*).[4]

Aristotle's conception of the soul is much broader than this. He takes the view which Descartes castigates, that the nutritive processes are a function of the soul. Plato and others had attributed a soul to plants.[5] Plato had coupled this view with another current view, that plants had sensations and desires.[6] Aristotle retains the first idea, that plants have souls, but sensibly rejects the second, that they have sensations and desires. Instead, he makes sensation the distinguishing mark of animals. But how, then, does he justify continuing to attribute a soul to plants? By extending the concept of soul, so that the non-conscious processes of nutrition and growth will now count as an activity of the soul. This extension may sound strange to us. But appeal to a (non-conscious) soul is needed, Aristotle thinks, to do justice to such facts as that a plant does not expand haphazardly, but preserves, or develops, a certain distinctive organisation.[7] The resulting conception of the

---

3. It is easy to understand Aristotle's idea that our capacity for desire explains our moving from place to place (*De An.* III 9-10). But it is harder to see how the capacity to perceive can *explain* our perceiving, or how the capacity to retain a certain distinctive organisation while we grow can *explain* our retaining this organisation while we grow (*De An.* 415b23-8, 416a8-9, b21-2).

That the soul is a cause (415b8-28) helps to explain why Aristotle could not accept the view, which is often said to be like his, that the soul is related to the body as its harmony to a lyre (407b27-408a30). A harmony is not a causal agent in the right way.

4. Reply to objections brought against the 2nd *Meditation*, §4, in the 5th *Objections*, translated Haldane and Ross, Vol 2, p.210.

5. Plato *Timaeus* 77A-B. Empedocles believed he had in a previous incarnation been a bush (fragment 117 in Diels, *Die Fragmente Der Vorsokratiker*). It may have been because of his belief that souls could be reincarnated in plants that Empedocles forbade the eating of beans (fr. 141). But members of the Orphic sect allowed that some or all vegetable food lacked a soul (Euripides, *Hippolytus* 952).

6. Plato, *Timaeus* 77A-B. Put into the mouth of Protagoras by Plato, *Theaetetus* 167B. Asserted, if we can believe our late sources, by Empedocles, Democritus and Anaxagoras (see pseudo-Aristotle, *De Plantis* 815a16, b16; Sextus Empiricus, *Adv. Math.* VIII. 286, using as evidence Empedocles, fr. 110; cf. fr. 103).

7. See, e.g., *De An.* 416a6-9. A plant also produces seed for the next generation. And this must be done by converting the nutriment it draws from the soil (see *GC* I 5; *De An.* II 4). An excellent account of Aristotle's biological extension of the concept of soul is given by Solmsen in [53].

soul makes it coextensive with life, that is, with all life. The conception of soul is a biological one, and it encourages Aristotle to stress the continuity, rather than the differences, between processes in plants and processes in humans. Descartes was wrong, in the passage referred to at the beginning of this paragraph, when he ascribed the connection between the soul and nutritive processes to the earliest men. The connection is in fact an innovation of Aristotle's, though it may well be true that Aristotle's predecessors, other than Plato, already ascribed to the soul functions which were not mental ones.[8]

Though Aristotle makes plant growth a function of the soul, he does not take the next step. He does not attribute the movements of earth, air, fire and water to a soul within them, presumably because the four elements are   **67** lifeless things. But although the four elements do not have souls to move them, there are analogies between the movement of elements, the growth of plants, and the movement of animals. All three are processes directed towards an end, and all three are due to nature, which in *Physics* II 1 is defined as an internal cause of change (192b20). There is the difference that the nature, or internal cause, is not a soul or a desire, in the case of the four elements. But this only raises the question how the nature that resides in the elements differs from a plant soul or from the desire of animals, a difficult question which we shall encounter again (below, p.59). The *Physics* offer no satisfactory answer, but an answer can be pieced together from Aristotle's later works.[9]

(iv) *The contrast with Descartes.* We can now return to the rival interpretations of the body-soul relation in Aristotle. Some of the interpretations attribute to Aristotle a Cartesian stand. Solmsen and   **68** Barnes attach importance to the fact that Aristotle makes perception an act

8. A major function of the soul, among early Greek philosophers, was to cause motion (*De An.* 403b26, 405b11, 409b19). Did the soul always cause motion by means of some mental activity? Aristotle implies not in the case of Democritus (*De An.* 406b24-5), though in this particular instance Aristotle's testimony is suspect. According to another conception, the function of the soul was not connected with consciousness in this life, but was simply to survive, perhaps with a very low level of consciousness, when a man died (see R.B. Onians [57] for such a conception in Homer). For Plato, one function of the soul was to cause motion, but it caused motion by means of some mental activity (*Laws* 896E-897A). I do not believe that *Timaeus* 36E says otherwise.

9. The *Physics* hints at analogies (192a22, 250b14). But it fails completely when it tries to spell out the disanalogies (255a5-20, b29-31). A good account of this failure is again given by Solmsen in [54]. According to later writings, desire in animals differs from the nature of a stone, in that it involves a physiological process in virtue of which desire is a cause of motion (*De An.* I 1; *MA* 6-10). It also differs in being intimately linked with other soul capacities, with nutrition, which maintains the organs in the right state, and with perceiving, imagining, conceiving and judging. For (*MA* 6-8, 11; *De An.* III 9-11) an animal must perceive, imagine, or conceive the end desired, and, in some cases, the means to its realisation. A human being may also make a judgment that the end or means conceived is to be pursued, or not. Desire differs again, in that desires have varying ends (*Meta.* IX 5; *Cael.* II 12), some of them conflicting (*EN* VII 3, Bekker's numbering), some changeable by training (*EN* II 1), some being only apparent goods, not real goods (*EN* III 4).

of the soul. But given Aristotle's biological conception of the soul (which Solmsen has done so much to bring out), this tells us that perception manifests life, not that it manifests consciousness. G.R.T. Ross finds significance in Aristotle's calling perception an *energeia* and *entelecheia*. But when Aristotle insists that perception is an *energeia* and an *entelecheia*, rather than a *pathos* (cf. Barnes, above, p.38), he has in mind that it is an actualisation of a disposition and that the subject of this actualisation is not destroyed but preserved and fulfilled (*De An.* 417a14-16, b2-12). When Aristotle says that perceiving is an *energeia*, rather than a *kinêsis* (*Meta.* 1048b18-36; *EN* 1174a14-b9; *Sens.* 446b2-3), he means that processes are incomplete until they reach their end, but with activities like perceiving one can say 'I have perceived' right from the very beginning. These points do not imply that perceiving is 'something mental' (G.R.T. Ross [49], p.5) or 'an act of mind' (p.6). Living can be called an *energeia*, even when we are talking of the non-mental life of a plant. W.D. Ross and Barnes attach importance to the passage we shall discuss below where Aristotle says that smelling is something else besides (*para*) a physical change (*De An.* 424a32-b18). But they assume without warrant that if there is 'something else', it can only be conceived of as distinctively mental or non-physical. Ross' second piece of evidence is that Aristotle sometimes speaks of perception as involving discrimination. But here too he assumes without warrant that discrimination can only be conceived of as something distinctively mental. Barnes and Hicks think that the faculty of desire is made wholly non-physical at 433b19, where Aristotle contrasts it with the organ which is physical (*sômatikon*), and which is therefore to be discussed in another work that deals with the body as well as the soul. But I believe Aristotle means no more than that the organ differs from the faculty in being a *part* of the body, and that the *De Anima*, though concerned with states that belong to the body and soul alike, is not interested in *parts* of the body as such. Again, crude though the discussion of the soul is in Aristotle's early work, *Physics* VII, I do not see with Barnes any claim at 244b7-15 that the kind of qualitative change represented by sense perception is non-physical.

Turning to the case on the other side for a while, we should notice that Aristotle has no word corresponding to 'mental act', or to Descartes' *cogitatio* (consciousness). Charles Kahn has suggested that the nearest word is *aisthanesthai* (perceiving), for this covers a very wide range of mental acts.[10] None the less, as Kahn carefully points out, the word does not correspond to Descartes' *cogitatio*, for Aristotle draws a sharp distinction between thinking and perceiving. He never suggests that thinking is a kind of *aisthanesthai*. Nor, as we shall see, does he say of *aisthanesthai* the sort of things that Descartes says of *cogitatio*.

In a very un-Cartesian way, Aristotle insists that in some sense of 'is' every mental act is a physiological process. Thus anger is a boiling of the blood or warm stuff around the heart, in a sense of 'is' analogous to that in

10. In Aristotle, pleasure and pain (*PA* 666a12); awareness of memory-images (*Mem.* 450b14, 16, 18, 28); awareness of one's own acts of sense perception (*Som.* 455a17; *De An.* 425b12; *EN* 1170a29-b1); awareness of being asleep (*Insom.* 462a3). In other authors, desire, fear, and intellectual discernment. Kahn's article, reprinted as our Chapter 1, is basic reading for this subject.

which a house is bricks (*De An.* 403a25-b9).[11] The point is made about all **69**
pathê of the soul, the examples in this chapter being anger and calmness,
confidence and fear, loving and hating, appetite, pity, joy, perception and
thought,[12] though he sometimes prefers to call the last two actions (*poiein*,
403a7), or functions (*erga*, a10) of the soul, rather than *pathê* (a3). About
thinking he is at first hesitant, but, as we shall see, human thinking does not
seem in the end to differ in a way that seriously affects his point. The point
is not made about long-term states (*hexeis*), or capacities (*dunameis*) of the
soul.[13] And at one place Aristotle says it is thought to be a mark of the *pathê*
rather than of the *hexeis* that they are corporeal (*EN* 1128b14-15). None the
less, he does often speak as if *hexeis* and *dunameis* too had some kind of
physiological basis.[14]

The statement that anger is a physiological process does not initially
sound very Cartesian. But Cartesian interpreters of Aristotle may take
courage (cf. Barnes, above, p.37) from Aristotle's insistence that the
physiological process is only the matter, or material cause, of anger. There is
also a form, or formal cause, namely the desire to retaliate. And anger can
be said to *be*[15] this formal cause, or desire, just as a house can be said to *be* a
shelter. This statement in 403a25-b9 is reinforced at 424b3-18, where **70**
Aristotle says that exercising smell is something else besides (*para*, 424b17-
19) merely being affected by something. It is also a matter of *aisthanesthai*. In
view of the wide use of *aisthanesthai*, we may take the word as meaning
awareness. And we may take the point to be that smelling is not simply a
matter of being affected by odour, but is also an awareness of odour. The

11. Aristotle does not list this as a distinct sense of 'is', when he talks about the
different senses of the verb *to be*. But he still treats this use of 'is' in a distinctive way.
He notes that ordinary speakers prefer to say that a thing *is composed of wood* (*Meta.*
1033a16-19), or better (1033a19-22) *is wooden*, rather than that it *is wood*. And he has
reasons of his own, to be discussed on p.55, for doing likewise, and refusing to say that
a thing *is* its matter (*Meta.* 1035a7-10, 1041b12-16).

12. Other examples of *pathê* of the soul are envy, emulation, longing, shame and
shamelessness, kindness and unkindness, and indignation at unmerited prosperity
(*EN* 1105b19-28, 1128b9-15; *Rhet.* II 2-11; *EE* 1220b10-20). The semi-physiological
analysis is mentioned also at *Sens.* 436a6-10, b1-8; *Mem.* 450a27-30; *Som.* 454a7-11,
and is connected with yet other mental states, desire in general, pleasure and pain,
memory and memory images. For the claim that anger *is* a bodily process, see *De An.*
403a26. In making all *pathê* of the soul physiological, Aristotle is rejecting the claims
of Plato, *Philebus* 34B, 35C, 47E.

13. For the distinction see *EN* 1105b19-28, 1106a3, a5, 1157b28-31; *EE* 1220b13-
14; *Rhet.* 1378a20; *Cat.* 8b26-9a13, 9b33-10a10. *Pathê* of the soul (e.g. anger) are
accompanied by pleasure or pain, and affect one's judgment. We are said to undergo
change (*kineisthai*) when we have them. They are not the result of deliberate choice.
They are comparatively short-lived and easily removed. A *hexis* of the soul (e.g. good
temper) is something in accordance with which we are well or ill disposed in relation
to *pathê*. A *dunamis* of the soul (e.g. the ability to be angry) is that in accordance with
which we are capable of suffering *pathê*.

14. For examples, see Theodore Tracy [95], *passim*; Sorabji [50], notes on 449b6
and 453a19.

15. A *pathos* of the soul *is* an enmattered form (403a25), just as a house *is* a form
(403b6). Again, anger *is* a movement of a faculty (desire?), as well as *being* a
physiological movement (403a26-7).

Cartesian interpreter might now read into these two passages the idea that anger or smelling has two 'components'. The physiological process is one component; the other is a purely mental act of desire or awareness.

This interpretation is impossible for two reasons. First, the form of a thing is not a component in it. A shelter is not a component in a house. Aristotle explains this carefully in the *Metaphysics*. His examples are a syllable, a house, and flesh. These are composed respectively of letters, of bricks, and of the four elements. But the form is not a further component. The arrangement of the letters B and A, for example, is not a component in the syllable BA (*Meta*. 1041b19-33, 1043b4-6). On the contrary, it is matter, not form, which constitutes the components. This is how matter is defined (*Phys*. 195a19; *Meta*. 1032a17). There is a second objection to the Cartesian interpretation. Even if there had been a component in anger other than the physiological process, that component could not have been a purely mental act. For Aristotle, no acts are *purely* mental, since *every pathos* of the soul is, among other things, a physiological process.

The Cartesian interpreter must not look, then, for a purely mental component in anger. His only hope lies in finding Aristotle treating anger as a whole as a distinctively mental act, in spite of its also being a physiological process. But it is no longer very clear what it means to call something distinctively mental, if one is at the same time calling it physiological. It is true that many recent materialists, in talking of the identity of mental states and brain states, have spoken as if this were possible. But Richard Rorty is right in taking them to task.[16] The materialist view, as he points out, should be expressed by saying, 'what we thought to be mental acts may after all be physiological processes instead'. If one calls anger a physiological process, one cannot continue to call it distinctively mental. Or if one does, one is departing from a Cartesian concept of mental acts, and will then have to explain what one means by 'mental'. For Descartes, mental activities have no affinity (*affinitas*) with bodily activities.[17] And the mind itself has properties which are actually incompatible with those of the body, for the body is extended and divisible, the mind neither extended nor divisible.[18]

Aristotle is unlike Descartes in several fundamental ways. For one thing, the topic of self-awareness does not play the same role in his account of the soul. Descartes defines the mind as a conscious being (2nd *Meditation*, HR I, p.152), and consciousness (*cogitatio*) as 'all that is in us in such a way that we are immediately aware (*conscii*) of it'.[19] Because of this, the notion of self-awareness is central in Descartes' view of the soul. But Aristotle's remarks on self-awareness are brief, sporadic, and by no means centrally placed. The topic did not have the same interest for him. His most Cartesian remark is perhaps the one in the *Physics*, when he says that a change of quality in the sense organs of a living thing differs from a change of quality

71

16. Richard Rorty, 'Incorrigibility as the mark of the mental', *Journal of Philosophy* (1970), esp. pp. 399-406.
17. Reply to objection on the 2nd *Meditation*, in the 3rd set of *Objections*, transl. Haldane and Ross, Vol. 2, p.64.
18. 6th *Meditation, ibid.*, Vol. 1, pp. 190 and 196, and *Passions of the Soul*, article 30, p.345.
19. Reply to 2nd *Objections*, Definition I, *ibid.*, Vol. 2, p.52.

in a lifeless thing, in that it does not go unnoticed (*Phys.* 244b15-245a2). He also suggests, though sometimes only in an 'if-' clause, that one is inevitably aware of one's own perceiving, thinking, and remembering (*Sens.* 437a27-9, 448a26-8; *De An.* 425b12; *EN* 1170a29-b1; *Mem.* 452b26-8). But in several ways Aristotle's remarks on self-awareness are unlike Descartes'. First, he does not seem to hold consistently to the claims about self-awareness that we have just referred to.[20] Secondly, he is just as ready to entertain the idea that one is inevitably aware of one's own walking (*EN* 1170a30). And there is no attempt to make self-awareness a distinguishing mark of mental acts, by protesting, with Descartes, that awareness of one's own walking is not immediate (see note 19), or by distinguishing between the corporeal act of walking and merely seeming to walk.[21] Thirdly, Aristotle's view of how one is aware of one's own seeing is rather surprising. For *De An.* 425b12-25 equates the question of how we are aware that we are seeing (425b12, b13), or, in other words, how we are aware of our sight (425b13, b16), with the question of how we are aware of the organ that sees (*to horôn*, 425b19, b22). This implies that it is through awareness of the organ that we are aware that we are seeing. He goes on to remind us that the organ is coloured during the perceptual process (425b22-25),[22] and presumably we will be aware of its colouration.[23] This colouration is a physiological process, which could in

72

20. Processes (*kinêseis*) in the sense organs, and images (*phantasmata*) can after all pass unnoticed, according to *Insom.* 460b28-461a8, 461a19-22, and according to an argument (whose conclusion, however, Aristotle rejects) at *Sens.* 447a12-b6. Moreover, *Mem.* 451a2-5 admits that a man may be remembering, in spite of being in doubt whether he is.

21. 2nd *Meditation*, Haldane and Ross, Vol. 1, p.153; *Principles of Philosophy* I.9, *ibid.*, Vol. 1, p.222; Reply to objections on the 2nd *Meditation*, §§ 1 and 9, in the Replies to the 5th *Objections, ibid.*, Vol. 2, pp. 207 and 213.

22. For the view that the organ takes on colour when we see, see *De An.* 424a7-10, 425b22-4, 427a8-9, 435a22-4, 417a20, 418a3, 422a7, 422a34, 423b30, 424a18, 424b2, 429a15, 434a29. The first four passages suggest a literal taking on of colour. The theory has been misunderstood by modern commentators. Professor Hamlyn and Jonathan Barnes think such a theory absurd, and Barnes concludes that Aristotle cannot have held it (Hamlyn [78], pp. 9 and 11; [44], pp. 104 and 113; Barnes, above, p.38). But it is the *korê* which takes on colour (*De An.* 431a17-18; *HA* 491b21; *PA* 653b25), not the eye as a whole, which would indeed be an absurd theory. The theory would still be absurd, if the *korê* were the pupil, as all recent English translators of the psychological works suggest (Beare, Hamlyn, Hammond, Hett, Hicks, G.R.T. Ross, Smith). But the *korê* is in fact the eye-jelly inside the eye (*Sens.* 438a16, 438b5-16, *HA* 491b21, *De An.* 425a4, *GA* 780b23). And it would not have been obvious, with the instruments available to Aristotle, that the eye-jelly did not become coloured during the process of vision, nor yet (to take another example from Hamlyn and Barnes) that the *interior* of the ear did not become noisy. None of the perceptual organs would have been readily open to inspection during the perceptual process; all were internal.

One advantage of assuming a literal taking on of colour is that this explains (*pace* Barnes) how shapes and sizes can be received in the organ: the coloured patches in the eye-jelly have shapes and (small-scale) sizes. For further supporting evidence, see note 28 below.

23. This is part of a two-pronged answer to a puzzle set in Plato's *Charmides* 168D-E. Sight cannot see itself, for only what is coloured can be seen. Aristotle replies (i)

Richard Sorabji

principle, even if not in practice, be seen by other observers, using ordinary sense perception. So what one is aware of on these occasions does not sound like a Cartesian act of mind. The only concession to a Cartesian way of thinking – and it is not a very big concession – comes when Aristotle says that the perceiver does not simply *see* his own organ and act of seeing (*De An.* 425b17-22; *Som.* 455a17), but is aware of it in a different manner.[24]

There is another way in which Aristotle is fundamentally unlike Descartes. He does not divide up the world at the same points. We have already noticed that he does not treat mental acts as a single group, but makes a sharp distinction between perception and thought. Nor does he follow Descartes in trying to separate off from the group nutrition (see note 4), or in distinguishing between corporeal acts of walking or seeing, which do not belong to the group, and seeming to see or seeming to walk, which do belong (note 21). Aristotle groups together thought, perception and walking as activities of which we are conscious, and does not follow Descartes in protesting that we are not *immediately* conscious of corporeal walking (see note 19). Thought, perception and walking are grouped together again, on the grounds that they all belong to humans, none to plants. And they are grouped together with each other and with nutrition, on the grounds that all are due to the soul. Admittedly, walking, weaving and building are not things the soul does, but are merely due to the soul. But *De An.* 408b11-15 explains that this is no less true of thinking and being angry. All are things the man does with his soul, not things the soul does.

If Aristotle comes close to Descartes anywhere, it will be in his account of thinking. Indeed, God's thinking is a wholly incorporeal activity, so that here Descartes and Aristotle meet. But what about human thinking? This will always involve a physiological process, if it is always accompanied by imagery. It might be maintained (cf. Barnes above, p.40) that images are involved only in the *acquisition* of concepts, not in the use of them, not, that is, in thinking proper. But this would be hard to square with the statements of *De An.* 431a16, 431b2, 432a8. Moreover, Aristotle has *theoretical* reasons for wanting all human thinking to involve imagery. One reason (*De An.* 432a3-10) is his desire to refute Plato's view that the objects of dialectical thought are ideal forms, which exist separately from the sensible world. Aristotle thinks that very few things can exist separately from the sensible world; so the objects of thought need a sensible vehicle, and a vehicle is provided by the image in which (cf. also 431b2) the objects of thought reside. Thus Plato is wrong to suppose that dialectical thinking rises above

---

sight is not seen, but only perceived with the aid of sight. (ii) What is perceived on these occasions (the organ) is coloured, so on this score there would have been no barrier to its being seen.

For further references to the idea that, when seeing, one not only receives, but also perceives, processes in one's eye-jelly, see *GA* 780b32, and (in the course of an argument whose conclusion Aristotle rejects) *Sens.* 447a23-7.

24. The *De Anima* suggests that sight plays an indirect role in our awareness of our own seeing, just as it does in our awareness of darkness. We do not *see* darkness, but are aware of it through trying (and failing) to see *other* things. The *De Somno* – supplementing, but not, I think, contradicting the *De Anima* – says that we are aware of our own seeing through the central sense faculty (455a15-25).

the need for images (*Republic* 510B, 511C, 432A). Another reason for requiring images emerges in the *De Memoria*, which is an important source for Aristotle's theory of thinking.[25] If we are thinking of a triangle, we put before our 'eyes' an image of a triangle, but neglect the irrelevant fact that the particular imaged triangle happens to be, say, three inches across, and attend only to the relevant features, such as its having three sides. Similarly, if we are thinking of something non-spatial, we still put before our 'eyes' something extended, but ignore the fact of its being extended (450a1-7; cf. 452b7-15). Obviously such a process requires imagery (and hence a physiological process) at the stage of thinking, and not merely at the stage of concept acquisition. If we are to open a crack for a Cartesian interpretation, we would do better to raise the question whether the physiological process stands to the act of thinking as its matter, or merely as the matter of the imagining which is necessarily involved in human thinking. Similarly, we might ask whether the physiological process stands as matter, or merely in some other relation, to the act of attending to the relevant features of one's image. But a good many more steps would be needed, before we could move from these questions to the conclusion that Aristotle conceived of human thinking, or some aspect of human thinking, in a Cartesian fashion.

(v) *The contrast with Strawson.* This may be enough to make clear that Aristotle cannot be aligned with Descartes. But it should not be thought either than he can be aligned with present-day critics of Descartes. Present-day readers may be reminded of the anti-Cartesian arguments of Strawson,[26] when they see Aristotle refusing to make a sharp break between thinking or desiring on the one hand and walking, weaving, or building on the other. But Aristotle is further away from Descartes than modern critics are. For he equally refuses to make a sharp break between walking on the one hand and nutrition and growth on the other. All are equally due to the soul.

(vi) *The contrast with Brentano.* In 1867, Franz Brentano interpreted several Aristotelian passages as meaning that the object of sense perception or thought is not (or not only) physically present in the observer, but present in a non-physical way as an object of perception or thought (*Die Psychologie des Aristoteles* (Mainz, 1867), pp. 79-81, 86, 120, n. 23). In 1874, he suggested a new criterion of his own for distinguishing mental from physical phenomena. Mental phenomena are directed towards objects, and the objects have 'intentional inexistence'. That is to say, the object of a thought or wish exists in the mind, but does not have to have real existence outside of the mind (*Psychologie vom empirischen Standpunkt*, trans. L.McAlister, London, 1973). Brentano detected in Aristotle this idea of the 'mental inherence' of objects of thought and sense-perception, and he cited some of the same passages as before. The first publication merely spoke of colours and temperatures being in the perceiver as objects (*objectiv*). The later publication filled this out, finding in Aristotle objects of the kind which Brentano believed characteristic of mental acts. In connexion with sense

25. Sorabji [50], pp. 6-8.
26. Strawson, *Individuals* (London, 1959), Ch. 3, esp. §§ 5-6.

74   perception, Brentano cited as evidence for his interpretation Aristotle's
theory that the sense organs 'receive form without matter' (*De An.* 424a18,
b2, 425b23, 427a8, 429a15, 434a29, 435a22), the claim that using one's
senses is not the ordinary kind of *paschein* (*De An.* 417b2-7), and the claim
that the actualised object of sense is within the sense (*De An.* 426a2-4).

Of the three Aristotelian ideas that Brentano cites, the first two are used
also by Barnes (p.38 above), but neither idea seems to prove the point. I
have already commented on the second (p.46 above). The first concerns
receiving form without matter. It is nearly[27] always the sense organ, or the
perceiver, not the sense, which is said to receive form without matter.
Brentano takes it in his first publication that this reception of form involves
the object of perception being present in a non-physical way (pp. 80-1, 86),
and Barnes, following him, holds that it introduces a non-physical
component into perception. But there is good reason[28] to interpret the
reception of form without matter physiologically. It means that e.g. the
organ of sight (i.e. the jelly inside the eye, see note 22) takes on the colour of
the object seen, without taking on any material particles from the object,
such as Empedocles and Democritus had postulated. In that case, in talking
of the organ's reception of form without matter, Aristotle is so far talking
only of the physiological process.

The third Aristotelian idea that Brentano cites suits his case best. For
Aristotle does say that the actualised object of sense inheres in the sense (if
we read *têi*, the organ, at 426a4), and he adds that the actualised object of
sense lasts only as long as the act of sensing (426a15-26). This fits with

75   Brentano's first, and less explicit, claim that the object of perception for
Aristotle is in the perceiver in a non-physical way.[29] But Brentano's later
interpretation seems wide of the mark. For Aristotle does not agree that the
object of sense need not have real existence outside the mind. On the
contrary, the object of sense in its potential state does exist outside the
mind (426a15-26). Admittedly, Aristotle acknowledges that there are

27. The exceptions seem to be cases where Aristotle has misleadingly borrowed
the terminology of form without matter, to express the quite different doctrine that
the act of sensing is identical with the actualised object of sense.

28. Having declined to regard the reception of form without matter as a
physiological process, Barnes finds it difficult to attach any very precise meaning to
the idea. In fact, the idea is connected with the organ's becoming like the object
perceived (*De An.* 429a15-16), and with the taking on of colours or temperatures (see
De An. 424a7-10, 425b22-4, 427a8-9, 435a22-4). So it seems easier, and it is also
appropriate in the historical context, to interpret the reception of form without matter
in our way. This physiological interpretation has the added advantage of enabling us
to understand what Slakey could not understand, the second of two explanations at
424b1-3 of why plants cannot perceive. Plants cannot receive form without matter,
i.e. they can only take on colour and warmth by admitting coloured or warm matter.
Barnes' reason for refusing to regard the reception of form as a physiological process
of the organ changing colour or temperature is that the resulting theory would have
been 'open to devastatingly obvious attack' (above, p.38). Our answer to this is given
in note 22 where additional evidence is offered for the physiological interpretation.

29. Perhaps the actualised object of sense is something that *we* would characterise
as mental. And this would support Barnes, provided he does not say that Aistotle
himself would conceive the actualised object as mental. It does not support Brentano,
however, for Brentano believes that only the sense is mental; its object is physical.

mental states whose objects do not really exist. A wish, for example, can be directed towards something impossible, such as immortality. But this is not true of all mental states, nor even of all kinds of desire (*EN* 1111b10-30).

(vii) *The contrast with materialism.* Having failed to align Aristotle with Descartes or Brentano, we should not swing to the opposite extreme and treat him as a materialist. The fullest case for doing so was made by Slakey (note 1 above). But unfortunately Slakey rested his case mainly on an interpretation of *De An.* 423b27-424a10 which I believe to be mistaken. In this passage, Aristotle says that *aisthêsis* is a mean or mid-point (*mesotês*). Slakey takes this to mean that sense (the capacity to perceive) is the capacity of the organ to change to one extreme or the other, to hot or to cold for example. He infers that sensing will simply be the process of the organ's changing to hot or cold. There are several objections to this interpretation.

First, when Aristotle talks here of *aisthêsis*, he seems to be concerned not (or not directly) with sense, as Slakey requires, but with the sense *organ*.[30] For he describes it as changing temperature (424a6-10). Second, even if he had been directly concerned with sense, he would in any case have been assimilating it hereby to the organ, and not, as Slakey suggests, to a capacity of the organ. Aristotle, I believe, is concerned in particular with the organ of touch. He argues that this organ cannot lack temperature (etc.), in the way that the eye-jelly lacks colour. (This is the relevance of 423b27-31). He also argues that its natural temperature is an intermediate one, mid-way between hot and cold. (This is why he calls it a mean or mid-point, 424a4.) That its normal temperature is a mean one is inferred from the supposed fact that we have a blind spot for mean temperatures (*alla tôn huperbolôn*, 424a4). The inability of plants to perceive is explained (424b1, 435a20-b3; cf. 434a27) as due to their lack of an organ of touch, which is in turn due to their being too earthy and cold to have an organ with a mean temperature. We can thus explain three things which Slakey could not account for (for a fourth, see note 28). We see first why Aristotle uses the word *mesotês* which means mid-point, second how he accounts for the insensitivity of plants, and third what relevance he sees in lines 423b27-31.

But even if this particular passage does not support Slakey's materialist interpretation, we ought to take his suggestion seriously. For we could well expect Aristotle to be a materialist, seeing that so many of his predecessors were preoccupied with the physiology of mental acts. Many of their statements, at least if taken in isolation, could suggest that mental occurrences are simply physiological entities. And Aristotle, along with his successor Theophrastus, and later commentators who drew on Theophrastus, often interpreted early writers in this sense.[31] Moreover,

30. Either *aisthêsis* refers to the organ here, or, if it refers to sense, the sense is called a mid-point only derivatively, because the organ is one. The sense does seem to be called a blend (*logos*) later at 424a27, 426a29, b3, b7, but the point being made there is a different one which applies to senses other than touch.

31. See *Meta.* 1009b11 ff.; *De An.* 427a26, on Empedocles and Democritus. Also Parmenides fr. 6, lines 5-6, and fr. 16. Empedocles fr. 105. Anaxagoras, according to Theophrastus, *De Sensibus* §31. Democritus, according to Aëtius, A.30 in Diels. Some of Plato's *Timaeus* also lends itself to this interpretation. On Homer, see R.B. Onians,

many of Aristotle's own remarks, if taken in isolation, seem to suggest a materialist view. Of sense perception he says that it is a matter of being affected by something, that it is a change in the body, that it is a qualitative change, and that a certain change in the eye is seeing.[32]

77   Even more striking is his treatment of memory-images and dream-images in the *De Memoria* and *De Insomniis*. We are given every reason to think that Aristotle is discussing what we should call a mental image. It is a *phantasma*, is in our soul, and is contemplated by us.[33] None the less, at the same time, he gives this image a very physical interpretation, insisting, for example, that the surfaces within the body must not be too hard to receive it (*Mem.* 450a30-b10), and implying that the image does not depend for its existence on being perceived.[34] At *Insom.* 462a8-12, he says that we can confirm that we observe processes in our sense organs, if we attend to what happens when we are going to sleep or waking up. For sometimes on waking up, we can surprise the images (*eidōla*) that appear to us in sleep, and find that they are processes in our sense organs.

But these statements should not be taken in isolation. They must be read against the background of Aristotle's full theoretical statements in the *De Anima*. The two main theoretical statements are very prominently placed. One comes in the opening chapter of the first book (403a3-b19), the other in the closing chapter of the second book (424b3-18), where it rounds off the discussion of the five senses. We should remember these full explanations when we encounter the more hasty expressions which we have been looking at. Of the two theoretical statements the first is that which says that the physiological process is only the material cause of anger. There is also a formal cause. The second is that which says that smelling is something else besides (*para*) the process of being affected by odour.

The materialist interpreter may take heart when he sees that Aristotle uses the very same kind of analogy as some modern materialists have used. Anger *is* a physiological process in much the same sense as a house *is* a set of

---

op cit. For Aristotle's interpretation of some earlier views on pleasure, see *EN* 1173b7-9.

32. For these four statements, see (i) *De An.* 424a1, 427a9; (ii) *Phys.* 244b11-12; (iii) *Insom.* 459b4-5; *MA* 701b18; (iv) *GA* 780a3.

33. *Mem.* 450a25-451a17; *Insom.* 3. For the word *phantasma*, see *Mem.* 450b10, b24, 451a15, etc.; *Insom.* 461a18, 462a16, a29-31. For 'in the soul', see *Mem.* 450a28, b10-11, 451a3. (The expression 'a process *of* the soul' would have been less significant, since it could have been applied to plant growth, as well as to a mental entity.) For reference to contemplating and perceiving the image, to taking it as resembling, or as identical with, familiar objects, to its appearing and being noticed, see *Mem.* 450b15-18, 450b24-451a2; *Insom.* 460b10-11, b23-7, 460b31-461a8, 461a19-22, 462a8-12. The significance of the last point, however, the observability of the image, will be reduced, when we recall that Aristotle sometimes speaks of our observing physiological processes within ourselves (see pp.49-50).

34. *Insom.* 460b31-461a8, a19-22. A physical interpretation suggests itself also when Aristotle says that the changes left behind in us by earlier sense-images are located in the blood in our sense organs (461b12, b16-19, 462a9, a12). They can travel down with the blood towards the heart (461a5-7, a28-b1, b12). They may collide with each other (461a10-11), and change their shape (461a10-11, b19-21) like the eddies in rivers, or like figures in clouds (461a8-9, b19-21).

bricks. Some modern materialists have offered the analogy of a bucket of water *being* a set of H_2O molecules. But Aristotle is more accurate than these materialists. For they want to say that mental states may be *identical* with physiological processes. Aristotle sees that, at least for some purposes, it is misleading to say that a house is *identical* with a set of bricks, and in general that a thing is *identical* with its matter. He denies that the syllable BA *is*, or is *identical* (*to auto*) with, the constituent letters, or that flesh *is* its constituent elements. And he gives the excellent reason that the components can outlast the compound. Bricks can outlast the house.[35] The same reason has recently been given by Professor Wiggins for distinguishing between the relation of identity and the relation of composition.[36] By noticing that, at least for some purposes, it is wrong to say that a thing is identical with its components, Aristotle improves on some present-day materialists, and on Descartes.[37] He often relaxes his ban on saying that a thing *is* its matter. Very occasionally (in another kind of context, and for another purpose) he even lets us say that a thing is *one* with its matter (or rather he says that this way of speaking is 'better' than certain others he has been describing, which need not mean that it is in every respect all right, *GC* 320b12-14; cf. *Phys.* 190a15-16). But the important point is that he also has strong reasons against saying that anger is identical with, or one with, a physiological process. And this differentiates him from the modern materialists we mentioned.

There are other contrasts too. Aristotle would not agree that perception is *simply* a physiological process. For this 'simply' (Slakey's word) would ignore the formal cause. A house is not *simply* bricks; it is also a shelter. And this further description is a very important one. Indeed, the formal description of perception is, if anything, more important than the material description. For the body exists for the sake of the soul, in the sense that there would be no point in the existence of bodies and bodily processes, but for the existence of souls and soul states (*De An.* 415b15-21). Aristotle would reject the view of some materialists[38] that talk of sensations or houses could be replaced by talk of physiological processes or bricks, without impairing our ability to describe and explain. Formal descriptions cannot be replaced by material descriptions in this way.

It should now be clear why Aristotle disapproves of Empedocles and Democritus for making perception into a mere qualitative change (*Meta.* 1009b13). It also should be clear how we are to interpret the statements quoted earlier where Aristotle seems to talk as if perception or images were physiological processes. They are indeed physiological processes in a way, but only in a sense of 'are' which does not mean 'are identical with', and

35. *Meta.* 1041b12-16; cf. also 1035a7-10, 'the form, or the thing in so far as it has form, should be said to be the thing, but the material by itself should never be said to be so'. Presumably, in the case of anger, the physiological process can occur in sleep, without anger occurring, just as bricks can exist, when a house does not.

36. David Wiggins, *op.cit.* (above, note 2), pp. 10-25.

37. Descartes says in the 2nd *Meditation* that he *is* a mind, and in the 6th that he *has* a body. But he also says in the 6th *Meditation*, and elsewhere, that he is *composed of* (*compositus, composé*) mind and body.

38. See Richard Rorty, 'Mind-body identity, privacy, and categories', *The Review of Metaphysics* (1965).

with the proviso that they are not 'simply' physiological processes.

Aristotle's use of the matter-form distinction in his psychology has been called a strain, a misfit, and an obfuscation.[39] But it has the merit of steering us away from the idea that mental states may be *identical with*, or may be *simply*, physiological processes.

(viii) *What is the formal cause of desire?* A certain question now becomes urgent. We have seen that anger and smelling are not 'simply' physiological processes. But we have also seen that, whatever else they are, the something else cannot be a further component. Nor can it be a Cartesian act of mind. What else, then, can anger and smelling be? The further description should presumably be parallel to the description of a house as a shelter.

Aristotle tells us that anger can be further described as a desire to retaliate, and smelling as an awareness of odour (*De An.* 403a25-b9, 424b17-19). But neither answer is very helpful to people with our interests. For the new terms, 'desire' and 'awareness', are, like the original terms ('anger' and 'smelling'), the names of *pathê* of the soul. They therefore invite the same question all over again, 'What else are desire and awareness, besides physiological processes?' We would like a description that differs in kind, and is not simply the name of a *pathos*. Unfortunately, Aristotle has not addressed himself to this question. In what follows we can do no more than ask whether what he says provides the *materials* for an answer. I propose to take the example of desire.

On the material description of desire we are well informed. According to *MA* 6-10, it is a process of heating or cooling, which results in expansion or contraction of the gaseous stuff called connate spirit, and of the organs, and hence eventually leads to limb movements. The change of temperature involved in the desire to retailiate is not a second physiological process additional to the boiling of the blood around the heart (the material cause of anger). 'Change of temperature' is simply a more general description of the same process.

But what is the formal description of desire? Aristotle places a strong emphasis on the connexion between desire and *action*. One of the most interesting passages is the analysis of abilities in *Metaphysics* IX5. After analysing non-rational abilities, such as the ability of fire to burn, he passes on to rational abilities such as the ability to heal. These latter are connected with desire. Thus one who is able to heal under appropriate conditions necessarily (1048a14) will heal, if (a) he wants to, (b) of the two results, healing or withholding health, this is the one he wants predominantly, (c) he is in the appropriate conditions (e.g. he is in the presence of the patient, the patient is in a suitable state, and there are no external obstacles to action).[40] Although Aristotle's interest is in the notion of ability, his account commits him to a certain view of desire. For it implies that if a man desires to heal, and the desire to heal predominates over any desire to withold health, then necessarily he will heal, provided (i) he has the ability to heal under appropriate conditions, and (ii) he is in those conditions.

A similar view is expressed in Aristotle's account of *akrasia* or weakness of

39. W.F.R. Hardie [61], pp. 64-6; Jonathan Barnes, above, p. 36.
40. For a modern version of this analysis, see Nowell-Smith, *Ethics* (Pelican, 1954).

the will (*EN* 1145a15-1152a36). He distinguishes between two kinds of weak-willed man. One such man has not deliberated at all (*EN* 1150b19-22, 1151a1-3, 1152a19, a27-8). But one has deliberated about the best means to achieve his ends, for example about how best to keep fit. And having decided that a diet of chicken is the best means, he has come to want a diet of chicken.[41] The discussion, then, presupposes a man who desires some end, such as health, has worked out the best means to it, and desires to pursue that means. A man with such a desire, we are told, will necessarily (1147a27, a30) act accordingly and take some chicken, provided that (i) he has the ability (1147a30), (ii) he is not prevented (1147a30-1), (iii) he is fully aware of the relevant observational facts (1147a25-6, a29-30, b9-12), such as 'this is chicken', (iv) he links these facts to the fact that eating chicken is good for health (1147a26-7). Aristotle has added in (iii) and (iv) two extra conditions that were not mentioned in the *Metaphysics*. But the upshot of the two passages is the same, namely that, in certain circumstances, desire necessarily (1048a14, 1147a27, a30)[42] leads to action.   **81**

Aristotle links desire and action again, when he says (*EN* 1139a31-2) that the efficient cause of *praxis* (deliberate action) is *prohaeresis* (a certain kind of desire). More generally, the efficient cause of animal motion is desire.[43] Neither these, nor the preceding statements are offered as providing an analysis of desire. And in some cases the link between desire and action will be more indirect than that described here. For example, Aristotle distinguishes between *boulêsis*, desire for an end such as health, and *prohaeresis*, desire for something in our power which we have calculated to be the best means (in our earlier example, desire for a diet of chicken). Desire for the end, coupled with calculation, is said to be the efficient cause of desire for the means. And it is only desire for the means which is directly an efficient cause of action (*EN* 1139a31-3). Desire for the end, Aristotle explains, may be directed towards things which are not immediately in our

41. Thus he is described as having deliberated, and as having formed a desire (*prohaeresis*) based on this deliberation, but as not abiding by his deliberation and his desire (*EN* 1145b11, 1148a9, 1150b19-22, b30-1, 1151a2, a7, a26, a30-5, b26, 1152a17, a18-19, a26, a28). The chicken example is derived from 1141b16-21. For the meaning of *prohaeresis* see *EN* 1112a18-1113a14, where it is described as a desire for something in one's power (and having a chicken diet is presumably in one's power), which one has calculated to be the best means for achieving one's end. Desire (*boulêsis*) for the end is attributed to the weak-willed man at 1136b7, 1166b8.

One should not be put off by the statement that the weak-willed man acts without exercising *prohaeresis* (1111b14, 1148a17). This only means that when he incontinently seizes beef-steak, he has no *prohaeresis* for *beef-steak*. He still has his *prohaeresis* for *chicken*.

42. It would be anachronistic to ask whether the necessity is logical or physical, for Aristotle does not regard these as distinct kinds of necessity (Sorabji, 'Aristotle and Oxford philosophy', *American Philosophical Quarterly* 1969). The *De Motu Animalium* provides physiological grounds for postulating a necessity, while *Metaphysics* IX5 provides conceptual grounds, grounds, however, which relate to the concept of ability, rather than to the concept of desire.

43. The efficient cause of animal motion is the soul (*De An.* 415b10, b21-2). It becomes clear that it is in particular one capacity of the soul, the capacity for desire (*De An.* III 9-10). The *De Motu Animalium* 6-10 explains the physical mechanism by which desire leads to action.

power, such as health, or towards things which we can't bring about by our own efforts, such as victory for some athlete, or even towards things altogether impossible, such as immortality (*EN* 1111b19-30).

Perhaps we now have the materials for conjecturing what Aristotle might say, if asked for the formal description of desire. Would part of his answer be that desire is, in certain conditions, a necessitating efficient cause of action? By 'action' I mean not merely *praxis*, deliberate action, which is confined to humans, but the various doings of humans and animals. The statement of conditions would include such provisos as that action is in our power, and that we are fully aware of the relevant observational facts. This could not be more than part of Aristotle's answer.[44] Another part would be that every desire has a final cause (*De An.* 433a15). This is the object of desire. And desire, like other activities of the soul, must presumably be defined by reference to its final cause (*De An.* 403a27), and its objects (*De An.* 415a20-2, 418a7-8). Putting this together, we get a fuller, though no doubt still an incomplete, answer to our question, 'what else is desire, besides a process of heating or cooling?' The answer is that desire has an end, and is, in certain conditions, a necessitating efficient cause of our acting towards that end.

If this conjecture is accepted about the formal description of desire, we can draw conclusions for anger, which is a kind of desire. Anger will be not only a physiological process, but also an efficient cause of retaliation. And we can draw conclusions also for certain other *pathê* of the soul. For loving and hating are listed as *pathê* in the *Rhetoric*, and are there treated like anger as being desires (1380b35, 1382a8). They are wishes for good or for harm towards another person. We can expect, then, that they will be efficient causes of corresponding actions.

Our expectation that loving will be connected with action is confirmed in the *Rhetoric* passage. For Aristotle describes loving not only as wishing good to another person, but also as being a doer of good to him, so far as possible (1380b35).[45] But there is something here that we did not quite expect. Aristotle does not say that loving is an efficient cause of doing good to someone. He says that it is being a doer of good to him, i.e. presumably, it is a tendency to do good to him. Modern discussions have suggested that there is a big difference between a mere tendency to do good and an actual cause of doing good. Perhaps Aristotle does not see a distinction here. We shall return to this question shortly.

Though loving is classed as a *pathos* in the *Rhetoric*, friendship is assimilated to a *hexis*, or long-term state, in the *Nicomachean Ethics* (1157b29). For the difference between *pathos* and *hexis*, see note 13. It need

---

44. It is a commonplace to contrast Aristotelian explanations as teleological with Galilean explanations as causal (see e.g. Georg Henrik von Wright, *Explanation and Understanding* (London, 1971), Ch. 1; Charles Taylor, *The Explanation of Behaviour* (London, 1964), Ch. 1). Certainly, Aristotle favoured teleological explanations, but we should not forget (von Wright, p.92; Taylor, pp. 4, 20-5) that he thought teleological explanations compatible with explanations by reference to efficient cause. An action, for example, has some end as its final cause, and some desire as its efficient cause.

45. Similarly, kindness (*Rhet.* 1385a16) is defined by reference to action, as that in accordance with which a person is said to render a kindness.

be no less true of *hexeis* than of *pathê* that some are connected with action. Examples of *hexeis* are the virtues and vices discussed in the *Nicomachean Ethics*. And these are connected not only with *pathê*, but also with action, according to *EN* 1106b23-8. For example, hot-temper is not only a matter of being ill-disposed in relation to the *pathos* of anger. It also manifests itself in action in various ways. Consequently, a large number[46] of the virtues and vices are analysed by reference to action, and not, or not only, by reference to *pathê*. In many cases, *hexeis* and *dunameis* (capacities) are described not as mere tendencies to act, but as efficient causes of action, and as things 'from which' and 'through which' we act.[47]

83

If we have not gone too far beyond Aristotle's text, in our speculations, we now have some sort of answer to our question. The answer will only apply to desire and to some *pathê* or *hexeis* of the soul. For Aristotle shows no interest in connecting all *pathê* or *hexeis* with action towards an end. But at least for desire we can suggest a formal description which is not merely the name of another *pathos*.[48] The description is that desire has an end and is (with appropriate qualifications) an efficient cause of action towards that end. If this is the sort of thing that Aristotle would say, we can now understand how he can hold that desire is something else besides a physiological process, without thinking that the something else is a further component, and without thinking that the something else, or the desire itself, is a Cartesian act of mind.[49] Our suggested further description of desire is rather like the description of a house as a shelter, in that it does not name either a component or a Cartesian act of mind.

(ix) *The analogy with plant growth and elemental motion.* We can now return to the point made earlier that Aristotle stresses the continuity between processes in plants and processes in humans. Desire is treated as parallel to the growth of a plant. Neither is called mental. But just as the growth of a plant is not simply a physical process, but also a development towards an

46. Courage, Liberality, Magnificence, Great-Souledness, Friendliness, Truthfulness, Ready Wit, Justice, and the corresponding vices. Also Self-Indulgence, Hot Temper, Friendship, Technical Skill, Practical Wisdom.
There is a class of virtues (friendliness, truthfulness, ready wit) in connexion with which Aristotle deliberately plays down the rôle of emotion and emphasises the rôle of action. See *EN* 1108a9-31, 1126b11-1128b9 (esp. 1126b22-3), and William Fortenbaugh, 'Aristotle and the questionable mean-dispositions', *Transactions and Proceedings of the American Philological Association* (1968).
47. See e.g. *Phys.* 195a5-11, b23-4; *Meta.* 1019a15-1020a6, *EN* 1129a6-21, 1143b26, *GA* 726b21; *Rhet.* 1366b9, *De An.* 415b10, b21-2.
48. This is not to deny that the notions of having an end, or of acting towards an end, might turn out to involve some indirect reference to *pathê* of the soul. And we have not made a positive suggestion as to how these further *pathê* might be analysed. But we have said enough to show how Aristotle could analyse desire without making it, or its formal cause, into a Cartesian act of mind, and without making its formal cause into a component.
49. D.M. Armstrong (*A Materialist Theory of the Mind* (London, 1968), pp. 11-12) and Barnes (*op. cit.*) ascribe to Aristotle the view that, in so far as man has a soul, he has some non-physical attributes. Is desire, as here defined, a non-physical attribute? Once we observe that it is at any rate not a mental attribute, by Cartesian criteria, the question loses much of its interest.

end, so desire is not simply a physical process, but also an efficient cause of action towards an end. We can also see more clearly the analogy between desire and the *nature* of the lifeless elements. Just as desire is an efficient cause of action towards an end, so the nature of a stone, according to the conception of nature in *Phys.* II 1, is an internal cause of its moving downwards towards an end.

84   (x) *The contrast with Ryle.* We must ward off a final danger. We have seen that in his divergence from Descartes, Aristotle does not side with the materialists, nor with Strawson. But it may now appear (and it has been suggested in recent literature)[50] that Aristotle takes the same path as Ryle, for Ryle, like Aristotle, stresses the links between mental states and action. This would be a mistake for at least two reasons. First, Aristotle has no general programme for analysing mental states by reference to action. He makes the link only in some cases. Secondly, in *The Concept of Mind*, Ryle analyses many mental states as dispositions or tendencies to act, and he argues that dispositions or tendencies are not causes of action. D.M. Armstrong opposes Ryle in *A Materialist Theory of the Mind* (pp. 85-8). He claims that a disposition necessarily has a 'categorical' basis (cf. Aristotle's boiling of the blood around the heart), with which it can be identified (Aristotle would reject the talk of identification). It is, Armstrong says, in virtue of the categorical basis that the disposition can be a cause of action. While Aristotle would not entirely side with either party in this controversy, some of what he says is closer to Armstrong. For he does speak of desire, and of various *hexeis* and *dunameis*, as efficient causes of action. And he might well agree that desire is an efficient cause of action partly because of its physiological basis.

(xi) It is tempting, when Aristotle says that anger and smelling are something else besides a physiological process, to suppose that the something else can only be a Cartesian act of mind. Conversely, if one notices that he postulates no such act of mind, it is tempting to suppose he must be a materialist. If one notices that these are not the only possibilities, the next temptation is to hunt among other current anti-Cartesian views, and to try and match Aristotle with one of them (with Ryle's or Strawson's perhaps). But so long as commentators hope to fit Aristotle into pigeon-holes of more recent make, they will continue to come out with such widely divergent interpretations as the ones we noted at the beginning.

2: *Implications for modern philosophical problems*

Aristotle's view of the body-soul relation has implications for various modern problems. Some of these problems arise for Aristotle only in a different form, and some do not arise at all. They do not arise for a number

---

50. See A.R. White, *The Philosophy of Mind* (New York, 1967), pp. 46-9, '... to possess some knowledge is to have a tendency or an ability to behave in certain ways'.

of reasons, as we shall see, but often because Aristotle's view of the body-soul relation *prevents* them from arising.

(i) One problem that has troubled modern philosophers is the problem **85** how a mind can possibly move a body. On Descartes' view, as we have seen, this involves interaction between two things that have no 'affinity' with each other. Aristotle is interested in the method by which the soul moves the body. In Book I of the *De Anima*, he attacks accounts which make the soul into a gas, or other kind of spatial entity, that moves the body by pushing or pulling. Aristotle's biological concept of the soul is not, as we have seen, the same as modern concepts of mind. But he comes fairly close to modern preoccupations in the *Physics*, when he worries about how the soul can move the body conformably with his principles of causation.

One such principle is the time-honoured requirement, first explicitly formulated by Aristotle himself, of no action at a distance.[51] In Aristotle's version, the principle says that what acts and what is acted on must be in contact. This in turn is interpreted as meaning that they must have their extremities or edges together. And 'together' is glossed as 'in one immediate place' (*Phys.* 226b21-227a7). But if a soul is not corporeal (*De An.* 414a20), nor spatially extended (*De An.* 407a2-3), it can have no edges. So how can it act on a body? Instead of concluding, like the Epicureans and Stoics,[52] that since body and soul do interact, the soul must be corporeal, Aristotle appears to be embarrassed into modifying his requirements of contact. At any rate, we find him suddenly switching at *Phys.* 243a3-6, a32-5 to the weaker principle[53] that what acts and what is acted on should be together, which is explained as meaning that there should be nothing in between them. There is no reference to contact or to edges. And when we ask why not, we notice that he is going on to discuss the case of animals who move themselves (243a11-15, a21-3). Now that his requirement is weakened, he is able to say that animals satisfy it. For what acts (and I take it he means the soul) is together with what is acted on (and I take it he means the body), since the former is, in a certain sense, *in*[54] the latter, so that there is nothing **86** in between them. Once again,[55] the *Physics* account of the soul seems to involve hasty improvisation.

By the time he came to write the *De Anima*, Aristotle would have had the means for showing how the stronger contact requirement is satisfied. And he might also have been in a position to answer modern perplexities about

51. *Phys.* III 2, 202a6-9, VII 1, 242b24-7, b59-63, VII 2; *GC* I 6. For the history of this variously interpreted principle, see Mary B. Hesse, *Forces and Fields, The Concept of Action at a Distance in the History of Physics* (London, 1961).

52. See Lucretius *De Rerum Natura* III 161-7. Cleanthes (Nemesius, *De Nat. Hom.*, p.33, in von Arnim's *Stoicorum Veterum Fragmenta* I 518). Iamblichus (quoted in Simplicius' commentary on Aristotle's *Categories*, ed. Kalbfleisch, pp. 302, 28 ff).

53. For a different improvised attempt to weaken the principle, by reference to a special kind of touching, see *Phys.* 258a20, with further explanation at *GC* 323a25-33.

54. In a weak sense of 'in', for the soul does not meet Aristotle's requirements for 'being in a place' (*De An.* 406a12-16). And this is presumably why reference to being in a place is dropped from the modified principle.

55. Cf. the attempt to distinguish animal motion from elemental motion: *Phys.* 255a5-20, b30-1, referred to above, note 9.

the mind moving the body, if he had further exploited his semi-physiological analysis of desire. Desire, as we have seen, is a physiological process of heating or cooling. And it is not philosophically puzzling how heating or cooling, by causing expansion or contraction, can lead to bodily movement. The details of the mechanism are given in *MA* 6-10. At no stage does the process violate Aristotle's requirement of contact, and at no stage do we have the Cartesian problem of interaction between two things that have nothing in common. That desire should cause movement is no more (and no less) puzzling than that heating around the heart should cause expansion. But if desires lead to movement, then there is a sense in which the *capacity* for desire is responsible for movement. For, as we have seen, the soul is a set of capacities, such as the capacity for desire.

Admittedly, in appealing to heating or cooling, we have not given a complete account of how the body is moved. For all non-compulsory animal motion is for an end (*De An.* 432b15). If we want a full explanation of animal motion, we shall have to appeal to this end, which is the object desired. But the end is a final, not an efficient, cause. So it does not raise the Cartesian problem of one thing acting as *efficient* cause upon another with which it has no affinity. Nor does it violate Aristotle's contact requirement, for this requirement too applies only to efficient causation (cf. *GC* 323a25-33).

(ii) We have been talking about how the soul acts on the body. But there is also a problem for modern Cartesians about how the body acts on the soul. How can a physical process in the eye lead to seeing? W.D. Ross (see above, n1), speaking of the physical process in the eye, says, 'it does nothing to explain the essential fact about perception, that on this physical change supervenes something quite different, the apprehension by the mind of some quality of an object'. Earlier on the same page, he speaks of 'the distinctively mental, non-corporeal nature of the act', and of 'a purely mental activity having nothing in common with anything physical'. For Aristotle, however, there is no question of how an act in the body can lead to a purely mental activity. For one thing, 'lead to' is not the right description, he would say, of the relation between the physical process and the apprehension of colour. Bricks do not 'lead to' a shelter, though they are necessary (*De An.* 403b3; *Phys.* II 9), if a shelter is to be realised.[56] For another thing, it is not a purely mental activity for which the physical process is necessary, either in the case of seeing, or in the case of desire. The physical process is necessary for the realisation of the formal cause. In the case of desire, we suggested, the formal cause is not a purely mental activity, but is having an end and being an efficient cause of action towards that end.[57]

87

56. Similarly, heating and cooling (even if they lead to action) do not lead to an efficient cause of action, but are merely necessary for the realisation of that cause.

57. The formal cause of seeing will be awareness of colour, if seeing is to be treated in the same way as smelling (see p.47). But the awareness is again not a Cartesian act of mind.

(iii) Aristotle's comparison of anger with a house has implications also for present-day questions about the predictability of states of mind. If I can predict what bricks there will be in the world, it does not follow that I can predict whether there will be houses. For that, I should need to know at least how the bricks were arranged, and perhaps also that the arrangements had at some time been used, or intended for use, as shelters. Equally, if I predict what physiological processes will be going on, it does not follow that I can predict whether people will be angry.

(iv) Throughout the discussion so far, we have been guilty of an over-simplification. For we have spoken as if Aristotle were giving a purely physiological description, with no implications for the mind, in his talk of the boiling of the blood around the heart. But in fact he is so impressed by the importance of a thing's function, that he believes a non-functioning heart, or non-functioning blood, is not a heart, or blood, in the proper sense of the word. This theory is applied to the body as a whole, and to many of its components.[58] Aristotle thus gives to the heart or eye a treatment that would be more appropriate for a scrap of paper used as a bookmarker. The scrap becomes a bookmarker, when so used, and ceases to be a bookmarker, when discarded. When it lies in the wastepaper basket, there is nothing distinctive to connect it, rather than thousands of other objects, with bookmarking; its use alone made it a bookmarker. Contrast the severed hand or eye. This still has a distinctive structure to connect it with its former activities, and so it should still (*pace* Aristotle) qualify as a hand or eye in the primary sense.[59] This is not to deny the important of function. Structure alone, unconnected with function, cannot make something an eye in the primary sense: the eye of a peacock's tail is not. But by making the link between the flesh and its function so tight, Aristotle runs into Ackrill's objection (ch. 4 below), that he is unable to pick out the matter in which soul resides in such a way that that matter could be conceived as existing without soul. If he had made the link looser, in the way recommended, he might have been able to avoid this objection.

For our purposes, the interesting thing is the implications of Aristotle's **88** theory for the problem of knowledge of other minds. If true, the theory would mean that the sceptic who doubts his knowledge of other minds cannot express his doubts by saying, 'I see many eyes around me, but I do not know whether they see. I see many bodies, but I cannot tell whether they feel'. According to Aristotle, in admitting the existence of eyes and bodies, he is admitting the existence of sight, which is the function of eyes, and of touch, the distinctive power of animal bodies.

It is interesting to find a similar argument put forward in recent articles by Douglas Long and John Cook.[60] Long points out that the sceptical doubt

58. See *GA* 726b22-4, 734b25-7, 735a8; *Meta.* 1035b16-17, b24-5, 1036b30-2, *De An.* 412b20-5, *PA* 640b34-641a7, *Meteor.* 389b31-390b2, *Pol.* 1253a20-2.

59. It does not need to be transplantable or reversable in order to qualify, as the modified Aristotelian view discussed by Ackrill would suggest (p.71 below).

60. Long, 'The philosophical concept of a human body', *Philosophical Review* (1964). Cook, 'Human beings', in *Studies in the Philosophy of Wittgenstein*, ed. Winch (London, 1969).

is often expressed as a question as to whether certain bodies are associated with minds. He claims that such philosophers as Price, Broad and Strawson have assumed the existence of other bodies in their discussion of the problem. And this assumption, according to Long, already implies the existence of other minds. So much is reminiscent of Aristotle. Long and Cook go further, and suggest that the sceptic cannot even reformulate his position.

It never occurs to Aristotle to raise doubts about other minds. Such doubts would fit very badly with his teleological attitude. If there were many 'eyes' around, but they had no sight, and many 'bodies', but they had no sense perception, then nature would have acted in vain. For as he says, the body exists for the sake of the soul (*De An.* 415b15-21). There would be no point in the existence of bodies, if there were not souls. Doubts about other minds would also fit badly with his dialectical method, the method of starting from opinions that have been accepted by *others*, and salvaging as much as can be freed from objections (*EN* 1145b2-7, 1146b6-8).

For Aristotle, seeing is, among other things, a physiological process, the colouration of the eye-jelly. And this process can in principle, even if not in practice, be observed by others. So there is an answer to the question how one can possibly know that another person is seeing. One can in theory observe the fact. Perhaps it will be objected that to observe the colouration of another man's eye-jelly is to observe only the material cause of his seeing, not the seeing itself. But this objection fails to do justice to Aristotle's position in two ways. First, in Aristotle's view, it is by this means that one is aware of one's own seeing (pp. 49-50 above). One perceives its material cause, the colouration of the eye-jelly. Secondly, it should not be supposed that after one has observed the physiological process, there is some purely mental act still waiting to be detected. The formal cause of seeing will not be, and will not involve reference to, a purely mental act, one having no 'affinity' with bodily acts. There are no such acts. If there had been, the sceptical doubt would have been easier to raise. As it is, we have not discussed the formal cause of seeing, but we have suggested that the formal cause of desire is having an end and being an efficient cause of action towards that end. And this is something with regard to which it is (not indeed impossible, but) certainly much harder, to raise a plausible doubt.

89

Aristotle is so far from entertaining doubts about other minds that, in his discussion of friendship, he almost reverses the sceptical position. Some of the benefits of friendship arise from the fact that it is easier to contemplate others than to contemplate ourselves (*EN* 1169b33-5).[61]

61. I acknowledge gratefully the helpful comments of William Charlton, David Hamlyn, Charles Kahn, A.C. Lloyd, A.A. Long, Norman Malcolm, Malcolm Schofield, and of my students, Bill Hartley and Philippa Mance. The writings which I have found most valuable are: Charles Kahn (ch. 1 above); Friedrich Solmsen [53]; Solmsen, 'Nature and soul', in [54], pp. 95-102. I am especially indebted to Solmsen's article in my section I (iii), and to Kahn's for the contrast with Descartes. I have taken the opportunity of making some revisions in this version, and I have slightly curtailed the footnotes.

4

J.L. Ackrill

Aristotle's Definitions of psuchê

In spite of the doubt he expresses as to the possibility or usefulness of giving $\qquad$ **119**
a general definition of *psuchê* Aristotle does offer such a definition in *De
Anima* II 1; indeed he offers three. In this paper I wish to develop (in a
simple, if not indeed simple-minded, way) a main difficulty his formulae
seem to involve, and to enquire into the root of the difficulty.

1.   Aristotle's three formulae are:
   (a)   'form of a natural body that has life potentially';
   (b)   'the first actuality of a natural body that has life potentially';
   (c)   'the first actuality of a natural body that has organs'.

What relation between *psuchê* and body is here intended? In his justly
admired monograph *Identity and Spatio-Temporal Continuity* Professor David
Wiggins suggests that 'the only logically hygienic way of sorting out
Aristotle's analogy' is to take '[living] body: soul' as equivalent to 'flesh and
bones: person'.[1] He offers Aristotle an interpretation of 'form' (or
'actuality') that makes form that which the matter constitutes: this wood,
iron, etc. is an axe; this flesh and bones is a person. 'What we have done
here is in effect to rediscover the "is" of constitution.'

I said that Wiggins *offers* Aristotle a certain interpretation. Indeed he
argues that Aristotle must, if pressed, accept it. He does not, I think, claim
that this is what Aristotle really meant; and he allows that 'Aristotle would
insistently repudiate this whole line of argument'. Let us then consider what
Aristotle does mean and whether he is open to the logical pressure Wiggins $\qquad$ **120**
seeks to exert.

In the *Categories* Aristotle treats individual things as the basic entitles –
'primary substances' – and their *species* and *genera* as secondary substances.
In later works he uses the distinction between matter and form in order to
explain what an individual thing is. Here is a bronze sphere; we can
distinguish what it is made of (bronze) from what makes that stuff a bronze
sphere (sphericity). Aristotle regularly distinguishes form, matter, and 'the
composite'. The last is the actual ('separable') thing, and to speak of form
and matter is to speak of the form and the matter *of* such a thing. Whatever
the obscurities or gaps in this Aristotelian account it is surely clear that he
has discovered 'the "is" of constitution'. Consider the following:

---

1.   p.48. I do not apologise for devoting some space to Wiggins' suggestion. I think
that it is wrong, and that in general his paraphrases and interpretations of Aristotle
are open to serious criticism. But his book is subtle and stimulating, and every part of
it deserves careful consideration.

(1)	(2)	(3)
bronze	sphericity	a bronze sphere
wood and iron	ability to chop	an axe
bread and cheese	a certain arrangement	a sandwich
bricks and timber	ability to shelter	a house.

An item designated under (1) is (constitutes) an item under (3) if it has the form (shape, character, power) indicated under (2). Under (1) will normally be found material- or stuff-words; under (3), sortals; and under (2), names or descriptions of properties, structures, powers, and the like.[2]

We need not, then, doubt that the 'is' of constitution is a main weapon in Aristotle's armoury. But it is equally clear that he does not think or wish to suggest that a body – or flesh and bones – *constitutes* a *psuchê*. For he quite consistently applies the above triadic scheme in the following way:

(1)	(2)	(3)
body	*psuchê*	animal

An animal, he is always saying, is (or is made up of) *psuchê* and body. Strictly the same is true of a plant, since a plant is *empsuchon* (living). If we confine ourselves to *man* we have the triad 'body, *psuchê*, man'. What makes a body a man is its having *psuchê* (its being *empsuchon*). It would make no more sense to say that a man *is* a *psuchê* than to say that an axe *is* an ability to chop. An item under (1) constitutes an item under (3) in virtue of its possession of the item under (2); part of the point of the triadic scheme is to *contrast* the term *psuchê* and *man* (or *animal* or *plant*).

How then does Wiggins come to think that Aristotle can be forced to a quite different account, one which actually identifies *psuchê* with *man* (or *person*)? Let us examine what he says (in note 58) in direct reply to an account like that just given. The following sentences contain the gist of Wiggins' argument. 'Aristotle gives the form of axe as *chopping* and that of eye as *seeing* … They [these concepts] come to much the same as *being an axe* or *being an eye*, but they are not strictly the same concepts as the concepts *axe* and *eyes*.' 'There is an *f* such that in virtue of *psuchê* Kallias is a particular *f*. What value can *f* take? *Chopping* makes this an *axe*. *Psuchê* makes Kallias a *what*? … If the answer be *man* that is fine, but if the form *axe* makes this particular axe this *axe*, surely *psuchê* makes Kallias this particular *psuchê*. And for Kallias then, *psuchê* and *man* must come to the same. The resolution which I shall offer Aristotle is precisely this – that the particular *f* is *this particular psuchê* or, equally good, *this particular man*.'

Now Aristotle certainly would give to Wiggins' question the answer 'a man'. Wiggins's claim that this commits him to equating *psuchê* and *man* depends upon the supposition that 'the form *axe* makes this particular axe this *axe*'. This presumably derives from the earlier passage where he says (a)

---

2. Notice that the form can equally well be called the form of the matter or the form of the composite: two aspects of the actual thing may be contrasted, or one aspect may be picked out.

that Aristotle gives the form of axe as *chopping*, and (b) that this concept comes to much the same as *being an axe*, although (c) it is not strictly the same concept as the concept *axe*. But (a) is incorrect, since it is not *chopping* but the *power* to chop (or, in the case of the eye, to see) that is the form or 'first entelechy'. Chopping and seeing correspond to being awake; what corresponds to being alive (*empsuchon*) is being able to chop and having sight (*De An.* 412b27-413a1). (b) is also unacceptable. *Chopping* and *being an axe* are obviously quite disparate concepts. But even *the power to chop* (which is what Aristotle actually gives as the form of *axe*) and *being an axe* are, though intimately related, easily distinguishable. Aristotle himself noted in the *Categories* that 'being deprived and possessing are not privation and possession ... Having sight is not sight nor is being blind blindness'. 'The **122** power to chop' and 'being able to chop' are not interchangeable expressions. Nor, moreover, are 'being able to chop' and 'being an axe': the former can, as the latter cannot, occur in a helpful answer to the question what makes this iron thing an *axe*. Finally, the admission in (c) is itself sufficient to destroy the argument Wiggins uses later to force on Aristotle the equation of *psuchê* and *man*. For if it is not after all the form *axe* (strictly speaking), but the form *being an axe* (or *being able to chop* or *the power to chop* or ...), that makes this an *axe*, there is not the slightest presumption that the form *psuchê* makes Kallias a *psuchê*.

What Aristotle says about axes is that some wood and iron (matter) constitutes an axe (composite) in virtue of its having the power to chop (form). Similarly, some part of the body is an eye because it has sight; and the body as a whole is a man because it has certain living powers, *psuchê*. *Psuchê* is the power a body must have if it is to be a man, as sight and the power to chop are what objects must have to be eyes or axes. There seems to be no justification for the suggestion that Aristotle either does or must identify *man* and *psuchê*.

It may be worth making two further remarks here to avert misunderstanding. First, it is of course true that Aristotle often speaks of man (horse, etc.) as an *eidos*, and that this is the very word translated 'form'. What is involved here, however, is not an implied identification of *man* with *psuchê* (his form), but a variation in the use of the term '*eidos*'. To speak of ambiguity might well be misleading, for the connexion between the two uses is exceedingly close. Nevertheless one can say that in some contexts '*eidos*' means 'form' and in other 'species'. The context usually makes perfectly clear which it means, but where necessary Aristotle adds a phrase to put it beyond doubt. Thus '*eidos* of a genus' (e.g. *Meta.* VII 4, 1030a12) plainly means 'species', whereas in '*eidos* and shape' (e.g. *De An.* II 1, 412a8) and 'actuality and *eidos*' (e.g. *Meta* VIII 3, 1043a32) 'form' is clearly intended. So the double use of the word '*eidos*' is no reason for confusing – or supposing that Aristotle confuses – form with species, or, more generally, form with composite substance.

Secondly, Aristotle says, especially in *Meta.* VII, some difficult things about 'what-it-is-to-be-*X*'. The following will serve as a rough but sufficient **123** reminder. To ask why an *X* is an *X* is, according to Aristotle, to ask why certain specified matter is (constitutes) an *X*; and to answer such a question one must give the form of *X*. The form is thus the 'what-it-is-to-be-*X*'. Not, of course, that an *X* is *identical* with its form – an *X* is a composite of form and matter.[3] But the form is what the matter has to get or have if it is to become or be an X; for the matter, to become or to be an X is precisely to get or to have the form. Now if an expression 'E' designates a form and not a composite there is of course no question corresponding to the question why an X is an X as construed above, and hence no clear meaning for the expression 'what-it-is-to-be-E'. Aristotle puts this contrast rather misleadingly when he says (in effect) that X is not identical with what-it-is-to-be-X, whereas E is identical with what-it-is-to-be-E. This last is misleading because it suggests what it is designed to deny, that E is the sort of term to which an analysis into matter and form can be applied. X must be distinguished from its formal defining character E; but E is neither the same as nor different from *its* formal defining character, since it *is* (and does not *have*) a form.

Aristotle thinks that it is not always obvious whether a word 'W' signifies, or on some occasion is used to signify, a composite or a form. He points out that in such a case one cannot give an unqualified answer to the question 'Is W identical with what-it-is-to-be-W?' For if 'W' signifies a composite, the answer is 'no', if a form, the answer is 'yes'. The examples Aristotle usually has in mind seem to be geometrical ('circle'); but he also makes his point by reference to 'man'. He says: 'For "soul" and "to be soul" are the same, but "to be man" and "man" are not the same, unless indeed the soul is to be called man; and thus on one interpretation the thing is the same as its essence, and on another it is not' (*Meta.* VIII 3, 1043b2-4). What Aristotle alludes to here, and in one or two other places, is the possibility that 'man' may sometimes be used to designate not, as usual, the composite of matter and form but the form alone, i.e. *psuchê*. It is far from clear what he has in mind. What is clear and immediately relevant is that the passages in question are few, whereas he constantly and systematically *contrasts* man as composite with *psuchê* as form. Moreover it is in the context of the distinction between *psuchê* and body that reference is made to a possible use of 'man' as equivalent to '*psuchê*': the use envisaged is not a use of '*psuchê*' to stand for the composite, but a use of 'man' to stand for the form. In other words, if one did use 'man' to stand for the form, to say of a body that it was a man would precisely not be to say what it *constituted*. This option therefore would not serve Wiggins' purpose.

2. Can we then say that Aristotle's account of *psuchê* stands in no need of any 'sorting out', that it is already 'logically hygienic'? Hardly. For it is not clear how the notions of form and matter or of actuality and potentiality are in this case to be understood. They normally find application where the relevant matter (or what is potentially an X) can be picked out and (re-) identified in both an unformed and an in-formed state (or both as potentially and as actually an X). Take first the concepts of form and

3. One can, of course, ask 'What is it for something to be an X?' and expect the answer to mention matter as well as form. Aristotle is well aware of this and indeed often asks and answers such questions. But his use of phrases like 'what-it-is-to-be-X' derives not from *this* question but from that indicated in the text. To put it otherwise, it depends upon the constitutive use of 'to be' – 'these bricks etc. are a house' – and not upon the classificatory use –'the thing in the drawer is a typewriter'.

matter. They are introduced by Aristotle to explain change. Certain matter
or material can be shaped or otherwise worked on (given a form) and made
into a so-and-so (the composite). In the simplest type of example the
material of which the composite is made is the very same material from
which it was made; and the same material will survive the destruction of the
composite. We can of course distinguish form from matter in regard to
things we have not made and things which may escape dissolution as long
as we like to think; but in making the distinction we are implying the
possibility of this material's not always having been (and not always going
to be) in-formed in this way. In order that the matter-form distinction
should be clearly applicable to anything, that a thing should be capable of
being seen as a composite of matter and form, it is necessary that the
material constituent should be capable of being picked out. 'Constituent' is
no doubt an unhappy word: it is because matter and form are not, in the
ordinary sense, constituents that no question arises as to how they combine
into a unity. We might speak of the material 'aspect'. To speak of a **125**
composite *qua* material or in its material aspect is to refer to some material
whose identity as that material does not depend on its being *so* shaped or in-
formed.

It is less easy to regard actuality and potentiality as two 'aspects' of an
actual thing. For to say that something is potentially an X seems to exclude
its now being actually an X. Aristotle distinguishes two very different types
of case in *Meta.* IX 6. (a) Unwrought material is potentially a statue, after
the sculptor's work it is actually a statue. Now in the statue matter and form
can be distinguished, and it seems to Aristotle not unnatural to speak of the
matter as potentiality (it is after all what was capable of receiving the form)
and the form as actuality (it is what had to be imposed on the matter if there
was to be an actual statue). Thus 'potentiality' and 'actuality' can come to
be used not only for successive phases but also for aspects of the composite
which are present simultaneously; but this is only because of reliance on the
idea of the matter as it was before being in-formed. This notion of
compresent potentiality and actuality involves the assumption that the
material of the actual thing was not always, or at least need not have been,
in-formed in *this* way. (b) The other type of case is that in which a power or
disposition is contrasted with its actualisation. What is implied in talk of
powers or dispositions is closely analogous to what was implied in talk of
matter. A particular performance displays or manifests a power or
disposition that could have been present before this performance (and
usually was) and can survive it (and usually will). Where '*dunamis*' means
'power' *dunamis* at *t* is not incompatible with actual exercise of *dunamis* at *t*.
Power is displayed in the exercise of it (whereas mere potentiality gives way
to its actualisation).

It seems then that both the matter-form distinction and the potentiality-
actuality distinction (in the two types of case just mentioned) depend upon
the idea that something that is actually the case might not have been: this
stuff might not have been so arranged, the capacity being now displayed
might have remained undisplayed. 'It is the nature of matter to be capable
both of being and of not being <such and such>' (*Meta.* VII 15, 1039b29).

The problem with Aristotle's application of the matter-form distinction to
living things is that the body that is here the matter is itself 'already' **126**

necessarily living. For the body is this head, these arms, etc. (or this flesh, these bones, etc.), but there was no such thing as this head before birth and there will not be a head, properly speaking, after death. In short – and I am of course only summarising Aristotle – the material in this case is *not* capable of existing *except* as the material of an animal, as matter *so in-formed*. The body we are told to pick out as the material 'constituent' of the animal depends for its very identity on its being alive, in-formed by *psuchê*.

There is a parallel difficulty with the notions of actuality and potentiality. Aristotle characterises the animal's body as 'potentially alive' and as 'having organs' – such organs, clearly, as eyes, hands, heart, etc. But to be such an organ is to have a certain power (as the eye has sight, *De An.* II 1, 412b18-22), and to be a body with a set of organs is to have certain powers – nutritive, perceptual, locomotive, etc. There is of course such a thing as the actualisation of any of these powers – their exercise on particular occasions; but it is not to that that Aristotle is referring when he calls *psuchê* 'the first actuality of a natural body that has organs'. He calls it the *first* actuality precisely to make clear (as he explains) that what he is trying to define is the life that a living creature has even when completely dormant, not active waking life – that would be the *second* actuality. If being alive, whether for an organ or for a whole body, is having certain powers (not necessarily exercising them) and to be an organ or a human body is to possess such powers, no distinction can be drawn for organs and bodies between their being potentially alive and their being actually alive. They are necessarily actually alive. If they lack the relevant powers they are just not organs or human bodies; if they have them they are *eo ipso* alive.

To sum up, Aristotle's definitions of *psuchê* resist interpretation because (i) the contrast of form and matter in a composite makes ready sense only where the matter can be picked out in such a way that it could be conceived as existing without that form, but (ii) his account of the body and bodily organs makes unintelligible, given the homonymy principle, the suggestion that this body or these organs might lack or have lacked *psuchê*. The complaint is not that Aristotle's concept of matter and form commits him to the impossible notion that what has form must lack it – that the same matter both has and has not the form; but that it commits him to something that he cannot allow to be possible in the case of living beings, namely that what has form might have lacked it – that the same matter both has and might not have had the form.

127

3.   What is the root of the difficulty? Is there something special about the concept of *living thing* that makes it recalcitrant to Aristotle's treatment? Or ought he just to give a different account of the matter of which *psuchê* is to be the form?

(A) It might be suggested that Aristotle could evade the difficulty simply by dropping the homonymy principle at least as regards living versus dead (or severed) organs or bodies. He could then allow an animal's 'organic body' after death to count still as a body (and the same body), and a dead or severed hand to count still as a hand (and the same hand). He would thus be able to give good sense – as we have demanded that he should – to the idea that this body, which is in fact living, *might not* be living; one day indeed it will certainly not be.

There are various ways in which this suggestion could be understood, but I shall mention only one. It involves raising a question about the interpretation of the homonymy principle. Let it be granted that if an organ *O* or a tool *T* is by definition something capable of performing a certain function, then it would in losing this capability cease to be an *O* or a *T* strictly speaking. (It might be a broken or a ruined *T*, but not therefore a *T* *simpliciter*.) But what counts as 'losing' the capability? Aristotle's position is not entirely clear. Consider first a blunt axe that can perfectly well be re-sharpened. Has this 'lost' its capacity in the required sense? It would seem more natural to hold that it is a permanent loss of power, not a temporary disorder or malaise, that causes an axe to be no longer an axe strictly speaking. Aristotle does not tell us what his principle requires us to say about a blunt axe, only what to say about an axe that has 'lost' its capacity. (Have I lost my pen if I have only mislaid it?) Consider next a faultless carburettor that has been taken from the car and lies on the bench. Is it disqualified from counting as a carburettor (strictly) because it cannot in this condition[4] inject fuel? Is a newly-made rudder not yet a rudder (strictly) because not yet installed in a boat? Aristotle argues warmly (in *Meta.* IX 3) against those who refuse to ascribe a power to anything unless it is actually being exercised. But his own account signally fails to make plain which of the circumstances and conditions that are necessary conditions of a thing's exercising a power are also necessary conditions of its simply having the power. A carburettor cannot inject fuel when dismantled; but are we therefore to say of a dismantled carburettor that it cannot inject fuel?

Because Aristotle does not discuss whether or how the homonymy principle applies to the blunt axe and the dismantled carburettor it is impossible to decide what he would say if confronted, as he might be today or tomorrow, with severed but re-usable limbs and organs or dead but revivable bodies. By the same token we cannot be sure whether to take him to be making a conceptual claim or asserting a depressing empirical proposition when he says (at *Cat.* 13a34-6) that 'one who has gone blind does not recover sight nor does a bald man regain his hair nor does a toothless man grow new ones'.

Here then is one suggestion we can offer Aristotle: that he should maintain the homonymy principle in a form that would not prevent a blunt axe and a dismantled carburettor from counting as an axe and a carburettor (strictly speaking), and that he should recognise as a possibility the re-use of severed organs and the re-activation of dead bodies. I am sure that this suggestion does not go to the root of the problem. But it would be a mistake to dismiss it off-hand on the ground that talk of reviving a dead body is simply contradictory, or on the ground that what Aristotle was seeking to elucidate was the old-fashioned concept of life and not the rather different one that after future medical advances our grandchildren may have.

4. Perhaps 'in this condition' is a bad phrase. What we are considering now is not a faulty state of the object but its separation from the environment that provides it with the opportunity to function.

(B) Could not Aristotle take as matter not the body as a set of organs but the body as made up of certain stuffs? The dead or severed hand is still, is it not, the same *flesh and bones*? Professor Wiggins is happy about this, treating **129** flesh and bones as parallel to the iron of which an axe is made. *His* only difficulty is over the competition that, as he thinks, arises for possession of the matter: this flesh and bones constitutes a human body, but also a person; and these (he argues) have different principles of individuation.

There certainly are places where Aristotle treats flesh and bone as matter in contrast to anhomoeomerous parts. 'The matter for animals is their parts – the anhomoeomerous parts for every whole animal, the homoeomerous parts for the anhomoeomerous, and those bodies we call elements for the homoeomerous' (*GA* I 1, 715a9-11). 'The homoeomerous bodies are composed of the elements, and serve in turn as material for all the works of nature' (*Meteor.* IV 12, 389b26-8). Where Aristotle discusses problems about form and matter in connexion with man he commonly mentions flesh and bone as matter rather than limbs and organs. See for example *Meta.* VII 8, 1034a6, X 9, 1058b7, and VII 10-11 – where it is instructive to notice that Aristotle mentions *organs* when arguing that form cannot be defined without reference to material parts, but *homoeomerous* parts when advancing the opposite point of view.

Nevertheless Aristotle regularly maintains that flesh and bone are defined by the work they do, and that therefore in a dead body they are only homonymously called flesh and bone. Thus in *Meteor.* IV 12, after he has spoken of organs and tools – 'all are defined by their function' – and has explained that the sightless eye or the wooden saw is an eye or a saw only homonymously, he goes on: 'So also with flesh; but its function is less obvious than that of the tongue' (390a14-15). Again, in *GC* I 5: 'That growth has taken place proportionally is more obvious as regards anhomoeomerous parts like the hand. For there the fact that the matter is distinct from the form is more obvious than in the case of flesh and the homoeomerous parts. That is why one would be more inclined to think that in a dead body there was still flesh and bone than that there was still a hand or an arm' (321b28-32). In *GA* II 1 a contrast between homoeomerous and organic ('instrumental') parts is combined with an insistence that the former too have a function and that the homonymy principle applies to both equally: 'For it is not face nor flesh unless it has soul: after their death it will **130** be equivocal to say that the one is a face and the other flesh, as it would be if they were made of stone or wood. The homoeomerous parts and the instrumental parts are produced simultaneously. We would not say that an axe or other instrument was made by fire alone: no more would we say it of hand or foot. The same applies to flesh, for it too has a certain function' (734b24-31, tr. Balme).

If then flesh and bone, properly so called, are necessarily living – or parts of what is living – to take them rather than eyes, hands, etc., as the 'matter' of an animal does not avoid the basic difficulty. The parallel with the iron of an axe is inexact. For though an axe must be made with iron (material with certain powers) iron can exist otherwise than in axes, whereas flesh is by definition in a living thing. We cannot therefore take much comfort from Wiggins' assurance: 'Of course we can specify the matter as "this flesh and bones".' Nor, by way of compensation, need we worry about his problem –

4. Aristotle's Definitions of *psuchê* 73

how flesh and bones can be (constitute) a living body *and* a person. For this is not a problem for Aristotle, who holds that to be a person (a man) *is* to be a living body (of a certain sort). Wiggins' problem arises from his ill-advised suggestion that '*psuchê*' means 'person' ('For our purposes it will not do very much harm to think of *psuchê* as much the same notion as *person*', p.46). The real difficulty for Aristotle is not how it can be true both that this flesh and bones constitute a living body and that this flesh and bones constitute a man (or a person); it is how it can be illuminating to say *either* of these – essentially equivalent – things if flesh and bones can occur only as constituents of living bodies.

(C) If neither the anhomoeomerous parts nor the homoeomerous parts of bodies seem able to play successfully the rôle of matter, because they are inseparable from *psuchê*, might inanimate materials like the four elements do better? Aristotle does of course think that the bodies of animals and plants are, like every other material thing, made up ultimately from the elements. In some places he actually refers to them as the 'matter' correlative to the form of man (e.g. *Meta*. XII 5, 1071a14); and he often mentions them by way of material cause when contrasting this with the formal or final cause. Nevertheless it is really quite clear that he would not be willing to say that a human body is (is made of) earth and water, or that the elements are potentially men. They are altogether too remote. In *Meta*. IX 7 Aristotle **131** raises the question *when* something is potentially so-and-so: 'E.g., is earth potentially a man? No – but rather when it has already become seed, and perhaps not even then ... A thing is potentially all those things which it will be of itself if nothing external hinders it. E.g. the seed is not yet potentially man; for it must be deposited in something other than itself and undergo a change. But once it has through its own motive principle got such and such attributes, then it is potentially a man' (1049a1-16).

If earth etc. are too remote to count as the matter of a human body, could they count as the matter of the *lowest* kind of living thing, plants? Does Aristotle's difficulty arise from the attempt, whose feasibility he himself casts doubt on, to give a *general* account of *psuchê*? Certainly he holds both that the different 'souls' or living powers form a logically developing series and that in the development of a man one power precedes another. For example, *GA* II, 3, 736a32-b8: 'One could not class the foetus as soulless, in every way devoid of life; for the seeds and foetuses of animals are no less alive than plants, and are fertile up to a point. It is plain enough that they have nutritive soul ..., but as they progress they have also the perceptive soul in virtue of which they are animal. ... For they do not become simultaneously animal and man, or animal and horse, and so on; for the end is the last to be produced, and the end of each animal's generation is that which is peculiar to it' (tr. Balme; cf. 736b13, 778b32-779a2). So it would make sense to say of a human body that it might have failed to grow to maturity, that it might have remained at the merely vegetable or merely animal stage. That a given body has *this psuchê* (the human) is contingent if it might have failed to develop beyond the animal stage.

It is quite likely that careful study of Aristotle's views on the actual processes of generation and growth would throw new light on some of his general doctrines. But talk of the lower forms of life or of early phases in a man's life cannot diminish our main difficulty. For even if plants and human embryos are 'nearer' to earth and water than men are, they are nevertheless alive; and for them too, therefore, the 'body potentially alive' of Aristotle's definition must be not earth and water but plant-fibre etc. and **132** flesh etc. Aristotle himself insists in an important passage of *De. An.* II 1 that 'it is not the body that has lost the *psuchê* that is "potentially such as to be alive"', but *the body that has it*; a seed and a fruit is potentially such a body' (412b25-7, cf. *GA* II 3). Seeds etc. are not yet 'potentially alive' in the sense this expression has in Aristotle's definition of *psuchê*, though they are potentially – they will with luck grow into – bodies that are potentially alive, bodies, in fact, of plants or animals. Until there is a living thing, then, there is no 'body potentially alive'; and once there is, its body is necessarily actually alive.

4.   It would clearly be wrong to say that the concepts of matter and form, or of potentiality and actuality, are improperly transferred by Aristotle from the account of process and change to the analysis of substance concepts. For they are perfectly clear and helpful analytic tools in many cases, even if their understanding and application does depend on presuppositions about change. The question is why they cause trouble elsewhere. I will end by mentioning two directions in which it may be useful to look.

We may be struck by the fact that artefacts provide the easiest and most straightforward examples of things whose ingredients or components evidently retain their character or identity from before (and also after) the 'lifetime' of the things. But not everything we can make is like this. The timber, hinges, and screws can still be seen when the cupboard is built, but the eggs and sugar are lost in the cake. If, as a result of cooking, *a* and *b* combine to form the homogeneous stuff *c*, *a* and *b* are no longer there to be picked out. We can refer to the *a* and *b* we started with, and perhaps we can recover the *a* and *b* again by some process. But *a* and *b* are present now, if at all, only potentially. Actual bricks constitute an actual wall, though those very same bricks might not have done so. But here is quite a different story: potential *a* and *b* are 'in' actual *c*, though they might have been actual *a* and *b*. Chemical change, in short, which yields a new sort of stuff, cannot easily accommodate an account tailor-made for other operations. (Compare the constant but often misleading use of mechanical terms and analogies for biological processes and events.) This is the difficulty for Aristotle with the basic living materials such as flesh and bone. They are produced, as he explains in detail in the biological works, by processes like cooking; and **133** they have powers and characteristics that, though explicable by reference to the powers of their ingredients, are new, emergent powers and characteristics.

This, then, may be one fairly deep source of trouble. Where things or materials are produced, whether in nature or by technology, by chemical action, the matter-form analysis is in difficulty. One can refer to the material that by such and such a process *became* this (and perhaps may be recovered *from* this); but this will not explain what it is that *is* this.

A second point, related but distinct, is this. Once Aristotle moves from examples like *bronze sphere* he gets to things that have functions, that can do specific jobs. As is well known, he likes to identify the 'end' or 'final cause' of an object with its essence or 'formal cause' (e.g. *Phys.* II 7, 198a25). But this creates a problem. For the job to be done determines the shape or structure or proportions as well as the material ingredients of the thing; and the thing's ability to do its job depends not only on what it is made of but also on shape, structure, etc. The thing's ability to do a certain job is not *identical with* its shape, structure, etc. So if this ability (*A*) is treated as the form of a functional object, what are we to count as its matter? If the ingredients alone, what has become of the shape, structure etc. (the original paradigm of form)? But if the ingredients plus shape, etc., i.e. the materials *thus organised*, then the matter (so understood) *necessarily* has *A*. Powers are surely consequential attributes in the sense that if one object has a power that another lacks this must be due to some other difference, an 'internal' difference of composition or structure. Aristotle would not, I think, wish to entertain the idea that two things might have different powers without their being any basis for this difference in their material constitution.

Here, therefore, is another source of trouble. A thing's power is not related to its material constitution (ingredients plus structure) in the same way in which a thing's structure is related to its ingredients; and the distinction between matter and form that works for ingredients and structure cannot be expected to do so for constitution and power. Somewhat the same may be said of potentiality and actuality: it is easy to distinguish the possession of a power from its exercise, but not easy to construe the possession of a power as itself the exercise of one.

5

Richard Sorabji

Aristotle on Demarcating the Five Senses

1. Senses and their objects

In the *De Anima* Book II, chapter 6, Aristotle tells us that sensible qualities are related to the senses as *kath' hauta*. In other words, one is defined by reference to the other.[1] I believe that Aristotle has no special interest in defining sense objects by reference to senses.[2] If he has not, then his point must be rather that the senses should be defined by reference to their
56 objects. But the interpretation of *kath' hauta* here may be controversial.[3] And we have no need to rest our case upon it, if we want to establish Aristotle's interest in defining senses by reference to sense objects.

That he wants to define (and in general to get clear about) the senses by reference to their objects is evident, if we consider the structure of the *De Anima*. Here Aristotle sets out to give an account of the soul. It emerges by Book II, chapter 3,[4] that if one wants to give an account of the soul suitable

---

1. *De An.* 418a8-25. For this sense of *kath' hauta*, see *A.Pst.* 73a34-b24. There are admittedly other senses.
2. If one looks at his definitions of colour, light, sound, odour, flavour, hot, cold, fluid, dry, one will find that they very seldom mention the senses. (*De An.* 418b9-10, 418b16-17, b20, 419a9-11, 420a8-9, a21-3, b11; *Sens.* 439a19-20, b11-12, 441b19-21, 443a7; *GC* 329b26-32; *PA* 648a20-650a3.) Much less do the so-called common objects, properties perceptible by more than one sense, get defined by reference to the senses (e.g. unity: *Meta.* 1015b16-1017a3, 1052a15-1053b8; change: *Phys.* 201a9-15). This is the more surprising, in view of the theory of actually functioning colour at *De An.* 425b26-426a26, which links colour closely to sight.
   Admittedly, the definitions of colour and light bring in the notion of transparency. But the connection between transparency and sight is stressed only in the definition of light (not strictly a sense object at all) at 418b9-10. Here light is defined by reference to the idea that when the air or water around us is dark, it is only potentially seeable-through whereas when it is light, we can actually see through it.
   Allowance should be made, of course, for Aristotle's purposes, which vary considerably in these different passages and which can influence the content of his definitions. But, none the less, it should not be supposed that he thinks the best or most scientific definition of sense objects, or the one that gives their essence, will mention the senses. The essence of colour is stated at *De An.* 419a9-11, without any very direct reference to sight.
3. In a valuable series of publications, Professor Hamlyn has argued that the point is that sense objects must be defined by reference to senses, either instead of, or as well as, the other way round. [78], *passim*; [92], esp. p.205; [80], esp. p.12; [44], esp. pp. 105, 108, 117.
4. 415a12-13.

for a specialised treatise, and not merely an account in very general terms, one should describe one by one the powers of which the soul consists; the power to think, the power to perceive, the power to absorb nutrition, and so on. And in the next chapter,[5] it turns out that in order to say what one of these powers is – for example, the power to perceive – one should first say what the corresponding activity is – the act of perceiving. That in turn requires that one should first study the object of the activity – for example, the objects of the senses. This point is made in Chapter 4, and in Chapter 6 of Book II.[6] It is this latter chapter which contains the statement that sensible qualities are related to the senses as *kath'hauta*. And though this statement, taken on its own, may be ambiguous, the closing sentence of the chapter is not. It says that qualities like colour, which are perceived by only one sense, the so-called *proper* objects of the senses, are the things to which the very being of each sense is naturally related.[7] It is already clear that Aristotle means to analyse the senses by reference to their objects, and the next five chapters (II 7-11) carry out the analysis, each chapter being devoted to one of the five senses. The analysis gives prominence to the sense objects throughout. The account of vision, for example, begins with an investigation of its object.[8] And when the account of the five senses is complete, and we move on to Book III, we there get our first, and on some views our only, conception of what the so-called *common* sense is, from hearing about its objects, motion, rest, shape, magnitude, number, unity.[9]

We should expect this pattern to be continued in the other psychological treatises. For whatever the date at which they were first drafted, the treatises included in the so-called *Parva Naturalia* are, in their final form, so presented that they will read as a continuation of the *De Anima*. Sure enough, we do find there the same tendency to define, distinguish, and identify sensory powers by reference to their objects. Thus, for example, in the *De Sensu* and *De Somno* Aristotle speaks of a central sense faculty which is responsible for various functions that a single sense could not perform on its own. This central sense faculty has a certain unity because it is dependent on a single bodily organ, the heart. But it differs in its being and in its definition, says Aristotle, according to the different *objects* that it perceives.[10]

Another example of the importance of sense objects for identifying senses is to be found in Aristotle's insistence that since fish and other animals perceive odour, we must allow that they exercise smell.[11] Evidently, the perception of odour is to be counted as smell, in spite of considerable differences in the mechanism involved. For the medium through which water animals perceive odour is not air, as it is for us, but water.[12]

5. II 4, 415a14-20.
6. 415a20-2, 418a7-8. It had already been mentioned as a possibility in I 1, 402b14-16.
7. 418a24-5. Compare the statement at *Meta.* 1021a29-b3, that sight is a relative term, related to colour or to something like colour.
8. 418a26.
9. 425a14-30.
10. *Sens.* 449a16-20; *Som.* 455a21-22.
11. *Sens.* 444b10, b15, b16; *De An.* 421b21.
12. *Sens.* 442b29-443a3; *De An.* 421b9-13.

Correspondingly, the organ they use for perceiving odour contains water, in Aristotle's view, not air.[13] Nor is the organ used at all like our nostrils in structure. Fish use their gills, dolphins their blowhole, and insects the middle part of their body, according to Aristotle.[14] And neither fish nor insects, he says, inhale when perceiving odour.[15] In spite of these **58** differences, their perception of odour is to be counted as smelling.[16] Similarly, the perception of sound is to be counted as hearing, and the perception of flavour as tasting, in spite of large differences in the mechanism involved.[17]

We have been arguing that Aristotle puts considerable stress on the sense objects in defining, distinguishing, and identifying the senses. In this, he shows himself faithful to a claim that Plato makes in the *Republic*.[18] For before asserting that knowledge and opinion have different objects, Plato maintains that in general different capacities have different objects, and different objects imply different capacities. Sight and hearing are adduced as examples of capacities.

We must not, however, exaggerate the unity of the passages cited from Aristotle. We should distinguish several different things he wants to do.

(i) Firstly, he wants to get clear about what sight is, what hearing is, and so on, by means of a protracted discussion. For this purpose, the sense objects are important. And one needs to consider them in detail, not merely to mention them. However, it is not only the sense objects that one needs to investigate. One should also know, for example, how the sense objects interact with the environment, so as to affect the sense organs, and what the process in the sense organs is (*De An.* II 7-12).

(ii) Different from a protracted discussion is a definition. Assuming Aristotle had not abandoned the scientific method described in the *Posterior* **59** *Analytics*, he would have hoped eventually to obtain a definition of sight, of hearing, and so on. The definition would mention only some of the facts about sight and hearing, but it could be used in deducing and explaining other facts about them. Evidently, his definition of sight and hearing would mention their objects, colour and sound. But we know it would not be confined to this. For in the *De Anima*,[19] he says that one should refer to the physiological process involved, when one defines any mental *pathos*. Thus in

13. *De An.* 425a5.
14. *PA* 659b14-19.
15. *Sens.* 443a4-6, 444b15-28; *De An.* 421b13-422a6.
16. The differences of mechanism must not be exaggerated. For gills and the middle part of insects' bodies, though different in structure from nostrils, are analogous in function, according to Aristotle, who thinks they serve to cool the body. Again, the fact that we need to inhale in order to smell is due merely to the need to open a certain lid, which in some animals is not present. Inhalation is clearly then only an incidental feature of our smelling. Nor will every difference of mechanism be permissible. For all smelling must involve an organ becoming smelly. And all smelling must be done at a distance from the object smelled.
17. *HA* IV 8. And for differences of mechanism: *PA* 656a35-7, 657a17-24, 658b27-659b19, 660a14-661a30, 678b6-13; *HA* 492a23-9, 503a2-6, 504a20-3, 505a33-5, 532a5-14; *GA* 781b23-4; *Resp.* 473a25-7.
18. 477C-478B.
19. 403a25-b9.

the definition of sight, he would mention nòt only the sense objects, but also the colouration of the eye-jelly, which is, in his opinion, the physiological process involved.[20] His reason for including mention of the physiological process is probably not so much to help in distinguishing sight from other things, as to produce a definition fitted for scientific purposes, one which can be used in generating deductions and explanations.

(iii) Different again from giving a scientific definition of sight is the process of simply distinguishing sight from other things, and of showing what cases are to be counted as cases of sight. For this purpose, Aristotle puts a very heavy stress on the sense objects and attaches much less importance to other criteria. We should, however, make a disclaimer on his behalf. For he is not particularly interested in giving us logically necessary and sufficient conditions for something's counting as a case of sight. And so he is not suggesting that reference to the sense objects would supply such conditions. He is interested in demarcating the sensory powers that a zoologist can expect to find in this world, rather than ones which could exist in logically possible worlds. So in assessing the criteria by which he demarcates the senses, we ought to consider whether they are adequate for this zoological purpose.

Enough of exegesis, for the present. I want now to raise a philosophical question, which may appear to take us away from Aristotle. Is it good advice, that we should stress the sense objects in defining the senses? The question may appear to take us away from Aristotle, because obviously our concept of definition is not his. But I should want of a definition some of the things that he wants. A definition of sight should include and exclude the right cases. And it should also bring out what, if anything, unites the various cases of sight. To answer the question, I propose to see how far one could get toward defining the senses, if one took things to an extreme and sought to define the senses solely by reference to their objects. Let us try defining hearing simply as the perception of sound, taste simply as the perception of flavour, smell simply as the perception of odour, and sight simply as the perception of colour and other properties.[21] We need not expect that these definitions will prove adequate. But in seeing where they do and where they do not fail, we may learn what value there is in stressing the sense objects. And this in turn may help us to see whether Aristotle is well advised to emphasise the sense objects, as he does.

Concentrating on the case of sight, I shall consider three objections to this kind of definition. The first objection is that there is such a large variety of objects that can be perceived by sight. Consequently, it would be laborious to define sight by reference to its objects. Moreover, it would conceal what

60

20. For my defence of this interpretation, see Chapter 3 above. Notice that reference to the physiological process will reimport reference to the sense objects. For according to Aristotle, the physiological process involved in sense perception is one in which the sense organ takes on the sense object. For example, the eye-jelly takes on colour.

21. This is a more promising kind of formula, I think, than the kind studied by Grice in 'Some remarks about the senses' (*Analytical Philosophy*, ed. R.J. Butler, Series 1, Oxford, 1962). The latter kind is couched in terms of perceiving a material object to have such and such properties.

80   *Richard Sorabji*

unity there is in the concept, and make it a mystery that the single name 'sight' should be used to cover such a heterogeneous list. Certainly, sight has many more objects than the two which Aristotle lists as its proper objects – namely, colour and the brightness of things that can be seen in the dark.[22] (By calling these proper objects he means that they can be perceived by no other sense.) In addition to these two properties, one can also see other kinds of brightness. One can see size and shape, motion or rest,

61   texture, depth, or the location of things. One might be said to see darkness or light,[23] the warmth of a fire or, somewhat less naturally, the sweetness of a ripe fruit.[24] How could an Aristotelian reply to this objection, that the objects of sight are too many and various?

One line of reply would be to say that the objects of sight just listed fall into two, possibly overlapping, groups. Firstly, there is a group that includes such properties as colour, brightness, and darkness. This group is small, and its members are somewhat akin to each other, both phenomenologically and, as is now known, in their physical basis, since they are all effects of the behaviour of light. Secondly, there are objects of sight like size and shape, some of which are not at all like colour, but which are perceived *by* perceiving colour or what is like it. If this is so, then sight, as it operates in the everyday world, will be firstly the perception of colour and of things like colour,[25] and secondly the perception of other things by means of perceiving these.[26]

The expression 'by' or 'by means of' here covers a variety of different
62   relations.[27] If anyone objects that the words are being stretched too far, we

22. *De An.* 418a26-9, 419a1-9.

23. I am here following Aristotle's distinction between brightness and light. By light he means that state of the air or water around us in which we can actually see through to colours at a distance from us. His idea is that when it is dark, we cannot actually see colours through the air or water. So the air and water are only potentially transparent. Light is the state in which they are actually transparent. This is all he means by the formidable sounding definition of light as the actualised state of the transparent (*De An.* 418b9-10, 419a11). It should be clear from this that light, a state of the surrounding medium, is quite different from brightness.

24. These cases are not very like each other. For warmth consists of such powers as the power to melt things or make them red hot. And the fact that something is melting or red hot is something I can be said to see. Sweetness does not in the same way consist of powers whose exercise can be seen.

25. Under 'colour' I include the three aspects of colour: hue, saturation, and brightness. Under 'hue' I include black and white along with the other hues. Under 'things like colour' I include brightness and darkness.

26. When I say that one sees shape (etc.) by *perceiving* colour (etc.), I do not mean that one has to *notice what colours are present*, in order to see the shape.

27. Thus, in the case of three-dimensional shape, often colours, highlights, and shadows serve merely as clues to the shape of something. But in the case of two-dimensional shape, the relation between colour and shape is often closer than this. For example, if there is a sharp boundary between an area of one colour (hue, saturation, or brilliance) and an area of another, and if we see where the boundary runs, this *is* to see (part of) the shape of the areas.

Seeing sweetness is more like the first case, in that colour and shine serve merely as clues to sweetness. Seeing warmth is, in some instances, more like the second case. For the relation between red (hot) and warmth is a much closer relation than that between a clue and what the clue points to.

can drop them from our account of sight altogether. And we can simply say that one sees, if and only if one perceives colour, brightness, or darkness. The idea that one cannot see shape and so forth without perceiving colour, brightness, or darkness is put forward as applying at least to any cases that Aristotle was likely to encounter in his zoological enquiries. Whether it is a logically necessary truth is something that the reader may decide for himself.

This account of sight, if correct, will meet the present objection. For the list of objects of sight will be a short one. One probably need not mention more than colour, brightness, and darkness. Moreover, the account reveals what unity there is in the concept of sight. For colour and brightness or darkness have a certain kinship with each other.

The materials for such a reply can be found in Aristotle himself. Brightness he mentions as being like colour (*Sens.* 439b2). By light, as distinct from brightness, he means that state of the air or water around us which permits us actually to see through it (*De An.* 418b9-10, 419a11), and this could be treated in either of the two ways proposed. For on the one hand, he insists that light is very like colour (*De An.* 418b11; *Sens.* 439a18); indeed, like white colour; darkness, like black (*Sens.* 439b14-18). But on the other hand, he would prefer to deal with the present question by saying that we perceive light by perceiving that we are successfully perceiving colour through the air or water around us. And we perceive darkness by perceiving that we are unsuccessful (*De An.* 422a20-1, 425b20-2). He might wish to add that it is better not to talk of *seeing* light and darkness, but more non-committally of perceiving them by means of sight (*De An.* 425b20-2). As for the use of sight to perceive size and shape, he explicitly says that size and shape are perceived through the perception of other properties such as colour. And in general the common objects are perceived by perceiving the proper objects (*Sens.* 437a5-9, perhaps *De An.* 425a19). The same point is made about the use of sight to perceive sweetness (*De An.* 425a22-4, a30-b4). In these cases, we see a colour and know from past experience that sweetness is associated with it. All this suggests the view that to see is to perceive colour or properties akin to colour, and other things only through the perception of these.

I have said that the *materials* for this view are present in Aristotle. But I must add it is not clear that it is quite the view he states. For he seems to think he can get clear about what sight is without referring to sense objects other than colour (which is seen in the light) and the brightness of phosphorescent things (which is seen in the dark). Why does he not mention other kinds of brightness? Surely he would have to do so if he took the view just outlined. One possible (though far from certain) answer is that he includes the brightness of things that shine in the light under the heading of colour and therefore does not need to mention it separately. This would not be a normal way to use the English word 'colour'. But Greek colour words often did double duty, and were used as much to denote degrees of darkness and brightness as to denote hues.[28] So it is just possible that under the heading of colour Aristotle means to include certain kinds of brightness.

63

---

28. See Platnauer, 'Greek colour perception,' *Classical Quarterly* (1921). Also Cornford, *Plato's Cosmology*, p.277.

Before we leave the present objection, we should notice one further point. The suggested solution claimed to be able to exhibit the concept of sight as having a certain unity. It did so by insisting on the kinship between colour and brightness or darkness. But part of this kinship was a phenomenological one. And to appeal to phenomenology is to appeal to the kind of experience to which these sense objects give rise. It becomes a question, then, whether the suggested definition of sight in terms of colour, brightness, or darkness appeals only to sense objects. Is it not also appealing to something other than sense objects – namely, to the kind of experience to which these sense objects give rise?

I now turn to a second objection that may be raised to the idea of relying on sense objects in defining the senses. For may not senses other than sight **64** sometimes perceive colour? If so, we cannot define sight simply as the power to perceive colour and so forth, for other senses will fall under the description. An unfanciful example is provided by the ability of some people to tell the colours of flowers by smell. In the typical case, however, what happens here is most naturally described by saying that an odour is smelled and is known to be correlated with a certain colour, not that a colour is smelled.[29] Aristotle discusses such cases in the *De Anima* at 425a22-4 and a30-b4. He calls such perception a merely incidental perception of colour. And with a view to meeting the present objection he could rule that such incidental perception of colour does not count as seeing.

But what if we turn to the more unusual kind of case reported by psychologists, or resort to imaginary examples? Cannot we then expect to find cases in which there is non-incidental perception of colour without their being an exercise of sight? A case that excited some interest recently was that of Rosa Kuleshova, reported in *Time* (25 January, 1963, p.58). She allegedly distinguished colours and read ordinary print with her fingertips, without relying on the texture of the paper. Later the case was declared by TASS to be a fraud. She peeped. But meanwhile other psychologists had reported that similar capacities were known in man and in other animals. May not cases such as this supply counter-examples to the claim that the non-incidental perception of colour is always an exercise of sight?

65   It is by no means so easy to find counter-examples as one might at first

29. No doubt, this description would be preferred in fact. But is there good reason for preferring it? A partial answer can be gained by comparing the relation between odour and colour with that between, say, being red (hot) and warmth, or between the shape things look and the shape they feel. Different as these latter two cases are from each other, they both involve a relationship such that we do not feel obliged to say merely that one property is seen and the other is known to be correlated with it. The first case has been mentioned in notes 24 and 27. Excellent discussions bearing on the second case can be found in H.P. Grice, *op. cit.*, and in Jonathan Bennett, 'Substance, reality and primary qualities,' *American Philosophical Quarterly* (1965). The point is that we do not have to talk of seeing visual shape and knowing that tactual shape is correlated with it. We can talk more boldly of seeing shape. For the shape things look and the shape they feel do not vary independently of each other. Nor is this a mere accident that could easily have been otherwise. If we try to imagine it otherwise, we will find we can no longer speak of there being physical objects and of these objects having a definite location in the imagined situation. For details, see the two articles mentioned.

suppose. Had the case of Rosa Kuleshova been genuine, we should have needed a lot of information about her before we could decide whether to say she was feeling colour, or seeing colour with an unusual part of the body, or feeling some such property as warmth and inferring to colour. Only if she was feeling colour would she supply a counter-example. To establish that she was feeling colour, we should have to show (a) that hers was a case of feeling, not of seeing with an unusual part of the body. (It would help to show this, if she could distinguish colours with any part of her body surface.) But we should also have to show (b) that her perception of colour was none the less non-incidental, in other words that she was not simply inferring to colour. And the trouble is that the performance of one of these tasks is liable to impede the performance of the other.[30]

We may add that if a case of feeling colour can be described at all, it will very likely not be a case that a scientist can expect to meet in the real world. And if not, it will not be a case of a kind that Aristotle is particularly concerned to classify.

Finally, we should raise a third objection against the appeal to sense **66** objects. May not people be said to see when they are subject to total hallucination, or when they have after-images, or when their eyes are closed and there is some stimulation of the optic nerve, or in other cases where there is no real colour, brightness, or darkness in the objective world which they are perceiving? If so, it is not true that all seeing involves the perception of colour, brightness, or darkness. Aristotle's own response would be to allow that in these cases no objective colour is perceived, but to deny that they are cases of seeing. Rather, they are exercises of *phantasia*, the faculty of imagination. At least, this is the usual trend in Aristotle, though there are faint traces of a different trend.[31]

30. Particularly important would be the question of what kind of experience she had. If the experience were too like that involved in seeing, we should be inclined to say she was seeing. If the experience were too like that involved in, say, feeling warmth, we might be inclined to say she was feeling, but that the perception of colour was merely incidental. The solution might seem to be to look for a case in which the experience involved was neutral – i.e. neither too like that involved in recognised cases of seeing, nor too like that involved in recognised cases of feeling. But it is not clear that even this would enable us to classify the case as one of feeling colour. For could we say her perception of colour was non-incidental if the colour did not give rise to the kind of experience normally associated with colour? The answer to this will no doubt depend in part on one's conception of colour, and on how closely one supposes the notion of colour to be linked to a certain kind of experience. One might argue that the notion of colour is connected not only with a certain kind of experience, but also with the behaviour of light. So if we can show she is reacting to the behaviour of light, and not to some by-product of light, such as temperature, we shall have reason to say her perception of colour is non-incidental. (For experiments ruling out reaction to temperature, see *Nature*, 29 August 1964, p.993.) But this suggestion in its turn creates a difficulty. For if she perceives by means of light receptors, this will make her unable to perceive by direct contact, and so cast doubt again on the idea that she is feeling. This is perhaps enough to indicate some of the difficulties.

31. For the predominant trend see, e.g., *De An.* 428a16 and *Insom.* 458b7-9, 459a1-21. For traces of a different trend see *De An.* 425b22-5, which is tempted by the idea that when one has an after-image, one does perceive real, objective colour – namely, the colour taken on by one's eye-jelly, as a result of looking at the bright object.

The Aristotelian answer is not satisfactory, for surely the examples in question are cases of seeing in the ordinary sense. Is there any other way of meeting the present objection, so as to preserve the idea that all seeing involves the perception of colour, brightness, or darkness? It may be urged that when one sees with closed eyes, one is at least perceiving subjective colour, even if there is no objective colour in the external world that one is seeing. But one who thus appeals to subjective colour should notice what he is doing. He is in effect appealing to something which initially we might have been inclined to distinguish from colour itself – namely, the kind of experience to which colour gives rise. He is saying that the experience is like that of perceiving objective colour. He is not wrong, for the character of the experience is part of the reason why seeing with one's eyes closed is counted as a kind of seeing. But on the other hand, it is not clear whether the definition can still be said to confine itself to the mention of sense objects only.

What conclusions can we now draw from our attempt to define sight as the perception of colour, brightness, or darkness? The definition goes a long way toward picking out the right cases, though, as the third objection shows, it does not, without special interpretation, cover quite all the standard cases of sight.

67   A more interesting point that has emerged *en route* is the importance of the kind of experience that is involved in sight. We found ourselves appealing to the character of this experience, firstly when we talked of the phenomenological kinship between colour and brightness or darkness, secondly when (in note 30) we argued against the possibility of feeling colour, and thirdly when we spoke of subjective colour. It looks as if the character of the experience is an important element in the concept of sight. And part of the reason why it is helpful to mention the sense objects in a definition of sight is that reference to the sense objects implies in turn a reference to the kind of experience to which the sense objects give rise.[32]

A further conclusion is that we should be cautious in claiming that the attempted definition confines itself to the sense objects. For not only does the mention of colour, brightness, and darkness import a reference to the kind of experience involved, but also there was an appeal to the notion of perception. Sight was treated as one species of the genus, perception. Now, if we were to analyse the generic notion of perception in its turn, we might well have to refer to the kind of physical mechanisms that distinguish sense perception from other forms of cognition. And if so, the attempted definition of sight in its turn involves an implicit appeal to these mechanisms.

Finally, we have been laying stress on two criteria, the sense objects and the kind of experience involved. But we should remember that it may be necessary to appeal to other criteria as well, at least when we leave the standard cases of sense perception and consider how to classify imaginary and logically possible cases. Here we may need to take into account the behaviour involved, the mechanisms within the perceiver's body, and the mechanisms in the surrounding environment.[33]

32. Grice arrives at a similar conclusion, travelling by a somewhat different route, in his valuable paper, *op. cit.*

33. These possibilities are discussed in detail by Grice, *op. cit.*

Where does this discussion leave Aristotle? It suggests that his stress on the sense objects is helpful. For reference to these does pick out most of the standard cases of sight and does bring out the unity of the concept. But reference to the objects alone, we have seen, will not suffice. And so we may be glad that in his protracted discussion of the senses, the emphasis on sense objects does not lead to the exclusion of other aspects of each sense. With some qualifications, then, the verdict so far is in favour of Aristotle. But I have hitherto excluded from discussion a certain one of the five senses – namely, the sense of touch. To this I shall now have to turn.   **68**

2. The sense of touch

There is an exception to what we have been saying about the importance of sense objects. This exception is the sense of touch. I have in mind the layman's conception of touch, rather than the refined concept of psychologists, which has been influenced by neuro-physiological discoveries. The layman's concept includes, roughly speaking, those perceptual powers which are called powers of *feeling* sensible properties, but only sensible properties of a kind that can belong to non-sentient bodies and not, for example, such properties as hunger or pain. In speaking of touch, I am using the noun 'touch', not the verb. The verb that goes with it is not the verb 'to touch', but the verb 'to feel'.

It would be unsatisfactory to rely heavily on the objects of touch in defining the sense. For one thing, the objects of touch are extremely varied.[34] Not only would it be laborious to define touch by reference to its many objects, but also knowledge of what these objects are would give no indication of what unites the varieties of touch, nor of why some kinds of sense perception are excluded. Again, given the diversity that already exists, one would meet less difficulty than in corresponding cases with other senses, in classifying under touch new perceptual powers which have quite different   **69** objects from any of those currently recognised as objects of touch. So one does not want a definition that restricts too much the list of objects. A further inconvenience (though a surmountable one) for someone who lays stress on the objects of touch is that so many of the objects apprehended by touch are apprehended by other senses too, as, for example, are size and shape, rough and smooth, sharp and blunt, and perhaps hot and cold.

---

34. Aristotle might be able to shorten the list of objects somewhat, thanks to his view that coarse and fine, viscous and brittle, hard and soft, come from dry and fluid (*GC* 329b32-34). In fact, he says all the other objects of touch are reducible to the basic four, dry and fluid, hot and cold (*GC* 329b34, 330a24-26). If this is so, might he not be able to specify the objects of touch as dry and fluid, hot and cold, and other properties reducible to these? Such a specification runs two opposite risks. It would let in the objects of other senses, if any of these are reducible to dry, fluid, hot, or cold. At the same time, it is not clear how it would accommodate heavy and light, rough and smooth. For he does not show how these are reducible to dry and fluid, hot and cold, though he does bring out some causal connections between them. In any event, he can at best shorten the list of objects of touch. He cannot eliminate the irreducible difference between the pair, hot and cold, and the pair, dry and fluid.

In view of these difficulties, it is not surprising to find people defining touch by reference to something other than its objects. We shall encounter two criteria that were canvassed in ancient times.

(a) *The contact criterion.* The criterion that impresses Aristotle is that touch, in his view, operates by direct contact with the body.[35] In saying this, he may be influenced by the etymology of the word for touch – namely, *haphê*, a word which was still often used with its original meaning of contact. At any rate, he says in the *De Anima* (435a17-18) that the sense of touch gets its name from the fact that it operates through direct contact.

Aristotle's appeals to the contact criterion are fairly numerous. Thus when perception occurs through direct contact, we quite often find him treating this as reason enough for classifying a perceptual power as a form of touch. In the *De Sensu*, for example (442a29-b3), he accuses Democritus of reducing all the senses to touch, apparently on the grounds that Democritus makes all the senses operate through direct contact between the body and the atoms that stream off the object perceived. Again, in the *De Anima*, at least on one interpretation of lines 434b11-18, he argues from the fact that an animal needs to perceive a thing when in direct contact with it, to the conclusion that it needs the sense of touch. In the immediately following lines, 434b18-19, again on one interpretation, he argues from the fact that taste apprehends something with which we are in direct contact – namely **70** food – to the conclusion that taste is a variety of touch. Elsewhere in the *De Anima*, at 424b27-8, we find the statement, 'And all things that we perceive when in contact with them are perceived by touch'.

An argument in the opposite direction is offered at *De Anima* 422a8-16. Not only does perception by direct contact indicate the sense of touch, but all exercises of taste (a form of touch, in Aristotle's view) are through contact. This is in spite of appearances to the contrary, which might suggest that fish taste food thrown into the water at a distance from them, or that we taste through the intervening liquid the sugar at the bottom of our drink. Aristotle's argument travels in the same direction when he says, 'What is perceived by touch is directly contacted' (*De An.* 434b12-13).

In these remarks, Aristotle has not abandoned the idea of distinguishing the other four senses by reference to their objects. On the contrary, he is presupposing it. And he thinks this way of distinguishing them fits in with the definition of touch by reference to direct contact. His idea is that sight, hearing, and smell (where these are defined as the power to perceive colour (and so forth), sound, and odour) are *never* exercised through direct contact (*De An.* 419a11-21, 419a25-30, 421b16-18, 422a14-15, 423b20-5). Taste, however (where this is defined as the power to perceive flavour and is regarded as a form of touch), is *always* so exercised (*De An.* 422a8-16). It is given these facts that we can, in his opinion, safely distinguish touch (including taste) as operating through direct contact with the body. He does not say how things would need to be classified, if some acts of perceiving

35. This is not to say that touch operates through direct contact with the sense organ. For the organ of touch is within, according to Aristotle, in the region of the heart (*Sens.* 439a1).

flavour were performed at a distance or some acts of perceiving colour were through direct contact.

Though Aristotle is wise to lay stress on something other than the *objects* of touch, his choice of the direct contact mechanism is difficult to work with. And this applies whether with him we take touch as including taste, or not. To bring this out, let us first notice which perceptual powers he lists under touch. He includes the power to perceive hot and cold, fluid and dry, hard and soft, heavy and light, viscous and brittle, rough and smooth, coarse and fine, as well as the power to perceive flavour. These lists are taken from the *De Anima*[36] and from the *De Generatione et Corruptione*.[37] Elsewhere, rough and smooth are distinguished from the others, as being objects of sight as well as of touch – in other words, as being common objects.[38] Other common objects are size, shape, sharp and blunt, motion and rest, number and unity.[39] It is only when these common objects are perceived by direct contact that Aristotle thinks of them as being perceived by touch.

There are several difficulties to be mentioned in applying the contact criterion. Firstly, one can by the sense of touch feel the heat of a stove while at a distance from it. Again, though one sometimes tastes by direct contact, one can sometimes also taste the olive at the bottom of the Martini without being in direct contact with it. Aristotle might wish to reply to the first example that one really is in direct contact with the flavoured object after all.[41] But if these are legitimate ways of showing that touch and taste always operate by direct contact, could they not have been used with equal plausibility to show that smell operates by direct contact? What makes Aristotle so sure that one does not smell the air intervening between oneself and the rose, or that one does not smell as a result of bits of rose dissolving and becoming mixed with the air?

This difficulty may suggest an alternative way of applying the contact criterion. Why did not Aristotle seek to distinguish touch (including taste) from the other senses by saying that touch is that group of perceptual powers that *can* operate by direct contact? Not every exercise of touch will involve direct contact, but those exercises which do not will be similar to those which do, in ways which justify our counting them as exercises of the same sense, touch. Unfortunately, this way of applying the contact criterion runs into an immediate difficulty. For hearing and smell would seem to be powers which *can* operate through direct contact,[42] even if they seldom do so in fact.

Finally, there is a difficulty of another sort in relying on a contact criterion. It is that taste will have to be counted as a form of touch. Aristotle is quite happy so to count it. But our own concept of touch does not include taste. Nor did the concept that Aristotle inherited. At any rate, when we

36. 422b25-7.
37. 329b18-20.
38. *Sens.* 442b5-7.
39. *Sens.* 442b5-7; *De An.* 425a16.
40. *GC* 327a3.
41. *De An.* 422a8-16.
42. One can smell the snuff lodged in one's nostrils, and hear the bath water trapped in one's ears, though Aristotle seeks to deny this in the passages mentioned on p.86.

discuss the main rival to the contact criterion, we shall notice that a number
of Aristotle's predecessors did not group taste along with the tactual
powers.[43] So the contact criterion does not pick out existing concepts of
touch. It seems more that Aristotle is making a recommendation – namely,
that we should follow the contact criterion to its logical conclusion and
include taste under touch. But the recommendation does not seem a very
good one, given the way in which, as we have seen, this criterion cuts across
other criteria for distinguishing senses.

Apart from the above difficulties involved in using the contact criterion,
there was another reason why it could not be employed by certain of
Aristotle's predecessors. For Empedocles, Democritus, and, according to
Aristotle,[44] most of the other early philosophers of nature had made *all* sense
perception operate by direct contact. The contact, in the case of some forms
of sense perception, was with particles that streamed off the thing perceived
and into the sense organs. Contact could not therefore be used as a criterion
for distinguishing one sense from others. It characterised all forms of sense
perception alike. Aristotle avoided this obstacle to using the contact
criterion.[45] For on his theory, the sense organs did not receive particles of
matter from the thing perceived. Rather, they received form without
73 matter.[46]. The eye-jelly, for example, took on the colours of the thing
perceived but did not come into contact with material particles from it.[47] It
may be urged that the early philosophers of nature still could have used a
contact criterion for drawing distinctions between senses. For there is a
difference between being in contact with the main mass of the thing
perceived, and being in contact with particles that have streamed from it. So
why should not touch be distinguished as involving contact with the main
mass? This new criterion no longer turns on the question of whether contact
is employed, but rather on the question of what it is that is contacted.
Assuming that it still deserves to be called a contact criterion, it does meet
the latest objection to contact criteria. But it is not the contact criterion that
Aristotle himself uses for touch, since he does not require contact with the
main mass.[48] Nor, of course, would it escape the objections raised earlier
against contact criteria.

(b) *The non-localisation criterion.* There is evidence that some of Aristotle's
predecessors had used another criterion instead of the contact criterion. The
clearest example of this comes in Plato's *Timaeus*, 61D-65B. Here Plato
groups together various properties that we should count as objects of touch
– namely, hot, cold, hard, soft, heavy, light, smooth, and rough. But he does
not use a contact criterion for grouping them, nor does he use one of the

43. See pp. 89-90.
44. *Sens.* 442a29-30.
45. On this subject, see the useful article by Solmsen [86].
46. *De An.* 424a18, 424b2, 425b22, 427a8, 429a15, 434a29, 435a22.
47. In another sense, Aristotle did accept that all sense perception involved
contact. The object seen must be in contact with the air, and the air in turn with the
eye (*Phys.* 245a2-9).
48. Thus, he allows that fish exercise taste, a form of touch, when in contact not
with the main mass of their food, but with that part of their food that has dissolved in
the water.

names for the sense of touch that is etymologically connected with contact –
namely, *haphê* or *psausis*. Rather, he groups these properties together
because, in his words, they are affections 'common to the body as a whole'
(64A, 65B). What he means is that they are perceived without the use of a
localised organ, such as eyes, nose, ears, or tongue. Rather they can be
perceived through any part of the body.[49]

Plato does not always avoid the names that are connected with contact.   **74**
Thus in the *Republic* (523E) we find him using for the sense of touch the
name *haphê*. This time he is talking of the perception of thick and thin, hard
and soft. He uses a related word for the sense of touch at *Phaedo* 75A, and
perhaps at *Theaetetus* 186B, 189A, 195D-E.

There is another author who combines the non-localisation criterion with
the use of terminology that is connected with contact. In *Regimen* I 23, a
treatise which was written perhaps around 400 BC., and which belongs to
the Hippocratic collection of medical writings, there is reference to a sense
called *psausis*, a name which is connected with contact. But the author goes
on to add a reference to the non-localisation criterion, saying that the whole
body is its organ.

For a use of the non-localisation criterion without terminology suggesting
contact, we may refer to Theophrastus' report (*De Sensibus* 38) on
Cleidemus, a Presocratic who was perhaps contemporary with Democritus.
According to this report, Cleidemus distinguished between perception
through the tongue and perception through the rest of the body.

This last example is important for an additional reason. Not only does it
use the non-localisation criterion for distinguishing a sense. But also by its
treatment of what we should call taste, it implies a rejection of the contact
criterion. For both perception through the tongue and perception through
the rest of the body operate by direct contact. Yet for all that, they are not
grouped together as forming a single sense.

The same is true in the passage cited from the Hippocratic treatise,
Regimen. Even though this passage uses the name *psausis*, which is connected
with contact, it does not include taste as falling under *psausis*. On the
contrary, it distinguishes between perception through the tongue and
perception through the whole body. And it is the latter that is called *psausis*.
In spite, then, of using a name connected with contact, the author does not
treat contact as a sufficient ground for including a form of perception under
the heading of *psausis*. He seems to have preferred the non-localisation   **75**
criterion to the contact one.

The same seems to be true of other authors. At any rate, on the most
natural interpretation, Democritus lists five senses in fragment 11 of Diels'
collection – namely, sight, hearing, smell, taste, and touch. Though he uses
a contact word, *psausis*, for touch, he agrees with Cleidemus and with the
author of *Regimen* I, in refusing to subsume taste under the heading of touch.
And he thereby implies rejection of the contact criterion. Admittedly, an

49. Aristotle would not agree that touch lacks a localised organ. The organ is in
the region of the heart (*Sens.* 439a1). He could still have distinguished the recognised
tactual powers, if he had chosen, however, by saying that the other senses have either
a localised organ at the surface of the body (ears, eyes, nose) or at least a localised
channel at the surface (tongue).

alternative interpretation has been suggested for the passage. Solmsen[50] remarks that the word *psausis* might be being used not to refer to the sense of touch, but to emphasise that the other four senses named operate, in Democritus' opinion, by contact. This interpretation is very much less natural. But even if it be correct, we still get a result of some interest. For if contact characterises the other four senses, then Democritus is not free to distinguish a fifth sense, touch, as the sense which employs contact. So, as was remarked before, if he wished to use the contact criterion, he would have to use a version of it different from Aristotle's.

Aristotle himself seems to have been influenced by the tradition which treats taste as distinct from touch, in so far as he devotes separate discussions in the *De Anima* to sight, hearing, smell, taste, and touch. He does not treat taste and touch together, in spite of his recommendation that we should subsume taste under touch.

Let us summarise these findings. On the one hand, we do encounter among Aristotle's predecessors the names *psausis* and *haphê*, which are connected with contact. On the other hand, a good many authors, including ones who used these names, seem to have rejected the contact criterion as a way of distinguishing the sense of touch. This rejection comes out in their insistence on treating taste as distinct from touch. (Moreover, their view that all the senses operate by direct contact commits them to rejecting Aristotle's own version of the contact criterion.) In place of the contact criterion for distinguishing touch, a number of them used the non-localisation criterion. It looks as if, in spite of their choice of nomenclature, the non-localisation criterion answered more faithfully to the conception which they actually had.

Certainly, the non-localisation criterion is the one that corresponds most closely to the present-day concept of touch, at least if we take the layman's conception, which I referred to before. The powers that the layman groups under touch (and here the power of taste is not included) are distinguished by the fact that they operate without any obvious localised organ. If modern research has discovered localised organs, these were not apparent at the time the concept was being formed. The absence of an obvious localised organ is the only feature that is common and peculiar to the very diverse powers that are grouped under the heading of touch. This is not to say that the feature is logically necessary or logically sufficient for making a perceptual power count as a variety of touch. But at least it has served as a principle of collection for the familiar varieties. And newly encountered or imaginary perceptual powers will be classified on the basis of their similarity to these familiar ones (even though the similarity will not necessarily be in respect of non-localisation).

We get a strong indication of the influence that the non-localisation criterion has had, if we ask ourselves the following question. What else has led to taste being excluded, and to the perception of temperature being included, under the heading of touch? It looks, then, as if the non-localisation criterion, to be found in Plato and others, has retained its influence to the present day.

50. *Op. cit.*

Two related points of clarification need to be introduced, however. The non-localisation criterion does not on its own enable us to classify individual acts of perception. For one can, for example, feel the texture of something with one's tongue or ear. So we must not suggest that each individual exercise of touch will be carried out without the aid of a localised organ. Rather, the point is that the same quality, texture, can be apprehended by the same kind of mechanism and the same kind of experience, through a quite different part of the body, at least in the case of a healthy human being. And these considerations warrant our saying that, even if a given exercise of the power is confined to a localised organ, the power itself is not so confined.

The point could be put like this. The non-localisation criterion is used to classify not individual acts of perception, but perceptual powers. And in deciding which individual acts fall under a given power, we may have to appeal to criteria other than the non-localisation one.

This brings us to the second point of clarification. We have been saying that under touch we include at present those perceptual powers which operate without any obvious localised organ. But the truth of this statement depends on what counts as a distinct perceptual power. Is the power to perceive shape, for example, whether visually or tactually, to be counted as a single power? If so, we will get an unfortunate result. For when we ask whether or not this single power is confined to a localised organ, either answer will be unsatisfactory. Suppose, for example, it is said that the power to perceive shape is not confined to a localised organ, on the grounds that tactual exercises of the power are not so confined. Then the entire power of perceiving shape, even the power to perceive it visually, will have to be classified under touch, which is not the result we want. The moral is that the non-localisation criterion can only be used to classify powers under the heading of touch, if we have adopted the right kind of procedure for individuating powers in the first place.

Now that we have introduced the non-localisation criterion, we are in a better position to evaluate two arguments of Aristotle's. In *De Anima* II 11, he introduces several imaginary situations. One of these situations involves people being able to perceive flavour with any part of the body.[51] In this situation, he says, people would identify taste with touch. Taken in one sense, Aristotle's claim is perfectly correct, as our discussion of the non-localisation criterion will show. For in the envisaged situation, the perception of flavour would not be through a localised organ. Taste in that case would have at least as good a claim as the perception of temperature to be classified under touch. Admittedly, this is not the kind of point that Aristotle himself is intending to make in the passage.[52] So all we should say

51. 423a17-21.
52. Aristotle's own point is that in the imaginary situation described, we would fail to notice that taste is a distinct kind of perception in its own right, distinct from, say, the power of perceiving fluid and dry. For there would be no differerence of organ or medium to attract our attention to its distinctness. Aristotle does think, however, that taste is a distinct kind of perception, and that it would remain so in the imaginary situation. This is not to retract his view that taste is a kind of touch, and would remain so in the imaginary situation. It is to insist that taste is, and would be, only

78   is that our discussion of the non-localisation criterion reveals one sense in which his remark is correct.

The second Aristotelian argument which we can now profitably recall is his objection to Democritus, that Democritus reduces all the senses to touch.[53] The ground of this charge is apparently that Democritus makes all the senses operate through contact. Aristotle is right about one thing. The name *haphê* originally meant, and still often meant, contact. Consequently, if all the senses operate through contact, the name *haphê* is not a very appropriate one to reserve for one of them. Rather, it should be applied to all. This point is only one about nomenclature, however. There is a much more important point on which Aristotle cannot fault Democritus. He cannot say that Democritus is debarred from distinguishing between the sense that is called touch and the other four senses. For Democritus is free to draw this distinction by reference to the non-localisation criterion.

Retrospect

We have argued that Aristotle emphasises the sense objects in his account of four of the senses. And we found some good reasons for following such a policy. But we argued that the policy would not be a good one in connection with the sense of touch, and that Aristotle wisely stresses a different criterion in speaking of this sense. He goes wrong, however, in choosing the contact criterion for touch, rather than the non-localisation criterion that had been used by several of his predecessors. Although the name *haphê*, like

79   our word 'touch,' was often used to mean contact, it is in fact the non-localisation criterion that corresponds most closely to the conception of touch that people have actually had.[54]

---

one kind of touch. Aristotle suggests that just as in the imaginary situation we would fail to notice the distinctness of taste, so now perhaps we fail to distinguish different kinds of perception that are lumped together under the heading of touch.

53. *Sens*. 442a29-b3.

54. Earlier drafts were read at Cornell, Princeton, and London Universities, and at a weekend meeting of Birkbeck College. I benefited from many helpful comments at these meetings. But I should like to acknowledge in particular Hidé Ishiguro, Alan Lacey, and David Hamlyn, who prepared for me on these occasions valuable comments which have led to many improvements. Some of the work for this paper was done on leave, while I held a Howard Foundation Fellowship from Brown University, and a project grant, No. H68-0-95, from the National Endowment for the Humanities. I acknowledge these sources gratefully.

6

Richard Norman

Aristotle's Philosopher-God

In chapters 7 and 9 of *Metaphysics* XII, Aristotle argues that the activity of the Prime Mover is to 'think itself'. The way in which his argument has been interpreted by many recent commentators is exemplified in the following summary by Ross ([16], p.182):

> Now knowledge, when not dependent, as in man, on sense and imagination, must be of that which is the best; and that which is the best is God. The object of his knowledge is therefore himself.

This argument can be represented by the following syllogistic schema:

> A thinks B
> B is A
> _____
>
> Therefore   A thinks A.

I shall therefore refer to it as the Syllogistic Proof. What I want to suggest is that Aristotle does not use the Syllogistic Proof – that he does not say what Ross and others attribute to him, and that it is not the meaning he intended to convey. There is one point at which he is sometimes regarded as saying it; at 1074b34 there occurs the sentence: 'If it is best, it thinks itself, and the thinking is a thinking of thinking.' But I hope to show that, in order to regard this as a simple statement of the Syllogistic Proof, one has to isolate it from its context; and to do so is to make nonsense of, and render superfluous, the whole chain of reasoning that leads up to it. Indeed, I think that in general one is entitled to ask why, if Aristotle meant what Ross and others have understood him to mean, he chose such a long and complicated way of saying it.

A further point I wish to make is that this interpretation lends an air of unnecessary absurdity to the whole account. It suggests that the Prime Mover is a sort of heavenly Narcissus, who looks around for the perfection which he wishes to contemplate, finds nothing to rival his own self, and settles into a posture of permanent self-admiration. This, of course, is a caricature, but it merely exaggerates the impression that Ross and others do actually convey. And the reason why they convey it is that a central element in their misunderstanding of Aristotle's argument is their misconception of what he means by mind 'thinking itself'.

It is generally recognised that these two chapters of *Metaphysics* XII are connected in some way with certain remarks which Aristotle makes in *De*

Anima III 4. But I do not think that scholars have always recognised just what difference this makes to the interpretation of Aristotle's argument, and I therefore want to begin with a brief glance at the relevant chapter of *De Anima*.

De Anima III 4

In this chapter Aristotle begins his treatment of thinking soul, and his first step is to compare the operation of intellect with perception. If, he says, thinking is analogous to perception, it must consist in being acted on by the object of thought 'or something else of that sort'. Aristotle assumes that the analogy does hold (429a17-18), and suggests that the manner in which intellect is acted on by the objects of thought is in being 'capable of receiving the form'. Intellect has no positive nature of its own; it is pure potentiality. In itself it has nothing in common with the forms that are its objects, but it is potentially like them. When it thinks, it takes in the forms, and acts as a receptacle for them.

After elaborating the point that intellect differs from perception in being completely independent of the body, since its objects are not physical things but forms, Aristotle introduces an important new point at 429b5. 'When the intellect has become each of its objects in this way, as the man who actually knows is said to be, that is, when it is capable of acting on its own, even then it is in a sense potential (though not in the same sense as it was before it learned or discovered anything), but now it can think itself'.

Here we have the first indication of what I take to be the most important idea in this chapter – the theory of two sorts of thinking, the one a preliminary to the other. In the first sort of thinking, the intellect takes in the forms and, being itself mere potentiality, it is actualised by becoming those forms. And it is now capable of performing the second sort of thinking; having become the objects of thought it is now able to think itself. The manuscript reading *autos de hauton* ('itself') has been regarded as suspect, and Bywater's suggestion *autos di' hautou* ('on its own') has been preferred by some commentators. Ross, arguing for the emendation, says: 'There would be no point in a reference here to self-knowledge'. But this second kind of thinking just *is* self-knowledge. Intellect thinks itself, because it thinks those objects of thought which it has become through the earlier kind of thinking.

For the purpose of comparison with *Metaphysics* XII it is important to notice the precise terms in which Aristotle differentiates the two kinds of thinking. In the earlier stage, intellect is potentiality – 'it must have no other nature than this, that it is potential'. In the second stage intellect is (despite the mention of its being still in a sense potential) characterised principally by the fact that it is now actualised – '... it has become each of its objects, as the man who *actually* knows is said to be'. We can therefore most conveniently refer to the two kinds of thinking in the manner of the ancient commentators, as that of potential intellect and that of actual intellect. The second important opposition is this: the first kind of thinking is dependent upon something external – it is 'to be affected in some way by the object of

65

thought' – whereas the second is entirely self-sufficient and intellect thinks 'on its own'. And thirdly: in the earlier stage intellect *becomes* identical with the objects of thought, whereas in the second stage it *is already* identical with them and therefore thinks itself.

The remainder of the chapter is taken up as follows:

429b10-22: Aristotle reiterates that the objects of perception and intellect are physical things and their essences respectively.

429b22-430a9: Aristotle examines two difficulties. (a) To think something is to experience something, but how can intellect experience anything if it is incapable of being affected? This is solved by clarifying the special sense in which the activity of intellect is experiencing or being affected. (b) How can intellect think itself? This is answered by repeating that 'in the case of things without matter that which thinks and that which is thought are the same, since 'theoretic' knowledge is identical with what is known "theoretically" ... But in things that have matter, each object of thought is present potentially.' The importance of this section is that it introduces us to more of the vocabulary with which Aristotle differentiates the two kinds of thinking. The main addition is that of the phrase 'theoretic knowledge' to describe the second stage of thinking. We have also been given the opposition between things apart from matter, which are the objects of the second stage of thinking, and objects of thought immanent in physical things, the objects of the first stage of thinking.

66

The relevance of all this to *Metaphysics* XII 7 and 9 is that Aristotle's regular way of talking about the activity of actual intellect is in terms of 'intellect thinking itself'. It is interesting to see why this is so. Aristotle's talk about the nature of processes of thought is influenced by the use of a misleading model. Like so many philosophers, for example the British empiricists, he tends to take perception, and especially sight, as the paradigm of mental processes. The subject-object distinction in perception, between that which sees and that which is seen, is then carried over into consideration of the nature of thought and creates the assumption that thought is also susceptible of a subject-object analysis, into that which thinks and that which is thought.[1] It is easy enough to identify the objects of potential intellect. They are clearly the things in the external world, regarded as universals and not as particulars. But what about actual intellect? If its thinking is abstract and theoretical, what can the objects of this thinking be? Obviously they cannot be any visible entities in the external world. Therefore they must be invisible, purely mental entities – abstract matterless objects of thought (cf. Lockean 'ideas'). Where and what are these objects of thought? They are in the mind, of course, and in fact they must be that mental stuff of which the mind is composed. If, in this abstract thinking, mind thinks nothing outside itself, it must think itself. The pattern of error here is the one which has been all-pervasive in the history of philosophy: the preference for an ontological solution when what is called for is a conceptual solution. Unable to identify any entities which serve as objects to acts of abstract thought, Aristotle invents new 'metaphysical' entities to fill this rôle. But the reason why one cannot

1. As we have already noted, the analogy with perception is explicitly used in this way at 429a13-15 and 17-18.

identify any such entities is not that they are internal and immaterial, but that the whole subject-object analysis is inappropriate. What is really needed is an alternative model – for example, one which makes thinking less like perceiving and more like talking to oneself.

However, the fact is that Aristotle uses the phrase 'intellect thinking itself' as a regular way of describing pure abstract thought. And the points I wish to argue are therefore:

1. When Aristotle describes the Prime Mover as 'thinking itself', he is not referring to any activity that could be called 'self-contemplation'; he is simply describing the same activity that human minds perform when they engage in abstract thought.

2. Consequently he does not need the Syllogistic Proof in order to show that the Prime Mover thinks itself, and he does not use it. All he needs to show is that its thinking is entirely of the 'theoretic' kind and not at all of the 'receptive' kind.

3. Since 'self-thinking' is the same as ordinary human abstract thought, it is not this that characterises the Prime Mover, but rather the fact that it thinks of perfection, and does so eternally.

The argument in Metaphysics XII 7

In the first half of chapter 7, up to 1072b14, Aristotle shows that the Prime Mover is a final cause, in that it is good and the object of desire. He then states that the activity of the Prime Mover is that of thinking about what is best. Its activity is like the best which we humans experience, but we do so only for a short time, it does so eternally. Since thinking, as activity, is a pleasure, it must be about what is good, and pure thought (*hê noêsis hê kath' hautên*) must be about pure perfection (*tou kath' hauto aristou*).

The next sentence, at 1072b20, reads: *hauton de noei ho nous kata metalêpsin tou noêtou* – 'Intellect thinks itself through participation in the object of thought'. Ross comments: 'In order to find the connexion between these two sentences, it seems necessary to suppose that when Aristotle says that the divine *noêsis hê kath' hautên* is of *to kath' hauto ariston* he means the conclusion to be drawn 'and therefore of the divine intellect itself', which has been exhibited as the primary object of desire (a27), in other words as the perfect (a35). He then goes on to show *how* intellect knows itself ...' (*Aristotle: Metaphysics*, Vol. 2, p.379).

Now admittedly Aristotle's reasoning is often obscure, and at times the main argument becomes so submerged under qualifications and explanations that it is made to seem almost incidental to them. But can we really suppose that in this case the main argument has become so submerged as to have actually disappeared? We have represented the Syllogistic Proof as

A thinks B
B is A
———————
Therefore   A thinks A.

If Aristotle really uses it, this logical step ought to be the most important in **68** the whole argument, the drawing together of the different strands to produce the main conclusion. Yet we have to suppose that Aristotle requires us to supply the second premiss from twenty lines earlier, and to infer the conclusion for ourselves.

Before trying to explain 1072b20 ff., let me give the section in full:

> Intellect thinks itself, by way of its participation in the object of thought. For when it apprehends and thinks, it becomes that which is thought, so that intellect and its object are the same. For intellect receives the object of thought and the essence. And when it has it, it is actualised. Divinity, then, belongs to intellect as actualisation rather than to intellect as potential, and 'theoretic' thought is what is pleasantest and best.

Ross correctly recognises that this is a description not specifically of the Prime Mover but of intellect in general, and is a short summary of the theories we have seen stated in *De Anima* III. But in that case the obvious interpretation is to regard the section as following directly from the phrase *hê noêsis hê kath' hautên*, explaining, in terms of *De Anima* III, what this 'pure thought' is. The supposed syllogism would interrupt the sequence of reasoning, which is that the Prime Mover is pure thought, and therefore has the characteristics of human abstract thought, which 'thinks itself'. This interpretation makes for an overall continuity, following naturally from the sentence 'The life [of the Prime Mover] is like the best which we, for a short time, experience; for it is in that state always', and leading up naturally to the sentence: 'It is remarkable enough if God's happiness should be eternally what ours is sometimes, but still more remarkable that it is even greater.' God's happiness is not generically different from man's; it is like his. But it is greater in degree because in man 'theoretic' thought is mixed with the activity of passive intellect, in God it is completely pure. And God's happiness is superior in respect of duration, because man engages in 'theoretic' thought sometimes, God eternally.

So the sequence of the whole argument from 1072b15 to 1072b27 is:

> The activity of the Prime Mover is like the best that we engage in, but eternal.
>
> For us, thinking is pleasure, and the greatest pleasure is 'pure thought', because that is about pure perfection.
>
> This 'pure thought' is the abstract 'theoretic' thought which is the second stage in human thinking, and in which intellect and its object **69** are one.
>
> Therefore the Prime Mover is eternally engaged in this abstract thought.

And when it is said that the Prime Mover 'thinks itself', what is meant is not 'self-contemplation' but simply that identity of intellect and object of thought that characterises all abstract thought. This is why the phrase is introduced so unobtrusively, without any suggestion that it constitutes any new characterisation of the Prime Mover. The Syllogistic Proof is thus completely absent, because entirely unnecessary. Indeed, no proof at all is offered of the fact that the Prime Mover thinks itself. The only proof that could conceivably be offered would be a proof that the Prime Mover's thinking is entirely of the 'theoretic' kind and not at all of the 'receptive' kind. This is the proof that Aristotle offers in chapter 9.

The argument in Metaphysics XII 9

Chapter 9 begins with the assertion that the Prime Mover is 'most divine of the things which present themselves to us', and in the rest of the chapter Aristotle considers what this fact entails about the nature of the Prime Mover. One thing that clearly does follow is that the Prime Mover does not think about nothing, for then, so far from being most divine, it would have no more worth than a man asleep. What, then, does it think about? The question is posed in the form: which of the two kinds of thinking does it engage in? Is it intellect (i.e. the capacity for thought) or thinking, potentiality or actuality, is the object of its thought something external or the mental concepts that constitute its own mind? If the former – i.e. if its essence is not thinking but potentiality – then its state will be determined by something other than itself, viz. its external object of thought, and so it will not be the highest reality. This seems to indicate that the Prime Mover is pure thinking.

The argument is now restated from a different starting-point. What does intellect think? 'For either it thinks itself or it thinks something other than itself. And if it thinks something other than itself, either it always thinks the same, or its object varies.' The implication is that the possibility of *allo noein*, variety in the object of thought, arises only if intellect thinks something other than itself, and that if it thinks itself it always thinks the same. This may look as if it counts against the interpretation I have been offering; it seems to suggest that the intellect's own self is one object of thought alongside all the other possible objects of thought, and that its always thinking the same is guaranteed by its always thinking this particular object of thought. But, as the context shows, it is not in this sense that self-thinking intellect always thinks the same.[2] The relevant difference between the two sorts of thinking is this: what self-thinking intellect thinks about is determined by what conceptions it contains within itself, what potential intellect thinks is determined by what it encounters. Potential intellect can think 'any chance thing'. Actual intellect cannot; its thinking is bounded by the limits of its own contents, and it is in this sense that it always thinks the same. Thus if actual intellect always thinks 'that which is most precious', this will be determined by intellect itself and by the fact that the conceptions which it contains are of supreme worth. But if potential intellect always thinks that which is most precious, this will be determined by the fact that it

70

---

2. Cf. 1075a6, where it is stated that divine thought has a single object only in the same sense as human thought has. Its contents are indivisible, because 'everything which contains no matter is indivisible'.

always *encounters* that which is most precious, i.e. it will be determined by something outside itself.

The argument therefore proceeds as follows: Clearly the object of the Prime Mover's thought cannot be just any chance thing. It must think that which is most divine and precious, and it must do so eternally, without change. Now if it is not thinking but potentiality, this will mean that (a) the eternal continuity of its thought will not belong to it as a part of its essence, but only contingently, and therefore will involve effort and be tiring; (b) the Prime Mover itself will not be that which is most precious, but its object of thought will. For 'thinking will belong to it even if it thinks what is worst'; that is to say, if it is mind as potentiality then it is equally capable of thinking what is worst as well as what is best. 'So if this is to be avoided', if it is to think not what is worst but only what is best, it will not itself be what is best. The point seems to be that, if it is capable of thinking both the best and the worst, then, even if as a matter of fact it thinks what is best, it will do so only contingently, and will therefore not have as much worth as that which is most precious – which is its object. Hence if the Prime Mover is itself the highest being it cannot be potentiality; it must be pure actualisation, thinking and not intellect. It must think itself, and the thinking, as abstract thought, must be a thinking of thinking.

We saw that Ross regarded the sentence 'If it is best, it thinks itself ...' as a statement of the Syllogistic Proof. It should now be apparent that the sentence is in fact an integral part of the preceding argument and has to be set firmly in the context of the distinction between intellect and thinking. Ross summarises the argument as: **71**

> The PM thinks that which is best.
> The PM is that which is best.

Therefore   The PM thinks itself.

But, in so far as it can be summarised, the correct summary would be:

> The PM thinks that which is best.
> If the PM is intellect as potentiality, it could think both the best and the worst.

Therefore   If it is potentiality, that which it thinks is better than the PM itself.

> But the PM is that which is best.

Therefore   The PM is not intellect as potentiality.

Therefore   It is intellect as actualisation.

Therefore   It thinks itself.

This argument contains the two premisses and the conclusion of the

Syllogistic Proof, but the two premisses have completely different rôles here, and the conclusion 'It thinks itself' has nothing to do with any 'self-contemplation' but is simply a reference to that abstract thinking in which intellect 'thinks itself'.

Further confirmation of this interpretation is immediately provided by the next section. Having stated that 'its thinking is a thinking of thinking', Aristotle considers the objection that thought is always of something other than itself, and only incidentally of itself. He answers this objection by reminding us that in some of our thinking knowledge is its own object. These kinds of thinking are the productive sciences, whose object is 'the essence in abstraction from matter', and the 'theoretic' sciences, where the object is the thought, the mental concept – '*ho logos kai hê noêsis*'. This seems to me to establish beyond reasonable doubt that when Aristotle refers to the Prime Mover with the phrase 'it thinks itself' he wishes to indicate simply that activity of abstract thought in which humans also engage. The Prime Mover's abstract thought is of greater worth than human abstract thought. It is always of that which is most precious, whereas human abstract thinking is often also of the worst of things. But in so far as the Prime Mover thinks itself it is doing nothing different from what we do when we think in the abstract.

The difference between this and self-contemplation might be put in the following terms. In an act of thinking there is

(a)   the subject that thinks;
72   (b)   its 'object', i.e. the thought which it thinks;
(c)   its 'object', i.e. that *about which* it thinks.

To describe the Prime Mover's activity as 'self-contemplation' suggests that (a) and (c) are the same. But the sense in which intellect 'thinks itself' is rather that which amounts to an identity of (a) with (b). Another way of pointing the difference is suggested by Alexander Aphrodisiensis' treatise *De Anima*. Paraphrasing Aristotle's account of intellect thinking itself, he says:

> For that which is capable of thinking [i.e. intellect as a disposition] becomes something which 'thinks itself'; and it is [something which thinks itself] when it thinks, primarily and *per se* thinking of the form which is its object, but incidentally thinking of itself because that which it thinks of happens to occur to it when it is thinking.[3]

The difference between self-contemplation and the Prime Mover's self-thinking is the difference between intellect whose object is primarily itself and intellect whose object is only incidentally itself. Of course, as Aristotle is aware, there is a sense in which all conscious thinking is incidentally self-thinking: in thinking of something the mind is conscious of itself thinking it. Active intellect, in the Prime Mover and in the human mind, thinks itself 'incidentally' in this further sense: in so far as it has become the objects of thought it thinks itself incidentally when it thinks the objects of thought. But it does not think itself *as such*.

3. *De Anima* 86.19ff. (Supplementum Aristotelicum II, 1, ed. I. Bruns, Berlin, 1887).

One final point in favour of this interpretation: it is, so far as I can see, the only one which can make sense of Aristotle's assertion in Book X of the *Nicomachean Ethics*, that the activity of the Prime Mover is the *summum bonum* of human life. To suppose that in making this the ideal Aristotle is urging men to rapturous self-admiration is as false as it is ludicrous. The life that Aristotle is advocating is the life of the philosopher and of abstract philosophical thought.

It would be wrong to suggest that these passages in Aristotle have been universally misunderstood. The ancient commentators were less prone to error because they kept much closer to Aristotle's own words. For that very reason it is difficult to tell how far they really understood the significance of the arguments. But this is how pseudo-Alexander, for instance, reproduces Aristotle's argument:

> When our intellect (which is potentially the objects of thought) actually becomes the objects of thought as a result of supreme knowledge and of living well beyond all superlatives, then we live the life which is best and most blessed and beyond every pleasure, and which cannot be communicated in words, but is known to those who have experienced this blessed experience. Aristotle is saying, then, that the first cause always enjoys a life of the same quality as the best activity we engage in for a short time (not always, but when our intellect actually becomes the objects of thought). For it is impossible for us to live such a life always, but only on occasions, whereas for the first cause (as we shall learn a little later) it is possible. For its activity is nothing other than thinking itself; and its activity is its pleasure. On that basis, then, it lives always this life, viz. thinking itself. (*In Metaph.* 671.8-18 (*CIAG* I))

73

Pseudo-Alexander does seem to have grasped the point that the Prime Mover's self-thinking, though differing in duration, is of the same kind as our own normal abstract thought; and that the reason why the Prime Mover thinks itself is simply that the best form of life is that of active intellect, which thinks the objects of thought it has become. Among the modern commentators there is a general recognition that the passages in the *Metaphysics* which we have been examining are linked with those in the *De Anima*. The significance of this connection has sometimes been appreciated (see e.g. Hicks' note on *De Anima* 430a2), but more often it has gone unnoticed. I append a representative selection of quotations:

> T. Gomperz, *Greek Thinkers* (London, 1901-12, Vol. 4, p.220): 'His life is thought; but this thought can only be directed towards the best, that is Himself; and this self-contemplation fills Him with the highest bliss.'

> F.M. Cornford, *Before and After Socrates* (Cambridge, 1932, p.101): 'The activity of this Form must be of the highest kind conceivable – an eternal life of self-contemplation, for the only object adequate to God's contemplation must be God himself.'

W.K.C. Guthrie, *The Greek Philosophers* (London, 1950, p.139): 'God
.... is pure mind, which can contemplate in a single instant, and does
so eternally, the whole realm of true being. It is a splendid thought,
but unfortunately we have not finished with the philosophic
conscience. "The whole realm of true being" – yes, but of what does
this realm consist? The conclusion is that the only possible object of
the eternal thought of God is himself, the one full and perfect being.
... He is "wrapped in eternal self-contemplation".'

74   J.H. Randall [18], p.136: 'It does not "know" the world: it does not
"know" anything any more than the laws of nature can be said to
"know" anything. It is not "intelligent", as man has the power of
intelligence; it does not "think", as man can be said to "think" at
times.' And p.142: 'For Aristotle, indeed for any Greek, the perfect
functioning of *nous* must be a "life". It is "the life of *nous*", the "life of
reason": that is, *nous* eternally present to the highest object it can
conceive, itself.'

B. Russell, *History of Western Philosophy* (2nd ed., London, 1961,
p.180): 'God does not have the attributes of a Christian providence,
for it would derogate from his perfection to think about anything
except what is perfect, i.e. himself.'[4]

4. I am very grateful to Professor D.M. Balme and Dr A.L. Peck for their valuable
comments on an earlier draft of this paper.

7

Malcolm Schofield

Aristotle on the Imagination

Introduction

Every educated man knows that Aristotle invented logic. It is not so widely known that he contests with Plato[1] the distinction of having discovered the imagination. Men imagined things, just as they argued correctly and incorrectly, before the birth of the Old Academy; but it was Aristotle who gave the first extended analytical description of imagining as a distinct faculty of the soul, and who first drew attention, not least by the ambiguities and strains of his own account of the matter, to the difficulty of achieving an adequate philosophical understanding of imagination. I shall not in this essay attempt a survey of all Aristotle's uses of and pronouncements about *phantasia*.[2] I shall restrict myself to a set of fundamental problems in the interpretation of his official and principal discussion of it in *De Anima* III 3. In that chapter lurk most of the pleasures and puzzles which the student of Aristotle's views on imagination will want to savour.

It has been doubted whether Aristotle's *phantasia* should be rendered as 'imagination' at all. Plato in the *Theaetetus* (152AC) and *Sophist* (264AB) introduces *phantasia* into philosophical discourse about mental states as the noun corresponding to the verb *phainesthai*, 'appear'; and it is his doctrine that any belief which a man forms because of what he perceives with his senses is an instance of *phantasia*.[3] Now a clear connexion with the verb is preserved by Aristotle in talking of *phantasia* in *De An.* III 3 and elsewhere. Moreover, it has been noticed that the range of 'appearances' which Aristotle allocates to the faculty includes cases which are not obviously instances of mental imagery, but seem more like examples of direct sensory experience; and again, that in his causal explanation of *phantasia* Aristotle allows that a man may have *phantasia* of what he is at the moment actually

---

1. See in particular *Phil.* 38A-40E, *Soph.* 263D-264B. In the former passage, it seems hard to deny that Plato, in talking of the work of the painter in the soul, is identifying imagination (so e.g. Hackforth, *Plato's Examination of Pleasure* [Cambridge, 1945], p.72); the latter passage is too brief for very sure appraisal, but its account of *phantasia* is not dissimilar enough from that of the painter's work in the *Philebus* nor from Aristotle's treatment in *De An.* III 3 for one to be able to share Cornford's brisk confidence in asserting that *phantasia* is not here imagination (*Plato's Theory of Knowledge* [London, 1935], p.319). But these are both late dialogues, which may owe something at this point to discussions in the Academy to which Aristotle contributed.

2. Useful surveys are offered by J. Freudenthal [109], Beare [55], pp.290 ff.; Ross [16], pp. 142-5; Rees [111].

3. So at least he seems to say at 264A4-6; but no doubt he would allow that 'because' (*dia*) requires elaboration and restriction.

perceiving (428b25-30), yet (as Wittgenstein remarked) 'while I am looking at an object I cannot imagine it'.[4] Some scholars have accordingly inferred that *phantasia* is for Aristotle, at least in some moods, a comprehensive faculty by which we apprehend sensory and quasi-sensory presentations generally.[5] Thus his view of *phantasia* is equated[6] *pro tanto* with a view of sensory activity (or rather passivity) more typically associated with phenomenalists and sceptics; or else he is taken to have succumbed temporarily to a Kantian conception, according to which 'sensation [i.e. sense perception] would ... be reduced to the level of a mere passive affection which has to be interpreted by *phantasia* before it can give any information or misinformation about objects' (Ross [16], p.142).

Its Kantian associations might justify continuing to call the *phantasia* of this latter interpretation 'imagination'. But it is recognised that to admit such a comprehensive rôle for *phantasia* as either interpretation envisages is hard to reconcile with Aristotle's treatment of the senses in Book II of *De Anima*. It is widely allowed, although not universally nor by me, that Aristotle's official designation of *phantasia* in *De An.* III 3 as 'that in virtue of which we say that a *phantasma* occurs to us' (428a1-2) implies that it is a faculty more narrowly but more usually named 'imagination', viz. one in virtue of which we can have mental images.[7] And we find Ross, for example, portraying Aristotle's usual view of *phantasia*, both in *De Anima* and in *Parva Naturalia*, in terms which call to mind Hobbes' 'decaying sense' and Hume's 'faint and languid perception': its characteristic sphere, on Ross' reading, is mental imagery ([16], pp. 143-4).

One conclusion one might draw from this apparently conflicting evidence of Aristotle's meaning is summed up in Hamlyn's glum verdict (*ad* 427b27): 'There is clearly little consistency here [sc. in *De An.* III 3].' My view is that the conflict in the evidence is in good part merely apparent. For it is a bit artificial to divide the work Aristotle assigns to *phantasia* between mental imagery and the reception of sensory or quasi-sensory presentations. If we are to attribute to him a concept of imagination, then without endowing it with a Kantian scope we can permit it to range beyond the confines of mental imagery, as several modern authors, writing in the wake of Ryle and Wittgenstein, would urge.[8] And although we must recognise a proprietary connexion between *phantasia* and the verb *phainesthai*, 'appear', we need not suppose that the use of the word Aristotle wishes to exploit is the

---

4. L. Wittgenstein, *Zettel*, ed. G.E.M. Anscombe and G.H. von Wright, trans. G.E.M. Anscombe (Oxford, 1967), no. 621.

5. So e.g. Beare [55], p.290; Ross [16], pp. 142-3; K. Lycos [110], p.496 and n.1; D.W. Hamlyn [44], pp. 129, 131, 133-4.

6. E.g. by Hamlyn and Lycos.

7. See e.g. R.D. Hicks [43], *ad* 428a1; Hamlyn, p.129 (although it was Professor Hamlyn who in discussion sowed the seeds of doubt in my mind about this interpretation).

8. See e.g. H. Ishiguro, 'Imagination', *Proc. Arist. Soc.*, Suppl. Vol. 41 (1967), pp. 37-56; P.F. Strawson, 'Imagination and perception', in *Experience and Theory*, ed. L. Foster and J.W. Swanson (London, 1970), pp. 31-54; R. Scruton, *Art and Imagination* (London, 1974), pp. 91-120. The basic texts in Ryle and Wittgenstein are: *The Concept of Mind* (London, 1949), ch. 8; *Philosophical Investigations*, trans. G.E.M. Anscombe (Oxford, 1958), II xi (cf. also *Zettel*, nos. 621 ff.).

phenomenalist appropriation of it as the universal, basic, neutral term to report on one's any and every sensory or quasi-sensory experience without ever yet committing oneself to a claim about how things are in the external world. Commentators who have supposed just this have been too little sensitive to the Protean character of 'appears' and cognate expressions, so irresistibly exhibited by Austin.[9] I shall argue that in the contexts which concern us Aristotle has his eye on the more everyday use of *phainesthai* to express scepticism, caution or non-committal about the veridical character of sensory or quasi-sensory experiences, on those comparatively infrequent occasions when for one special reason or another it seems inappropriate in a remark about one's own or another's experience to claim that things are as they seem: 'it *looks* thus and so [– but is it really?].' This usage is not unnaturally associated with the imagination, for 'imagination involves thought which is unasserted, and hence which goes beyond what is believed'.[10]

According to the view which I shall advance, then, we need not charge Aristotle with the radical inconsistency in his treatment of *phantasia* diagnosed by Hamlyn. None the less, we should be wary about assimilating *phantasia* and imagination. Grant that a conceptual link between imagination and a use of 'appears' can be forged: even so, the link is not nearly as close as the morphologically grounded connexion between *phantasia* and *phainesthai*, nor does 'appears' supply the obvious, natural entrée to the study of the imagination which *phainetai* provides to that of *phantasia*. A little lexicography will show that the syntactic behaviour and the semantic range of *phantasia* (not to mention *phantasma* and *phainesthai*) are markedly different from those of 'imagination'.[11] And if for a moment we

9. See *Sense and Sensibilia* (Oxford, 1962), esp. chs. 3 and 4; also R.M. Chisholm, *Perceiving: A Philosophical Study* (Ithaca, N.Y., 1957), esp. ch. 4.

10. Scruton, *Art and Imagination*, p.97.

11. *Phantasia*, like *phantasma*, derives from the verb *phantazō* (found only in its middle and passive forms before the Hellenistic period), which means 'to make apparent', 'to cause to *phainesthai*'. Now nouns of the *-sia* type formed from *-zō* verbs tend in the first instance to connote the action signified by the verb; nouns of the *-sma* type so formed regularly connote the result of the action, or what is done by doing the action. One might therefore expect that *phantasia*, in its primitive sense, would signify just that action which consists in producing *phantasmata*: that if *phantasmata* are (say) 'presentations' (in the sense 'what is presented'), *phantasia* will be 'presenting' (or 'presentation' in an active sense) and likely to behave syntactically not unlike 'imagining' or 'imagination'. But this expectation is largely disappointed in Greek before Aristotle: and the reason is not far to seek. We have noted the absence of active forms of the verb *phantazō* in pre-Hellenistic texts. What this means in practice is that we read not of persons *making* things appear thus and so, but of sights, dreams, etc. *being presented* or *presenting themselves* to persons. This fact no doubt explains both the relative rarity of *phantasia* compared with *phantasma* (cf. LSJ s.vv.) and the near absence of an active force in *phantasia* when it does occur in writers before Aristotle. If human agents do not *phantazousin*, actively make apparent or present things, if *phantasmata* are rather made to appear by the chances of life, then there will not be much scope for the *nomen actionis phantasia* as 'presenting', 'making apparent', although *phantasma* will find a place naturally enough. Contrast other pairs of nouns similarly formed from *-zō* verbs whose active voices are, however, employed: *diadikasia, diadikasma; eikasia, eikasma; skeuasia, skeuasma*. Here it is invariably the latter

banish the rendering 'imagination' from our minds, then in one section of
De An. III 3, at any rate (the discussion whether *phantasia* is a faculty of
judgment, 428a1-b9), reflection on the range of phenomena Aristotle
assigns to *phantasia* and on the way he introduces them into his argument
suggests a rather different physiognomy for the concept from that conveyed
by 'imagination'. Aristotle seems to be concerned with a capacity for having
what I shall compendiously call *non-paradigmatic sensory experiences*[12] –
experiences so diverse as dreams and the interpreting of indistinct or
puzzling sense data, which may be held to resemble the paradigm of
successful sense perception in one way or another, yet patently lack one or
102 more of its central features, and so give rise to the sceptical, cautious or non-
committal *phainetai*. One merit of this interpretation of *phantasia* is that it
makes immediately intelligible Aristotle's ensuing causal analysis of the
faculty, which takes as its crucial premiss the fundamentally sensory
character of *phantasiai*, and proceeds to define them in terms of sense
perception proper, as causal traces of actual perceptions (428b10-429a2).
Nor is the immediate intelligibility of that analysis all that is salvaged. For if
we read it as an account not of imagination but of non-paradigmatic sensory
experiences, it is readily taken as a not implausible attempt to give a single
general explanation of an extremely interesting feature of human
psychology, namely the operation of our sensory equipment in a variety of
non-standard ways. As a theory of the imagination, on the other hand, its
very generality renders it disappointingly jejune, aside from its pre-echoes of
the unilluminating view of imagination familiar to readers of the British
empiricists. This is not, of course, to deny that mental imagery would be
reckoned by Aristotle as one type of non-paradigmatic sensory experience.
It is simply to argue that the focus of his attention, in these sections of *De
An.* III 3, is not imagery or imagination as such.

   These considerations should not lead us to abandon altogether a direct

----

member of the pair which is the rarer. When *phantasia* does gain what one might call a
natural toehold in the language, it does so in a secondary sense, 'presentation' as
corresponding not to the active but the passive of the verb – a frequent use in Aristotle
(cf. Bonitz, *Index Aristotelicus* 811a38-b11).

   Not only *phantasma* and *phantazô*, then, but *phantasia* too has a natural passive
tendency in the language as we find it, at odds with the active force of 'imagination'.
This certainly leaves its mark on Aristotle's treatment of the faculty of *phantasia* in *De
An.* III 3 – notably in his predilection for *phainetai*, 'appears', as an index to the
operation of *phantasia*, a predilection which suggests that he thinks of the mind in
phantasia as the passive recipient of experiences, not as actively imagining.
Nonetheless, the very fact that Aristotle (like Plato before him) presses *phantasia* into
service as the name for a mental disposition or act, comparable with thinking and
perceiving, reveals a philosophical impulse to force the word in a more active sense
(latent, of course, within it). Again, he occasionally refers to *phantasia* the faculty as *to
phantastikon* (*De An.* III 9, 432-a31; *Insom.* 1, 458b30, 459a16), which must be either
(following Plato in the *Sophist* 236C) the capacity for producing *phantasmata*, or the
capacity for *phantazesthai* in the novel Aristotelian sense, attested (though in the
passive) in two places at least (*Phys.* I 9, 192a15, *De An.* III 10, 433b12), of 'making
(something) appear for oneself' – i.e. a middle usage predicable of persons, with a
force approximating to that of 'imagining'.
   12. On this notion see further n20 below.

equivalence between *phantasia* and imagination. For in a passage from the opening section of his discussion of *phantasia* in *De An.* III 3 (427b16-24), Aristotle offers two criteria to distinguish it from belief (*doxa*) which fit the concept of imagination so perfectly, and are so fundamental to it, that it would be perverse to take the topic to be anything other than imagination. He tells us that *phantasia*, unlike belief, is up to us when we wish, or, in modern parlance, is subject to the will;[13] and that, whereas we are immediately affected by fear if we believe we are confronted by something alarming, in the case of *phantasia* it is merely as if we saw something alarming in a picture.[14] I do not say that these marks of imagination are not true also of some non-paradigmatic sensory experiences (if not of others, such as after-images or hallucinations). But it seems pointless to invoke the latter notion here unless the context demands it. And in the immediate context there is no trace of the concerns characteristic of the sections we considered briefly in the previous paragraph – the use of *phainetai* as signally appropriate to cases of *phantasia*, its emphatically sensory character (certainly *phantasia* is treated at 427b16-24 as rather like seeing,[15] but the criteria employed to distinguish it from belief make it analogous to thinking rather than to perception). Moreover, the whole section 427b6-26 bears signs of being composed separately from the sections which follow.[16] So they cannot be held to constitute a wider context sufficiently intimately connected with 427b6-26 to require our importing the idea of non-paradigmatic sensory experience into the section. Here at least, then, there seems every reason to identify *phantasia* with imagination.

103

But it was no doubt Aristotle himself who was responsible for putting together Chapter 3 of *De An.* III in the form in which we have it. He gives no sign that he is aware of changing subjects in the course of the chapter. We owe it to him, therefore, to try to understand how the concept of imagination which figures pretty clearly at the beginning of the discussion of *phantasia* could reasonably be treated as one and the same concept as the rather different notion which seems to be in question from 428a1 onwards. I

13. Cf. e.g. Ryle, *The Concept of Mind* (Penguin edition, London, 1963), p.233; Wittgenstein, *Philosophical Investigations*, p.213; *Zettel*, nos. 621, 626-8, etc.

14. Cf. Ryle's construction of imagining as a sort of pretending, *The Concept of Mind* pp. 244-57 (criticised by H. Ishiguro, 'Imagination', in *British Analytical Philosophy*, ed. B. Williams and A. Montefiore (London, 1966), pp.161 ff.); Scruton, *Art and Imagination*, p.97, etc., who treats imagination as unasserted thought (and will, no doubt, come under fire for doing so). In mentioning Ryle and Scruton, I do not mean to subscribe to their views on imagination, only to point up parallels between Aristotle and some of the best contemporary work.

15. This is because Aristotle thinks of imagination first and foremost as visualising, on which see B. Williams, *Problems of the Self* (Cambridge, 1973), ch. 3; Scruton, *Art and Imagination*, pp. 100-6.

16. The principal ground for this claim is that the discussion of the relation of *doxa* and *phantasia* at 428a18-24 makes no reference to the arguments already offered at 427b14-24 (cf. Hicks [43], p.456). Freudenthal thought the passage 427b14-24 was not only hard to relate to what preceded and followed, but also in contradiction with Aristotle's usual views on the topics it discusses ([109], pp.9 ff.); but he received a magisterial (if not entirely convincing) rebuke from G. Rodier [42], Vol. 2, pp. 408-13.

shall suggest (and have already hinted) that Aristotle can be fairly interpreted as adopting different but complementary vantage points on a more or less coherent family of psychological phenomena. But it would be a triumph of generosity over justice to pretend that he manages to combine his different approaches to *phantasia* with an absolutely clear head.

In the body of the essay I shall devote most of my space to the themes broached in this introduction. But first a word or two on my method and its limitations. In seeking to establish what Aristotle understands by *phantasia* we shall have to try to build up a picture chiefly from relatively isolated remarks tossed off in the course of the argument of *De An.* III 3, which must then in turn be tested against them. In the chapter Aristotle makes many distinctions between *phantasia* and other dispositions of the soul, sometimes (but not often enough) with clearly articulated examples. What he fails to do is to draw the threads of his discussion together, to provide a synoptic view of *phantasia* as he interprets it. This tempts one to examine other texts in the hope of achieving a more definitive impression of his conception, particularly from *Parva Naturalia* and elsewhere in *De Anima*. But these require cautious employment. For *De An.* III 3 remains Aristotle's one concentrated, extended theoretical discussion of *phantasia*;[17] elsewhere he is mainly concerned with its rôle in particular mental operations – dreaming, remembering, thinking, and so on. An account of his view of *phantasia* which relies too heavily on his treatment of these related phenomena runs the risk of distortion, the risk either of taking the way *phantasia* works in memory, dreams, and so on, as its mode of operation *tout court*, or more insidiously of putting the emphases of the description in the wrong places. Ross fell into this trap, so much so that he was forced to doubt whether some of the more important things Aristotle says in *De An.* III 3 really 'represent his deliberate view' ([16], p.143). If that chapter does not give us Aristotle's considered opinion, it is doubtful whether he had a considered opinion and certain that we could not with any confidence reconstruct it.

Of course, the persuasiveness of the account of *phantasia* in *De An.* III 3 which I am offering would be much weakened if it seemed not to correspond with what Aristotle has in mind when he talks of *phantasia* in other contexts. In this essay I have not attempted to show that my account will work for his handling of *phantasia* elsewhere. And it may consequently be objected, for example, that in Aristotle's theory of animal movement *phantasia* cannot be associated with sceptical, cautious, or non-committal *phainetai*, since the point of making *phantasia* a necessary condition of movement is to require that the moving animal positively fix upon some object of desire.[18] Or, more generally, it might be thought implausible that Aristotle should wish to specify a faculty of the soul in such negative terms, in view of the constructive work he puts *phantasia* to do not only in action but in remembering, thinking, etc., too.[19]

I offer some general considerations in reply, in lieu of the detailed

17. Notice the references to the chapter as Aristotle's official account at *Mem.* 1, 449b30-31 (where *De An.* III 7-8 is also in Aristotle's mind), *Insom.* 1, 459a15 (possibly an editorial addition), *MA* 6, 700b21-2.

18. This objection I owe to Profs. D.J. Allan and D.J. Furley.

19. This point was put to me by Fr. E. de Stryker.

investigation which a proper answer would entail. It will be evident from
what I say in the main body of the paper, and particularly from its third
section, that I take Aristotle's chief problem in *De An.* III 3 to be that of
providing conceptual room for an independent notion of *phantasia*, between
thinking on the one side and sense perception on the other. If this is so, then
we might reasonably expect two things: first, that Aristotle will take as
fundamental to *phantasia* in *De An.* III 3 features which will not necessarily
receive much emphasis in other contexts where he is not particularly
concerned with the demarcation problem of that chapter; second, that **105**
Aristotle will elsewhere, when concerned with other problems, be likely to
emphasise features of *phantasia* not given much prominence in *De An.* III 3,
or even to blur distinctions made or implied there. Thus, to take the first
point, it is principally in connexion with his attempt in *De An.* III 3 to
distinguish *phantasia* from sense perception as faculties of judgment that he
links *phantasia* so closely with the particular use of *phainetai* which I have
tried to isolate. This aspect of *phantasia* continues to attract Aristotle's
attention in contexts where he is concerned with perceptual or quasi-
perceptual judgments, as in *De Insomniis*. But – and here I move to the
second point – in other contexts, notably in his accounts of thinking and
remembering, he is not concerned with *phantasia* as a faculty of judgment at
all. When he introduces *phantasia* or *phantasmata* here, he has in mind our
capacity for visualising, just as he does in that section (427b6-26) of *De An.*
III 3 where I interpret him as discussing the active power of imagination.[20] I
am inclined to believe[21] that much the same aspect of *phantasia* is what
Aristotle chiefly has in mind when he claims that *phantasia* is a necessary
condition of animal movement, although here he is certainly concerned with
judgment (even if only as assent to what one visualises). This at any rate is
suggested by the way he develops his view in *De An.* III 9-11. For he seems
to think that movement and the desire which is its principal cause require

20. In a memorable intervention in the discussion of this paper at the 1975
Symposium Aristotelicum (whose text she kindly showed me subsequently), Prof.
C.J. de Vogel took my interpretation of *phantasia* in *De An.* III 3 as *non-paradigmatic*
sensory experience to be in conflict with the evident fact that Aristotle elsewhere
treats *phantasia* as indispensable to thinking and as playing a *normal* part in the
acquisition of knowledge. But let us take the case where the *phantasia* we are
concerned with is a piece of visualising: I do not mean to deny that, according to
Aristotle, all thinking involves visualising or that that is the norm; what I mean is
rather that visualising is not normal sensory experience (for normal sense experience
requires, as it does not, that we keep our eyes and ears open, etc.), but is sufficiently
like and sufficiently closely connected with normal sensory experience to be thought
of as a non-standard form of it. Of course, one is not very often going to use sceptical,
cautious or non-committal *phainetai* in commenting on the visualisation one does in
the course of thinking, just because one is interested principally in the thought, not in
its accompanying imagery. But (as Mr Sorabji pointed out in the discussion) if one
did reflect on it one would certainly wish to report on it in terms which (as *phainetai*
does) make it clear that one is not necessarily making a claim about how one
confidently sees the world. The same would not be true of animal imagination; but
animal imagination is an obscure corner of Aristotelian doctrine (cf. nn.35, 41, 55).
21. *Contra* the interesting interpretation advanced by M. Nussbaum in her
Harvard thesis *Aristotle's De Motu Animalium* (1975); I am grateful to Prof. Nussbaum
for allowing me to discuss a draft of her material on *phantasia* with her.

either the *thought* of a desirable object *or* at least something like thought (*noêsin tina*, 'a sort of thinking'), namely *phantasia* (*De An.* III 10, 433a9-12). What he says elsewhere about the connexion of thought and *phantasia* makes it very likely that it is mainly imagination or visualisation that he is thinking of (see especially *De An.* I 1, 403a8-9; III 7, 431a14-17, 8, 432a3-14, *Mem.* 1, 449b31-450a7). Here, as in *De An.* III 3, he first suggests that *phantasia*, as opposed to *noêsis*, is the prerequisite of desire in non-rational animals and in what prompts the fevered or the weak-willed man to act (here we catch an echo of sceptical, cautious *phainetai*: 'it seems good [but principle forbids it]').[22] But later in the same discussion Aristotle simplifies his account by making *phantasia* the crucial factor in all desire, explaining that it can be prompted either by thought or by sense perception – evidently recalling his doctrine that all thinking involves visualising.[23]

106   I have slipped into discussion of particular issues of interpretation willy nilly. But my chief point remains this: Investigation of *De An.* III 3 indicates that Aristotle's *phantasia* is a loose-knit, family concept. So we should expect that in its appearances elsewhere in his psychology its different elements are variously picked out or woven into fresh patterns. And that, I contend, is just what we would find if we carried out a detailed investigation of those contexts.

Phantasia and phainetai

Ross states: '*Phantasia* is in its original meaning closely related to *phainesthai*, "to appear", and stands for either the appearance of an object or the mental act [or, we might add, disposition] which is to appearing as hearing is to sounding' ([16], p.142). He goes on to cite a number of passages in Aristotle where *phantasia* seems to him to be used in this way. They and others like them constitute the evidence for holding that Aristotle at least sometimes conceives of *phantasia* as a comprehensive faculty in virtue of which we apprehend sensory and quasi-sensory presentations in general. I shall argue that this evidence can and should be given an alternative interpretation.

The most promising text for a broad conception of the faculty of *phantasia* might be thought to be a passage not in the psychological treatises but in the *Metaphysics*. For in *Meta.* IV 5, 1010b1-14, Aristotle introduces the notion of *phantasia* in a context where the verb *phainesthai* is not merely used

---

22. Cf. *De An.* III 3, 429a4-8; 10, 433a10-12 (with 9, 433a1-8). *Phainetai* bulks large in the discussion of pathological conditions in *Insom.* 2, 460b3-16, used with its sensory connotation. The *phainetai* appropriate to mention of *to phainomenon agathon* (cf. *De An.* III 10, 433a26-30 with e.g. *EE* VII 2, 1235b25-9, *EN* III 5, 1114a31 ff.) need not, of course, of itself suggest a *sensory* appearance; but no doubt Aristotle would say that any thought of the form: 'this *seems* a good plan' must involve visualisation. (I owe an awareness of the importance of Aristotle's remarks about *to phainomenon agathon* in this connexion to Prof. Furley's paper in [41].)

23. *De An.* III 10, 433b28-9; *MA* 8, 702a17-19. As Prof. Nussbaum suggests, Aristotle may put such stress on *phantasia* partly because it (unlike thinking) has a material basis which renders it an appropriate component in a physiological account of movement.

but used in a phenomenalist style to express sensory and quasi-sensory 'appearing' in general. The passage constitutes part of his argument against Protagoras' view that all *phainomena*, appearances, are true.

It is perfectly plain that here, as indeed in the rationale of Protagoras' doctrine offered at 1009a38-b9, Aristotle is including under *phainomena* any sensory or quasi-sensory appearances whatever. Witness the beginning of his second objection in the passage, at 1010b3-9:[24]

> Next, one may legitimately be surprised that they should find perplexing the question whether magnitudes and colours are such as they appear (*phainetai*) to those at a distance or to those nearby, to the healthy or to the sick; or whether it is what [appears so] to the weak or to the strong that is heavier; or whether it is what [appears so] to those asleep or to those awake that is true.

What directly concerns us, however, is Aristotle's first objection to the thesis that every *phainomenon* is true (1010b2-3). The text is corrupt, but runs thus **107** in Bonitz's widely accepted and plausible reconstruction: 'Even if perception, at least of what is special, is not false, still *phantasia* is not the same as perception.' A proponent of the idea that a broad conception of *phantasia* is to be found in Aristotle might argue that this objection is naturally read as implying such a conception, as follows: Aristotle is in effect accusing the Protagoreans of fallaciously inferring from the true premiss:[25] 'All perception (or, all perception of proper objects, the fundamental sort of perception) is true' the false conclusion: 'Every *phainomenon* is true.' And it is clear enough that he means to challenge the inference by pointing out that it depends on an additional tacit premiss (which is false) to the effect that every *phainomenon* is a case of perception. But what he actually says is that *phantasia* is not the same thing as perception. The natural explanation of his putting the point this way is that he thinks of *phantasia* as the faculty in virtue of which any *phainomenon* is experienced, and speaks here of *phantasia* rather than *phainomenon* simply because he wants to refer to the mental disposition or act involved, and so to make the appropriate contrast with perception. Moreover, the evident influence of Plato's *Theaetetus* in this paragraph (Plato is actually mentioned at 1010b12) and elsewhere in the chapter makes it unsurprising that Aristotle should have used *phantasia* in this broad manner. For that is just how Plato uses the word in introducing Protagorean relativism (*Theaet.* 152A-C).

Despite its plausibility, this interpretation of *phantasia* is not the only one possible for an unforced reading of the text. This can be made clear by an example. Aristotle is prepared to grant to Protagoras that hearing is always of sound; his point is presumably that it is not true that wherever there is the appearance of a sound in our ears we are actually hearing (we may be dreaming, for example: cf. 1010b8-11) – and even if we are hearing a real

---

24. Translation adapted from C. Kirwan, *Aristotle's Metaphysics*, Books Gamma, Delta, Epsilon (Oxford, 1971), whose version and interpretation (p.110) are, however, spoilt by the assumption that *phainetai* is to be rendered 'is imagined'.

25. On the interpretation of this premiss (and on its text), see the excellent discussion by Kirwan, pp. 110-11.

sound, it may appear to us other than as it really is (as coming from the
right, for example, when it actually comes from the left: cf. 1010b4-8). Now
in saying that *phantasia* is not the same as perception, Aristotle *might* mean
(as someone who held the interpretation sketched above would probably
argue) that perception (i.e. of proper objects) is only one sort of *phantasia*, to
be compared with interpretation of perception, dreaming, and further sorts
108   of *phantasia*. He would then be suggesting that, while the *phainomena*
experienced in perception may always be true, those experienced in other
sorts of *phantasia* need not be. But observe that he may equally well mean
that some *phainomena* are indeed cases of perception of proper objects, and as
such true, but that others (e.g. those we experience in dreams) involve the
coordinate faculty of *phantasia*, imagination or non-paradigmatic sensory
experience, which of course admits of falsehood. In other words, Aristotle's
objection to Protagoras will be no less forcefully and naturally expressed if
phantasia is not the genus of which perception is a species, but a species,
coordinate with perception, involved like it in the apprehension of just a
part of the whole field of *phainomena*. Nor does the comparison with the
Theaetetus give the former alternative unequivocal support. For Aristotle is
denying precisely what Plato makes Protagoras affirm, viz. that perception
and *phantasia* are one and the same. If his concept of perceiving has a
different scope from Protagoras', then his concept of *phantasia* may very well
do so too.[26]

We must conclude that it is hard to know how to understand the denial
that *phantasia* and perception are identical without further evidence of
Aristotle's teaching about them. For that we have to turn (as Aristotle
would surely expect us to turn) to *De Anima*, and in particular to the passage
in which he elaborates his reasons for distinguishing between *phantasia* and
perception (*De An.* III 3, 428a5-16). I consider first such indications as it
contains that the word *phainetai* ('appears') is a specially appropriate and
significant vehicle for describing what we experience in virtue of *phantasia*.

There are three occurrences of the word in the passage. In one of these
Aristotle's argument explicitly turns on the bearing of its use on the
character of *phantasia*; and in consequence the other two, although less
important in themselves, gain in interest and significance. Here is the telling
example, in the fourth argument of the set (428a12-15):[27]

> Further, it is not when we are exercising [our senses] with precision
> on the object of perception that we *say* that this appears (*phainetai*) to
> us [to be] a man, but rather when we do not perceive it distinctly.

Hamlyn complains that this argument 'is concerned with imagination in the
sense of appearances only and as these are perceptual phenomena they do
not serve to mark a distinction from perception' ([44], p.131). But if an
interpretation makes an Aristotelian point as irrelevant as that, the fault

26. We should observe how *very* much wider the concept of *aisthêsis* ascribed to
Protagoras in the *Theaetetus* is than Aristotle's perception of proper objects. It includes
feeling cold or hot, pleasures, pains, desires, fears (156B2 ff.).
27. With most editors and commentators I reject the words *tote ê alêthês ê pseudês*
(428a15) as a gloss.

may very well lie in the interpretation. And it is not difficult to find a **109**
genuine contrast between perception and *phantasia* expressed in Aristotle's
sentence. Aristotle is surely pointing out that if we clearly *see* a man, we do
not say: 'It looks like a man', since the caution, doubt or non-committal
implied by that form of words is out of place. It is when our eyes let us down
that *phainetai* becomes an appropriate location; and the judgment we make
by employing it is not straightforwardly a report of what we perceive, but a
more guarded statement of how what we perceive looks to us, how we
interpret it. 'How it looks to us', 'how we interpret it': Aristotle puts it the
first way, in the language of what I am calling non-paradigmatic sensory
experience, in essentially passive terms. But the appearance of 'to us' in his
formulation reveals his awareness of the subjectivity of the judgment, and so
suggests that he would not object to the idea that in *phantasia* we consciously
or unconsciously interpret the data of our senses. It is natural to assign such
interpretative activity to the imagination. This is particularly the case where
the interpreting is conscious. Suppose you and I are looking at a distant
object in murky light: we may have to exercise our imaginations, comparing
and contrasting what we *can* see with the way familiar middle-sized things of
our everyday acquaintance look, before we are able to conclude that it looks
like a man; we may have to try seeing it under different aspects before we
succeed in seeing it as a man.

> Whatever is placed beyond the reach of sense and knowledge,
> whatever is imperfectly discerned, the fancy pieces out at its leisure;
> and all but the present moment, but the present spot, passion claims
> for its own, and brooding over it with wings outspread, stamps it with
> an image of itself.[28]

But even if the indistinctly perceived object immediately and irresistibly
looks to me like a man, even if I have not consciously engaged in a moment's
reflection about what it is that I see, there is still reason to account my
judgment the product of imagination. For as in the earlier case I do not just
perceive a man, but see something as a man,[29] and if I say 'it looks like a
man', I employ a form of words which indicates an appreciation that I am
going beyond what I actually perceive.[30] If I am wrong, I may reasonably be
accused of merely imagining that it was a man;[31] right or wrong, I may be
held to have *decided* what it looked like no less than if I had had to make my
mind up slowly. The instantaneous character of my verdict does not tell
against my having actively engaged in imagination: imaginative leaps may **110**
notoriously occur in the twinkling of an eye. Notice, too, that the two
criteria of imagination proposed by Aristotle at 427b16-24 are satisfied in

28. W. Hazlitt, *Why Distant Objects Please* (from *Table Talk*).
29. For discussion, after Wittgenstein, of the close relation between imagining and
'seeing as', see e.g. Strawson, in *Experience and Theory*, pp. 44-52; Scruton, *Art and
Imagination*, ch. 8.
30. On going beyond the evidence as a criterion of imagination, see Scruton, *op.
cit.*, ch. 7.
31. For some remarks on this use of 'imagine', see Strawson, *op. cit.*, pp. 53-4; also
Ryle, *The Concept of Mind*, pp. 244-5.

the relevant way in this case as in the one where imagining takes time. Just
because imagination is here employed as an aid to perception, not in free
fantasy, one's attitude to the appearance in question is not likely to
resemble much one's attitude to a picture; but neither is it probable that
someone to whom it merely looks as if there is an enemy soldier in the
distance will be immediately affected by the spontaneous emotion
appropriate to perceiving an enemy clearly – the caution, doubt or non-
committal signalled by *phainetai* will tend to act as a brake. Again,
imagination remains subject to the will in these cases, inasmuch as it makes
perfect sense to ask a person to exercise his imagination upon what he
imperfectly sees.[32] The fact that he has no psychological option but to see
what he sees as a man no more counts against this being an instance of
imagination than the obsessive, haunting character which mental images
may exhibit, pleasantly or unpleasantly, debars them from being products
of the imagination.

Aristotle in his argument at 428a12-15 alerts us to a use of *phainetai* which
is appropriate only in special perceptual circumstances. He takes it to show
that men exercise *phantasia* precisely where sense perception fails them. It
would be perverse to read him as tacitly allowing[33] (indeed insisting) that
none the less *phantasia* has a broad Protagorean scope, and is in fact present
in all sense perception. If Aristotle had meant us to make this inference, he
should have phrased his argument differently; and he should have
introduced the concept of *phantasia* as an essential tool of his analysis of
sense perception, instead of omitting virtually all mention of it throughout
Book II of *De Anima*.

Phainetai occurs, probably as an index of *phantasia*, in the first and fifth
arguments of the set designed to show that it cannot be identical with sense
perception (428a6-8, 15-16). In the latter case Aristotle has in mind a
special phenomenon – after-images seem the likely candidate (cf. Hicks, *ad.
loc.*); this suggests a sceptical as much as a Protagorean use of the verb. The
same is true of its use in his first argument, which is more general in scope:
'Perception is either a capacity (e.g. sight) or an activity (e.g. seeing); but

111 something can appear (*phainetai*) even if neither of these is in question[34] (e.g.
dreams).' I submit that we should be guided by the results of our
examination of the fourth argument, and take it that in both these further
arguments Aristotle means to point to *phantasia* conceived as a faculty for
non-paradigmatic sensory experiences.

His other arguments at 428a5-16, in which *phainetai* does not occur, are
best interpreted upon the same assumption. Certainly they are hard to

32. For this interpretation of what it is for imagination to be subject to the will, see
Scruton, *op. cit.*, pp. 94-5.
33. Perhaps in something resembling the manner of H.P. Grice, 'The causal
theory of perception', *Proc. Arist. Soc.*, Suppl. Vol. 35 (1961), pp. 121-68.
34. *Huparchontos* is usually translated not 'in question', but 'present', which is
perhaps an easier rendering of the Greek. But the idea that the faculty of perception is
not present in sleep is not only not Aristotelian doctrine, but in direct contradiction
with what Aristotle is most naturally taken as saying in the next sentence (428a8-9),
when he states: 'sense perception is always present'. My translation attempts to
capture what Aristotle (as the Greek commentators saw) must have been meaning to
say: see Rodier and Hicks *ad loc*. I suspect a similar use of the word at *PA* I 1, 642a5.

marry with a broad Protagorean conception of *phantasia*. Consider the rather opaque second argument (428a8-11). Aristotle there claims (a10-11) that all animals have perception, but apparently not all *phantasia*. But on a Protagorean or typically phenomenalist view of 'appearances', these are the raw materials of which all perception, in however lowly an animal, is constructed.[35] The third argument is likewise easy to square with the interpretation of *phantasia* I am advancing, difficult with the broader interpretation. Aristotle says (428a11-12): 'Next, perceptions [sc. in the strict sense, of proper objects] are always true, but most *phantasiai* turn out false.' Aristotle's point is perhaps best expanded in terms of imagining: if someone has an image of an *F* thing, or sees *X* as *F*, what he imagines – an *F* thing – may not and probably will not exist (be a real contemporaneous *F* thing) at all. '*Probably* will not?' Perhaps Aristotle had run his mind over some of the main sorts of non-paradigmatic sensory experience -- e.g. dreams, memory-images, after-images, fantasy, hallucinations, the seeing of aspects – and reckoned that correspondence to truth was on the whole a rarity among these phenomena; perhaps his trust in common forms of speech suggested to him that the scepticism or caution or non-committal implied by the use of *phainetai* he associated with *phantasia* was usually likely to be justified. In any event, the claim that most *phantasiai* are false is not implausible, so construed. Yet if *phantasiai* were here in effect a mere synonym for Protagorean *phainomena*, it would surely be a highly improbable, if not indeed in the end unintelligible, thesis.[36]

But if those who believe that Aristotle sometimes gives *phantasia* a broad Protagorean scope cannot sustain their interpretation relative to these arguments for the non-identity of sense perception and *phantasia*, they may yet turn for support to his attack on Plato's view that *phantasia* is a blend of perception and belief. Aristotle's argument there (428a24-b9) has recently **112** been well analysed by Lycos [110] (whose account is lucidly summarised by Hamlyn, *ad loc.*); and since I am concerned simply with the scope *phantasia* is allowed by Aristotle to have, I refer the reader for a detailed treatment of the reasoning to these authors.

Aristotle first expounds Plato's view of *phantasia*, according to which 'appearing (*phainesthai*) will be believing what one perceives (and that not just coincidentally)' (428b1-2). He then offers a counter-example to this thesis, a case where one experiences a false 'appearance' about what is before one which conflicts with the true belief one holds about it (428b2-4): 'But things also appear (*phainetai*) falsely, when one has at the same time a true supposition about them (e.g. the sun appears (*phainetai*) a foot across, but is believed to be bigger than the inhabited world).' Now as we have

35. At the same time it is difficult to be confident of just what conception of *phantasia* does lie behind Aristotle's denial of it to some animals. Is it that only more sophisticated organisms like the ant and the bee have the capacity for interpreting and misinterpreting the world, but not the worm or grub (I follow Torstrik's reading at 428a11-12)? Aristotle's whole treatment of *phantasia* in the non-rational animals is puzzling. See further nn.41, 55 below.

36. Cf. J. Bennett, 'Substance, reality, and primary qualities', in *Locke and Berkeley*: A Collection of Critical Essays, ed. C.B. Martin and D.M. Armstrong (London n.d.), pp. 104-18; *Locke, Berkeley, Hume* (Oxford, 1971), pp. 89-102.

remarked, Plato, in the passage of the *Sophist* to which Aristotle's discussion relates (264A-B), holds that any belief which is formed as a result of perception is a case of *phantasia* and can properly be expressed by a form of words which includes *phainetai*. He seems to opt for a generously Protagorean range for *phantasia* and *phainetai*, even if he does not identify perception and *phantasia*. But in producing his single counter-example to Plato's thesis, Aristotle does not commit himself to accepting a similarly broad conception of *phantasia*. All he needs to do is to produce a case which he himself accepts as a case of *phantasia* and which Plato too might reasonably be expected to accept as such. So if the particular use of *phainetai* involved in the statement of the counter-example is one which is indicative of *phantasia* for both Plato and himself, that is sufficient for Aristotle.

I submit that Aristotle accepts the sun example as a case of *phantasia* just because it involves a use of *phainetai* which is naturally read ('appears ... but is believed') as implying scepticism. This accords not only with the results of our examination of 428a5-16, but also with the context in *De Insomniis* in which this example is used a second time. Aristotle argues at 460b3ff. that we are easily deceived with respect to our senses when we are in pathological conditions – in emotional states like love and fear or physiological disturbances like fevers. He points out that the coward in his fear thinks on the basis of a slight resemblance that he sees the enemy, the amorous man in his passion that he sees his beloved; and he comments that the greater the sway of the emotional state, the more tenuous the resemblance needed to make these things appear so (*phainetai*: the word is used four more times of deceptive appearances in the next sixteen lines). This, then, is the context in which Aristotle produces the sun example to show that in a normal frame of mind we are well able to resist and contradict a false appearance, exercising another faculty besides *phantasia*.[37] Notice the company which *phainetai*, used of the sun's misleading appearance, and in consequence *phantasia*, are made to keep – sceptical employments of *phainetai*, non-paradigmatic sensory experiences which we may think of as hallucinations, or as the seeing of unreal aspects.

The sun's looking a foot across would in truth be a rather unconvincing example of a Protagorean *phainomenon*. Someone who pronounces that the sun looks to him a foot across may be endeavouring to offer a report of his perceptual field sufficiently cautious to satisfy a sceptic or a phenomenalist that no illegitimate inferences from the perceived to the real are being made. It is one thing to aver that the sun looks small in comparison with the other items in one's perceptual field. It is quite another to make an estimate of *how* small it appears to be. For judgments of size take into account perspective, yet the very problem with the sun is that one's normal procedures for coping

---

37. Beare, the Oxford translator, takes the actual word *phantasia*, used here at 460b19-20, to refer not to the faculty but to the presentation of the sun as a foot across. This may be right; but there is no doubt that the faculty to which Aristotle does refer is *phantasia*, as is shown e.g. by the mention of *to phantastikon* as the faculty involved in cases of this sort at *Insom.* 1, 458b30, and by *De An.* III 3, 429a7-8, where Aristotle says that men act in accordance with their *phantasiai* (again, the translation is doubtful) because their reason is sometimes clouded by emotion or sickness or sleep.

with perspective break down. So the assertion that the sun looks a foot across seems to presuppose some tacit, and no doubt highly questionable, assumption about how far the sun looks to be from the earth. It in fact embodies an imaginative comparison such as: the sun looks like a foot wide beach ball kicked high in the air (but not *very* like – for the sun looks much higher than that). Compare Austin's observation on 'The moon looks no bigger than a sixpence':[38] 'It doesn't look as if it *is* no bigger than a sixpence, or as a sixpence would look if it were as far away as the moon; it looks, of course, somewhat as a sixpence looks if you look at it at about arm's length.' There is no sign in the text either of the *De Anima* passage or of the *De Insomniis* passage that Aristotle had reflected on the oddity of his example or on its non-paradigmatic perceptual circumstances. But it helps to make the texture of the analysis of *phantasia* in *De An.* III 3 the richer; and it does something to reinforce the identify of *phantasia* and imagination, albeit beneath the surface of the argument.   **114**

A final passage in *De An.* III 3, at the end of the causal analysis of *phantasia*, helped to persuade Ross that Aristotle in this chapter construes the faculty in the broad manner I have been denying. He states that at 428b18-30 Aristotle

> distinguishes between *phantasia* with respect to the special sensibles, the incidentals, and the common sensibles, and points out that while in the first case *phantasia* is infallible so long as the sensation is present, in the other two it is fallible even in the presence of sensation. This amounts to throwing on to *phantasia* the work of apprehending the incidentals and even the special sensibles as well as the common sensibles; and sensation would accordingly be reduced to the level of a mere passive affection which has to be interpreted by *phantasia* before it can give any information or misinformation about objects. ([16], pp.142-3).

Ross' statement of Aristotle's doctrine is seriously misleading, and his gloss on it the product of oversight and faulty inference. He omits to mention that in the first part of the passage to which he refers, Aristotle has restated his view (cf. *De An.* II 6) that there is sense perception not merely of special or proper objects (e.g. white) but of incidentals (e.g. that this white thing is Coriscus) and common objects (e.g. movement and magnitude). This view of perception is offered in Book II of *De Anima* as an adequate account of the matter; and even if sense perception, *aisthêsis*, is there treated very much as a passive affection, in the present chapter Aristotle is keen to stress that it is a capacity in virtue of which we *judge* (cf. Hamlyn [78]). Nor does there appear to be a general need for a special interpretative faculty performing the job Ross assigns to it; for however bare Aristotle's conception of perception of incidentals may be, it is (I take it)[39] an interpretative sort of perception. It would therefore be surprising if in his causal analysis of

---

38. *Op. cit.* p.41; cf. S.R.L. Clark, *Aristotle's Man* (Oxford, 1975), pp. 75-6..

39. Following Hamlyn in his commentary, pp. 107-8, 119; and see now the excellent discussion of S. Cashdollar, 'Aristotle's account of incidental perception', *Phronesis* 18 (1973), pp. 156-75.

phantasia Aristotle meant to abandon the relatively self-sufficient theory of perception reiterated in the course of his argument at 428b18-25. The only evidence Ross appears to rely on in believing that he is committed in the passage to a new theory is that cited in his first sentence – the distinctions made between sorts of *phantasia* (428b25-30). Yet those remarks could suggest that the work of apprehending sensibles is now assigned to *phantasia* only if what Aristotle has said in the immediately preceding lines about perception is forgotten, as of course it is forgotten in Ross's description of the passage; as it is, we can only understand Aristotle's doctrine here about *phantasia* by reference to his reasserted doctrine about *aisthêsis*.

115

None the less, the account of *phantasia* at 428b25-30 reported by Ross does present an embarrassment for my own interpretation. If *phantasia* is imagination or non-paradigmatic sensory experience, it is easy enough to see how it is possible to have *phantasia* of incidentals or common sensibles while one is still engaged in the relevant sort of perception. Aristotle's examples of an indistinctly perceived thing looking like a man and of the sun appearing a foot across are respectively cases in point – and cases which illustrate the fallibility of *phantasia*.[40] But what of the notion that while someone is perceiving a special object, e.g. seeing something white, he may also enjoy an infallible kind of *phantasia* of the self same object? It will not do to suppose (for example) that the perception in question is indistinct, leaving interpretative work for *phantasia* to do. For interpretation carries with it the possibility of error, especially if one cannot clearly *see* what colour one is looking at; it may look white, but be some other colour. I have no answer to this puzzle. All I can suggest is that Aristotle has here been overwhelmed by the scholasticism of this attempt to distinguish three sorts of *phantasia* corresponding to his three kinds of sense perception, which strikes most readers as a baroque extravagance. That is, he is so intent on constructing parallel subdivisions that he fails to notice that the idea of an infallible type of *phantasia* cannot bear scrutiny.[41]

40. I take it that these count as cases of *phantasia* just because the perception involved is non-paradigmatic: if in the first example one's perception was distinct, then it would be a straightforward instance of incidental *aisthêsis* (which might still, of course, be mistaken in its apprehension of the object in question); if in the second example the distance of the sun from the earth were such as our normal perceptual adjustments for perspective could accommodate, we should be dealing with a normal case of *aisthêsis* of a common object. Notice Aristotle's observation that *phantasia* goes wrong especially when the perceived object is a long way off (428b29-30).

41. Some members of the Symposium seemed in the discussion to feel that the schematism involved in Aristotle's distinctions between (for example) perception and *phantasia* of incidentals was so artificial that it might well break down in other contexts. We might then find Aristotle using the terms *aisthêsis* or *phantasia* indifferently to refer to any perception involving interpretation of the proper objects of perception, without any hint of the unreliability of *phantasia*. This would certainly suggest one explanation of why he treats now *aisthêsis*, now *aisthêtikê phantasia* as the condition of movement in the lower animals. Cf. e.g. *De An*. III 7, 431a8-10 (*aisthêsis*); *MA* 7, 701a29-36 *aisthêsis* or *phantasia* indifferently); *De An*. III 11, 433b31-434a7 (*phantasia*).

Phantasia and phantasma

In *De An*. III 3 Aristotle specifies the faculty of *phantasia* as 'that in virtue of which we say that a *phantasma* occurs to us', and contrasts this usage with 'saying something with a metaphorical use (sc. of *phantasia*)' (428a1-2).[42] In the previous section we examined some texts which have suggested to some (wrongly, in my view) that *phantasia* is sometimes given an extremely broad Protagorean scope by Aristotle. Here, by contrast, is a considered statement prominently placed in his official treatment of *phantasia* which has often been taken to restrict the faculty to experience of mental images (for *phantasma* is standardly translated 'image'). If the text really does mean this, it will require considerable ingenuity to explain on Aristotle's behalf why examples such as those of the sun appearing to be a foot across or of an indistinctly perceived thing looking like a man are pertinent to a discussion of *phantasia*. In neither of these examples does it seem plausible to suppose that the contemplation of mental images is involved; nor does Aristotle in presenting them suggest that it is.

I hold that it is a mistake to interpret *phantasma* at 428a1 as meaning 'mental image'.[43] 'Image' is not the root meaning of the word, nor is it a very frequent meaning in Plato; and there are strong contextual reasons, supported by a crucial piece of evidence in the passage of *De Insomniis* to which I have already alluded, for taking it otherwise here. I do not deny that in many Aristotelian contexts the *phantasmata* of which he speaks *are* what we would call mental images, nor that the word *phantasma* may conveniently and aptly be translated and understood as 'image' (as e.g. in *De Memoria*); only that that translation is inappropriate in *De An*. III 3.

Phantazô, the verb from which *phantasma* derives, means 'make apparent',

42. I take the metaphorical use of *phantasia* which Aristotle has in mind to be what Simplicius thought: he wrote (*ad loc.*) that Aristotle distinguished the use of *phantasia* he was concerned with from that derived metaphorically from it 'when we use [the expression] *phantasia* for *to phainomenon* (what appears [to be the case]), both in sense perception and in belief' (cf. the common use of the word recorded by LSJ s.v.1, Bonitz, *Index* 811a38-b11). In short, Aristotle is concerned with the employment of 'appears' peculiarly appropriate to imagination or non-paradigmatic sensory experience, and treats its applications in ordinary perceptual reports or in statements of belief ('that seems to me a dangerous course of action') as extensions of that usage. His justification would presumably be that it is preeminently in cases of non-paradigmatic sensory experience that *phainetai* (and so *phantasia*) has distinctive force: it is most especially in these cases that one really needs an expression whereby one can convey that it *looks* so; in ordinary perceptual reports one can as well say: 'It's a dog' as : 'It appears to me to be a dog,' and in voicing one's beliefs: 'That is a dangerous course of action.' Contrast the way Grice would handle the question of basic sense and metaphor: *op. cit.*, pp. 121-68.

43. In addition to the considerations I adduce in the text, I might add that it would be hard for anyone to maintain that the basic sense of *phantasia* had to do with mental images, when its commonest meaning in Greek is 'presentation', in the sense of 'what is presented'. If, on the other hand, Aristotle means to claim that the word is used in its basic sense in connexion with just a particular sort of presentation, viz. non-paradigmatic sensory presentations, then his position is a very much more plausible one.

'make show', 'present'. Only passive and middle forms (in particular contexts it is often hard to tell which) occur in pre-Hellenistic literature;[44] we find these used both absolutely and with a complement or predicate. Thus in Herodotus Artabanus reminds Xerxes that God smites with his thunderbolt not the small animals but the 'excessive' ones, and does not allow them to 'make a show of themselves' (*phantazesthai*); the Scythians 'made themselves no longer apparent' to Darius (*ouketi ephantazonto sphi*); a dream 'is presented' to Xerxes (*oneiron phantazetai moi*), (VII 10; IV 124; VII 15). Plato supplies numerous examples of the verb with a complement. God is not a magician who presents himself or makes himself appear in different guises on different occasions (*phantazesthai allote en allais ideais*) (*Rep.* 380D); the beautiful will not present itself to the philosophic lover as beautiful in the way that a face is (*oud' au phantasthêsetai auto to kalon hoion prosôpon ti*) (*Symp.* 211A); some pleasures 'present themselves as great and numerous, but are in fact jumbled up with pains' (*megalas ... tinas hama kai pollas phantastheisas, einai d'autas sumpephurmenas homou lupais*) (*Phil.* 51A); and so on (cf. Ast, *Lexicon Platonicum* s.v.). Notice how in these Platonic examples the guises described by means of the verb are all deceptive guises, guises which are at odds with reality.

We should consequently expect *phantasma* to mean 'appearance', 'apparition', 'guise', 'presentation', often with the strong implication of unreality. The pre-Aristotelian evidence in general bears out this expectation, although the range of the noun is narrower than that of the verb: I have not met with an instance of *phantasma* as 'guise', and 'presentation' never seems a very apt translation. In its earlier extant uses in the tragedians the word is used of ghosts or apparitions in dreams; and both Plato and Aristotle so use it on occasion (see LSJ, s.v. 1a). Plato, however, more often employs *phantasma* to talk of unreal appearances more generally; he treats it as the abstract noun corresponding to *phainesthai*, 'appear' (which perhaps helps to explain why in him, at least, the meanings 'guise' and 'presentation' available from *phantazô* are not exploited). Examples of this usage are particularly frequent in contexts where Plato is developing his metaphysics of copies and paradigms or where he is concerned with artificial representations.[45] It certainly hardens on occasion in such a way that *phantasma* can almost be said to *mean* 'image' or 'representation' in context. A notable psychological instance, which is very like Aristotle's favourite usage, occurs in the *Philebus* (40A). But Plato himself makes the basis of his own usage quite plain in the *Sophist*. He there defines sophistry as a species of image-making, viz. *phantastikê*, appearance-making (or as Cornford translates, semblance-making); and he is naturally concerned with *phantasmata* that are images. But his word for image is *eidôlon*, not *phantasma*, and he explains why he calls one species of *eidôlon phantasma* – because there are some *eidôla* which *appear* to be faithful likenesses or copies (*eikones*) of an original, but are not really: *âr' ouk, epeiper phainetai men, eoike de ou, phantasma*? (236B). And elsewhere (e.g. in the seventh deduction of the *Parmenides*) Plato uses *phantasma* as the noun corresponding to *phainesthai* when he has no concern with images: if you approach nearer to *the others*,

44. LSJ s.v. II say 'in early writers only in Pass.'; but this is clearly wrong.
45. E.g. *Rep.* 510A, 532C, 598B, 599A; *Soph.* 234E, 236C, 240D.

then contrary to your first impression they appear many and different, and because of this appearance of difference (*tôi tou heterou phantasmati*), different in character and unlike.[46] Again, in the *Cratylus* Socrates insists against **118** Protagoras and Euthydemus that things have a fixed being of their own, and are 'not dragged up and down relative to us or by us through private appearance' (*tôi hêmeterôi phantasmati*) (386E).

It is with these last two examples of *phantasma* in Plato that one in our *De Insomniis* passage (2, 460b3ff) is most closely comparable. In view of the Protagorean reference of the *Cratylus* text this might suggest once again a broad Protagorean conception of *phantasia* in Aristotle. But what disposes Plato to use *phantasma* in these contexts is the unreality or unreliability of the appearances in question; and it is with just such appearances that Aristotle too is concerned at 460b3 ff., as my earlier references to the passage showed. After giving his examples of the way in which persons in pathological conditions are liable to be deceived by false appearances, Aristotle adds a qualification: if a man is not gravely ill (Aristotle is thinking of fever), he can sometimes realise that what appears to him is false; but if his affliction is greater, he may be so deceived that (for example) he actually recoils from the animals he thinks he sees. Then comes the crucial couple of sentences (460b16-20):

> The reason for these things happening is that the governing element (*to kurion*) and that to which the *phantasmata* occur do not judge in respect of the same faculty. An indication of this is that the sun appears (*phainetai*) a foot across, but often something else contradicts *phantasia*.

Here *phantasma* is plainly used simply as the noun corresponding to *phainesthai*, one of the verbs Aristotle employs in presenting and discussing his examples of false appearances throughout the passage, as well as in the sun example. For the frequent employment of *phainetai* to indicate unreal appearances is the only feature of the passage which adequately and naturally accounts for the mention of a part of the soul concerned with *phantasmata*. The most striking support for this reading of *phantasmata* is Aristotle's immediate employment of the sun example to illustrate and justify his distinction between *to kurion* and 'that to which the *phantasmata* occur'. But that distinction is, of course, introduced to help explain how it is that false appearances deceive some but not others – as we learn in chapter 3 of *De Insomniis*, it is when *to kurion* is enfeebled or incapacitated that deception is most likely to take place. There is no hint, on the other hand, that Aristotle is at all preoccupied with mental images in the passage. The **119** topic is 'being deceived with respect to our senses' (460b3-4). And although the phenomena Aristotle mentions are pathological in character, and might be dismissed as hallucinations, and so as mere mental imagery, by a modern writer, that is not how he describes them. In the sun example, there is even less room for imagery; the same is true of the example known as

46. *Parm.* 165D (cf. 166A); see in general LSJ s.v. II.

'Aristotle's experiment' which follows it in the text.[47] Could Aristotle, however, be using *phantasmata* to mean '*sense* images', what Hume would have called 'impressions'? That seems highly unlikely. Aristotle has a technical term, *aisthēma*, which at least in some contexts seems to denote an image-like sense datum.[48] But I do not know any text where it is very plausible to suppose that *phantasma* is used in this way; indeed, *phantasma* is sometimes contrasted with *aisthēma*, as being a term appropriate to occasions where there may be no actual perceiving going on.[49]

The similarities between this *De Insomniis* passage and *De Anima* III 3, 428a1-b9, make it hard to resist the conclusion that when Aristotle specifies *phantasia* as 'that in virtue of which we say that a *phantasma* occurs to us' (428a1-2), *phantasma* again does duty simply as the noun corresponding to cautious, sceptical, and non-committal *phainetai*. Here, too, Aristotle illustrates his arguments with examples employing the verb, twice as an explicit pointer to the nature of *phantasia*; he uses the same sun example, which we know from *De Insomniis* to constitute an instance of a *phantasma* in this sense of 'appearance'. Moreover, to read *phantasma* in this way allows us to see in the analyses which follow the fulfilment of a methodological promise held out by the formula at 428a1-2. For notice that *phantasia* is not stated to be the faculty in virtue of which *phantasmata* occur to us, but that in virtue of which *we say that* a *phantasma* occurs to us. I take Aristotle to be intending by this formula to distinguish cases of *phantasia* by the linguistic behaviour they prompt. Now the linguistic behaviour in question must surely be the utterance of factual statements about what is perceived (or as it were perceived) which include and rely significantly on *phainetai*, used in the cautious, disbelieving or non-committal way I have attempted to specify. That, at least, is the one type of locution which is prominent and is implied by Aristotle to be an important clue to the character of *phantasia* in the body of the section of the chapter that begins with the formula about *phantasma*.

Aristotle's choice of this linguistic criterion as the working guideline for his investigation of the connexion or want of connexion between *phantasia* and other faculties of the soul, perception, belief, knowledge, etc., is one of

120

---

47. *Insom.* 2, 460b20-2; cf. Ross' note on the passage in *Aristotle, Parva Naturalia* (Oxford, 1955), pp. 273-4.

48. For a good discussion of the evidence, see R. Sorabji [50], pp. 82-3.

49. Cf. *De An.* III 7, 431a14-15; 8, 432a9-10; *Insom.* 3, 462a29-30. In the second of these passages Aristotle says that '*phantasmata* are as *aisthēmata*, except without matter'. 'Without matter' has caused difficulty. Rodier said (*ad loc.*): 'En réalité, les *aisthēmata* n'ont pas plus de matière que les *phantasmata*, puisque la sensation ne saisit que la forme sans la matière. Seulement la sensation se produit en présence d'un objet matériel, tandis que l'imagination peut avoir lieu même en l'absence de cet objet.' I take Aristotle to mean that in imagining it is as if one were actually perceiving, but of course the physical basis of the sense image of actual perception, viz. the colouration of the *korē*, is not present – or at least, if it *is* present (as in the case of genuinely perceptual appearances, like seeing an indistinct object as a man), it is not the physical basis of *phantasia*: the matter of a *phantasma* even of a perceptual sort is a change or motion in the sense organ caused by the perception itself (cf. *De An.* III 3, 428b25-30; *Insom.* 2, 460b22-5). On the matter of *aisthēmata*, see Sorabji [50], p.83; and above, p.49, n.22.

the most impressive features of his treatment of the imagination. It provides a particularly clear and arresting testimony to his enthusiasm for philosophising on the basis of *endoxa*, of course.[50] But it is also evidence of deep insight into the problems of characterising a psychological phenomenon such as imagination. For in attempting to say what makes imagination different from sense perception or belief Aristotle steers clear of two opposite but equally fruitless modes of differentiation, with which he was none the less familiar. He does not make the distinction between imagination and perception in physical or physiological terms; he employs those terms in his causal analysis, at 428b10 ff., but only after he has sought to clarify in quite different terms what the two phenomena are that he wants to relate in a causal connexion. Nor, on the other hand, does Aristotle adopt the procedure associated with Hume, of reflecting on the presence of sensory features in imagining, and then attempting to give an account, based on introspection, of the difference in sensory quality between imagining and perception. He had once defined *phantasia* as a sort of weak perception, in the early *Rhetoric* (I 11, 1370a28); but that approach has been abandoned by the time of *De Anima*. Instead he opts firmly for behavioural criteria. Thus at 427b16-24 he asks: is believing a voluntary activity like imagining? Are the emotional consequences of imagining the same as those of belief?[51] And he divines that *linguistic* behaviour is of fundamental importance. Not only does he advert to it as a means of differentiating imagination from perception, as when he notices that the language a man characteristically uses when imagining – 'appears' – is not what one would expect if he were reporting what he could see without difficulty (428a12-15). He also hits on the propensity to say *phainetai* as giving a way of *identifying* instances of imagination or *phantasia*. Imagining is not the sort of thing one can in any interesting sense observe; and its intentional, thought-dependent aspects make language a peculiarly appropriate vehicle for its realisation, not only its communication.

It is true that within the section 428a1-b9, it is only at 428a12-15, in the example of an indistinctly perceived thing looking like a man, that Aristotle explicitly draws attention to the use of the *word phainetai*. But it is hard to see any more immediate reason for his taking the sun example to be a case of *phantasia* than that he has observed that people say: 'The sun looks a foot across', when they believe its size to be very much larger (cf. 428b2-3). The sceptical, cautious or non-committal implications of using the word may, as I have suggested, have led him to assert that 'most *phantasiai* turn out false' (428a12). And when he remarks that things appear (e.g. dreams) although sense perception is not involved (428a7-8), it may be the disposition people have to employ *phainetai* in their dream reports which is again for Aristotle the most immediate pointer to the presence of *phantasia* – or at least what governs his approach to *phantasia* in dreaming.

This last point deserves elaboration. Dreaming is a particularly

50. Cf. G.E.L. Owen, '*tithenai ta phainomena*', in [36], pp. 83-92, and reprinted in our Vol. 1.

51. At *Meta*. IV 5, 1010b9-11, he distinguishes between the action appropriate to perception and that appropriate to *phantasia*, unfortunately too briefly and obscurely: cf. Kirwan, *op. cit.*, pp. 109-10.

interesting sort of *phantasia*, not least because with dreaming neither of the
criteria for imagination laid down by Aristotle at 427b16-24 is satisfied:
dreaming is not subject to the will, except in Freudian ways which Aristotle
shows no sign of anticipating; nor is one always as emotionally detached
from the horrors of a dream as from a horrific picture – sometimes it is much
more as if belief were involved, as Aristotle recognises in chapter 3 of *De
Insomniis*. Consequently dreaming presents a challenge to my thesis that
there is a unity to Aristotle's treatment of *phantasia* which is compatible with
identifying *phantasia* with imagination.

One might perhaps suppose that, if a philosopher is going to associate
dreams with imagination at all, he will do so on the basis of the
consideration that dreams involve mental imagery. That is at any rate the
sort of interpretation a reading of Ross' account of Aristotle's treatment of
phantasia might suggest ([16], p.144); and certainly Aristotle's use of
phantasma with respect to dreams in e.g. the first chapter of *De Insomniis* is
compatible with such an interpretation. But in fact between dreams and
cases of *phantasia* which do satisfy the criteria for imagination spelt out at
427b16-24 Aristotle forges a different link. What he exploits in *De Insomniis*,
and indeed makes central to his account of dreaming, is the appropriateness
122 of *phainetai*, 'appears', both to descriptions of the content of dreams and to
the seeing of aspects.

He takes as the starting point for his analysis of dreams the phenomenon
of pathological appearances – the way marks on the wall look like animals
to the sick man, or the way that, from the slightest resemblance, the
amorous man takes a boy he sees in the distance or with back turned to be
his beloved (*Insom*. 2, 460b3ff.) This is not just the point from which
Aristotle happens to begin; in the first chapter of *De Insomniis*, after puzzling
over the relation of dreaming to sense perception and judgment, he seems to
despair of finding any other mode of attack on the problem of the nature of
dreaming (458b25-8):

> With respect to this whole matter, so much at least is clear, that the
> very same thing which is responsible for our being deceived while
> suffering from fever causes this phenomenon [sc. being deceived] in
> sleep.

The similarity between the two cases which leads Aristotle to suppose their
causal analysis must be the same is evidently that, as with the pathological
seeing of aspects, so in dreaming things appear to be what they are not, and
are often mistakenly taken to be what they appear. This is borne out not
only by his explicit concentration on the phenomenon of deception here and
throughout much of the treatise, but by the thoroughgoing character of the
parallelism he endeavours to establish in chapter 3 between dreaming and
pathological 'appearances'. He goes so far as to construe the *phainetai* of
dream reports as the *phainetai* appropriate to the appearance of an aspect.
What happens in a dream, according to him, is that *something* looks, in virtue
of some small resemblance, like something else (*Insom*. 3, 461b10-21): it is
not just that Coriscus appears to me, but that a trace of my sense datum of
Coriscus appears to me as Coriscus (*ibid*., 461b21-30). Coleridge was
wittingly or unwittingly a pretty faithful Aristotelian when he described

dreams as devices 'by which the blind fancy would fain interpret to the mind the painful sensations of distempered sleep'.[52]

Now the pathological seeing of aspects shares with dreaming an important difference from cases like seeing an indistinct object as a man, or (to take an instance from *De Insomniis*) seeing the shifting shapes made by clouds now as a man, now as a centaur (461b19-21). The difference in question is that very failure to satisfy the criteria of imagination proposed at *De An.* III 3, 427b16-24, which we noted with respect to dreams: the fevered **123** man's appearances are *not* subject to his will; and if his affliction is bad enough, not only his emotions but his actions will resemble those appropriate to belief (cf. *Insom.* 2, 460b15-16). But Aristotle's own unitary explanation of dreams and such pathological phenomena, on the one hand, and the similarity between pathological and normal seeing of aspects, on the other, put us in a position in which we can now exhibit the unity in Aristotle's conception of *phantasia* while retaining our characterisation of it as imagination. For the causal explanation of dreaming and of pathological appearances accounts for just those features of these phenomena which make them unlike cases of *phantasia* which satisfy the criteria of 427b16-24. It is evidently because sleep and fever impair the operation of our faculties in general, leaving *phantasia* alone efficacious, that the will has no control over what appears to us in such conditions (see *Insom.* 3, 460b28-461b5) – or to put it in a more Aristotelian way, we cannot *act* when asleep (cf. *EN* I8, 1098b31-1099a3). And as Aristotle himself labours to show, it is for the same reason that the 'governing element', the faculty we have for making judgments on the basis of what our senses tell us, is also stifled, so that appearances are taken as veridical by default (see *Insom.* 2, 460b13-16; 3, 461b5-462a8); and consequently *phainetai* can be employed to refer to the appearances in a sceptical manner only by an observer (or the patient himself upon recovery, the dreamer when he has woken). Should these differences incline us to withhold the name 'imagination' from dreaming and the pathological seeing of aspects? The question has by this stage, I hope, an artificial air. We could appeal to 427b16-24 and refuse the name if we wished: but we could also agree to be impressed more by the similarity between these phenomena and the central cases of imagination, and rule that the criteria of 427b16-24 apply to *normal* imagination, reflecting that in *De Insomniis* Aristotle has provided both a description and a causal explanation of the abnormality of what we might call *abnormal* imagination.[53]

52. *Biographia Literaria*, p.5 of the Everyman Edition.
53. Here I am attracted by the argument of Ryle (*The Concept of Mind*, pp. 244-5): 'Make-believe is compatible with all degrees of scepticism and credulity, a fact which is relevant to the supposed problem, 'How can a person fancy that he sees something, without realizing that he is not seeing it ... The fact that people can fancy that they see things, are pursued by bears, or have a grumbling appendix, without realizing that it is nothing but fancy, is simply a part of the unsurprising general fact that not all people are, all the time, at all ages and in all conditions, as judicious or critical as could be wished'. Ryle has been criticised for 'lumping together', as conditions in which people are particularly prone to be uncritical of their fancies, 'dreams, delirium, extreme thirst, hypnosis, and conjuring-shows' (p.233): see Ishiguro, in

In confinio intellectus et sensus

It is instructive to notice what occasions Aristotle's introduction of the topic
of *phantasia* in *De An.* III 3. By the beginning of that chapter he has
completed his account of sense perception, and he now turns to consider

124 thinking, reminding us of what his investigation of the opinions of his
philosophical predecessors in I 2 had revealed: that soul in animals is
defined by them in one of two ways above all, by reference to the capacity
for movement or to the capacity for judgment (criteria accepted by Aristotle
himself: III 9, 432a15-17; cf. I 2, 403b25-7 *et passim*, III 3, 427a17-21). The
fact that both in thought and in perception the soul judges and is
acquainted with things that are led the ancients, Aristotle tells us, to
identify the two faculties. And so in his attempt to determine the nature of
thinking he takes for his first task the demonstration that this identification
is a mistake. He observes that all animals have sense perception, but not all
think; and he moves immediately to forestall a possible counter-argument
based on the idea that animals *do* think in a way, because they have
phantasia, which is also a sort of perception.[54] The equation cannot be thus
circuitously reinstated. *Phantasia* (which, Aristotle agrees, nearly all
animals[55] do have) is different both from sense perception and from
thinking, although sense perception is indispensable to it as it is itself to
hupolêpsis (427b6-16). This thesis about *phantasia* evidently requires defence;
and in a way the whole of the rest of the chapter is just that defence, a
digression necessary for Aristotle's justification of his treatment of thinking
as a genuinely independent faculty in the chapters which follow (III 4-8).

British Analytical Philosophy, pp. 160-1, and more fully J.M. Shorter, 'Imagination', in
Ryle, ed. O.P. Wood and G. Pitcher (London, 1971), pp. 138-9, 142-3. And no doubt
it is indeed dangerous to suppose that, just because in all these conditions one can be
said to have imagined things (no less than if one visualised Helvellyn knowing
perfectly well that one was doing so), a genuinely unitary concept of imagination is
applicable to all the different cases. But where we apply a single word without evident
ambiguity to different phenomena, there is a case for assuming that there are
important conceptual connexions and affinities between them (why else should the
same word be used? and how is one to be sure that in differentiating distinct senses of
a word one is not merely extrapolating illegitimately from different contexts of its
use?). At any rate, it is plain that Aristotle thought that a single faculty of
imagination was involved in the very various phenomena he treats as cases of
phantasia; and I have endeavoured, in the manner of more recent students of
imagination such as Strawson, in *Experience and Theory*, and Scruton, in *Art and
Imagination*, to trace the similarities between the different phenomena noticed by
Aristotle which might have fortified him in this belief.

54. For this interpretation of the connexion of 427b14-16 with what precedes, see
Rodier *ad loc.*

55. 'Nearly all animals': the doctrine of this chapter (cf. 428a9-11, 21, 23), and
elsewhere (II 3, 415a10). At the end of the day he allows, notwithstanding his *aporia*
on the matter, that even 'incomplete' animals have an indeterminate sort of *phantasia*
(cf. II 3, 414b16, III 11, 433b31-434a5, with Rodier *ad* 413b22, 433b31, 434a4; Hicks
ad 434a1); or at least, those of them that move: presumably the stationary animals
(cf. I 5, 410b19-20, with Hicks *ad loc.*) do not.

The first sections of the discussion of *phantasia* (427b16-428b9) show that it cannot be the same as perception or thinking (at least in the sense of *noein* which most interests Aristotle and which he studies at III 4-8). The final section (428b10-429a9) shows how sense perception is indispensable to it (argument for the contention that thinking requires *phantasia* is reserved until III 8, 432a3-10).

Aristotle shows himself aware, then, of a real temptation to assimilate *phantasia* to perception on the one hand and thinking on the other (cf. also III 9, 432a31-b3). But he was intent on demonstrating why these temptations must be resisted rather than on exploring them. This preoccupation with refutation, as so often in Aristotle, has unfortunate consequences. His combative instincts give him a predilection for single short knock-down arguments which can leave the hungry reader unsatisfied. In stressing non-identities he does not pause to reflect on the equally important affinities between *phantasia* and the other faculties which incidentally come to light in the course of his arguments. Nor does he appear to have tried to formulate in his own mind a single statement about **125** what *phantasia* is like (as distinct from what it is not like), free from the inconsistencies which at least apparently result when we lay side by side observations he finds it natural to make in one context with opposed observations or ways of speaking which seem to come naturally to him in other contexts. For us these features of his treatment of *phantasia* are as interesting as his avowed aims and intended achievements.

Although at 427b14-15 and in a number of other places Aristotle states or implies that *phantasia* is not the same as thinking (*dianoia, noein*), it is perhaps significant that in his official account of *phantasia* in *De An.* III 3 he seems to waver on this point – as though when he came to consider *phantasia* at length on its own account, not briefly in the course of comments on thinking, he had found it more like thinking than his usual characterisation[56] of it as a *sine qua non* of thinking suggests. At any rate, he there states his favourite thesis about the indispensability of *phantasia* to thinking in the more restricted formulation: 'there is no *hupolêpsis* without *phantasia*' (427b16); his argument for the non-identity of *phantasia* and *dianoia* is billed as proof that *phantasia* and *hupolêpsis* are not the same (427b16-17), and actually confines itself to differences between *phantasia* and *doxazein*, believing (427b17-24); and he moves on to the next section of the chapter with the cautious observation 'thinking ... seems[57] to include on the one hand *phantasia* and on the other *hupolêpsis*' (427b27-28).

---

56. Cf. I 1, 403a9; III 7, 431a17; *Mem.* 1, 449b31-450a1. Imagination seems to be regaining some of the credit as handmaid to thought which it lost in the heyday of Oxford philosophy: see e.g. Z. Vendler, *Res Cogitans* (Ithaca, N.Y., 1972), pp. 73-80; D. Kaplan, 'Quantifying In', in *Words and Objections*, ed. D. Davidson and J. Hintikka (Dordrecht, 1969), pp. 225-31, with Quine's reply, pp. 342-3.

57. Rodier (*ad loc.*) took *dokei* here to mark an 'opinion courante' (i.e. an *endoxon*), not a view of Aristotle's own. This may be right; but (as we shall see) there is reason to think Aristotle found something tempting in the opinion. I have not put any weight on 427b16-17 in this connexion, since the text is doubtful and obscure. But emboldened by Prof. W.J. Verdenius, I would retain *noêsis*, and translate (with Prof. D.J. Allan): 'It is clear that *phantasia* is not the same sort of thinking as *hupolêpsis*.'

Hupolêpsis is 'taking something to be the case' or (in that sense)
'judgment', a general notion here including as its species *epistêmê*
(knowledge), *doxa* (belief), *phronêsis* (practical understanding) and their
opposites (427b24-26). The illustration of *phantasia* Aristotle gives is of
someone producing things before his eyes like the mnemonists (427b18-19).
It might seem natural to infer that Aristotle here supposes the relation of
hupolêpsis and *phantasia* as species of *noein* to be that of the disposition or act
of judgment and the piece of thinking from which the disposition or act
results.

But it would be rash to attribute to him the view that the activity of
thinking is *phantasia* on the basis of this evidence. He has not stated that
phantasia and *hupolêpsis* are the only forms of thought; and elsewhere he
126 shows himself ready to distinguish between *phantasia* and the process of
thinking. A passage from *De Memoria* (1, 449b31-450a5) is particularly
instructive, employing as it does language similar to that Aristotle uses
when speaking of *phantasia* at 427b16 ff.:

> It is not possible to think without *phantasma*. For the same effect
> occurs in thinking as in drawing a diagram. For in the latter case,
> though we do not make any use of the fact that the size of the triangle
> is determinate, we none the less draw it with a determinate size. And
> similarly someone who is thinking, even if he is not thinking of
> something with a size, places something with a size before his eyes,
> but thinks of it not as having a size.[58]

This passage makes it plain that not merely the *hupolêpsis* which results from
thinking, but the process of thinking itself is distinct from *phantasia*, which it
nevertheless requires. Aristotle, exploiting a point made by Plato in the
Republic (510D-511A), recognises that what one engages in thinking about
and what one imagines in so thinking may be distinct in the sense he hints
at.

It is perhaps not possible to demonstrate that the distinction between
phantasia and the activity of thinking adumbrated in this *De Memoria* passage
is presupposed in the treatment of thinking in *De Anima* (although it is
perfectly consistent with the doctrine of III 4-8).[59] But the fact that Aristotle
in III 3 makes his distinction merely between *phantasia* and *hupolêpsis* is not
enough to suggest that he has not yet seen that distinction between thinking
and *phantasia*. For we should recall that a principal concern of III 3 is to
show that *phantasia* is not any of the more familiar capacities in virtue of
which we *judge* and are acquainted with what is. It is enough for him to
demonstrate that *phantasia* is not *hupolêpsis* or any of its species. And if he
guardedly allows that *phantasia* may be reckoned a species of thinking, that
may in part be due to this overriding concern with judgment: he may be
prepared for the sake of argument to concede to the man who equates

58. Translated after Sorabji [50]; cf. his comments *ad loc.*, and pp. 5-7 of his first
chapter.
59. For in *De An.* Aristotle seems to be concerned with judgments, not with the
process of thinking, in passages in which the relation of thought and *phantasmata* is in
question.

phantasia and thinking *tout court* that *phantasia* is a sort of thinking, so long as it is distinguished from thought in the sense of judgment, *hupolêpsis*.

At the same time, Aristotle may have been the readier to make the concession because of a feature of the arguments by which he distinguishes *phantasia* from *hupolêpsis*. He notes that *phantasia*, unlike belief, is up to us **127** when we wish; and that the emotional responses appropriate to belief and *phantasia* are different – in the former case 'we are immediately affected', in the latter it is 'as if we were looking at terrible or enheartening things in a picture' (427b17-24). These criteria of *phantasia* do not distinguish it from the activity of thinking: that, too, is in our power when we wish (cf. 417b24); nor does the thought of disaster or success automatically inspire immediate gloom or cheer. Aristotle may well have been persuaded by these features common to *phantasia* and thinking to allow the claim of *phantasia* to be a sort of thinking at 427b28. Nor is that claim without plausibility. A mnemonist instructing his pupil might well ask him to *think* of a set of places in which mental images may be put.

So Aristotle is tempted to view *phantasia* as a form of thinking, or at least as a thought-like component of thinking. But as we saw earlier, he also speaks of *phantasia* in ways which suggest that, if pressed, he would have had to agree that the thought-like features which he takes to be characteristic of *phantasia* at 427b16-24 are not invariable features of it. Thus it seems unlikely that he would wish to allow that the persons in the grip of fevers or strong emotion described in *De Insomniis* are able to engage in *phantasia* or not as and when they wish: what appears to them is patently not under their control. And he obviously does not think such persons capable of maintaining the emotional detachment from their *phantasmata* seen as typical of *phantasia* at 427b23-4: they, like dreamers, are often helplessly deceived, even to the point of moving bodily towards or away from what appears to them. Moreover, in just this context in *De Insomniis* Aristotle permits himself to speak of *phantasia* as a faculty in virtue of which we judge (460b16-18). Here, evidently, *phantasia* is much more like perception (one might think of it as *mis*perception)[60] than thought.

So, too, in the remaining part of the discussion in *De An.* III 3, from 428a1 to the end of the chapter. It is, for example, striking that, for his causal analysis of *phantasia*, Aristotle draws from the considerations which have filled the preceding pages the single idea that it is thought 'not to occur without sense perception, but only in things which perceive and with respect to those things of which there is perception' (428b11-13); and the chief conclusion of the analysis is that the change resulting from actual **128** sense perception which he argues is *phantasia* 'must be like perception' (428b14). When he goes on to infer that it, too, must be capable of truth and falsehood, working out an elaborate comparison between the propensities of sense perception and *phantasia* for the one or the other (428b17-30), it looks

---

60. An interpretation given further licence by *Insom.* 1, 458b31-3. There, having referred in a general way to the *phantasmata* discussed at 460b3-27, Aristotle remarks that whether the faculties of sense perception and *phantasia* are the same or different, it is clear that sense perception is a *sine qua non* of *phantasia*: 'For mis-seeing and mishearing belong to the man who sees and hears something which is truly there, but not what he takes it to be'.

as though, having begun by treating *phantasia* as a form of thinking, he ends by taking sense perception to be the key to its nature.[61] In particular, in concentrating on its propensity to give true or false views of facts, Aristotle seems clearly to count *phantasia*, like sense perception, as a faculty of judgment – contrary to what the discussion at 427b16-24 might have led one to expect. It is worth stressing this point, since some scholars, adopting Ross' emendation at 428a3 (which turns the statement of the MSS. that *phantasia* is a faculty or disposition for judgment into a question), suppose that in rejecting at 428a5-b9 any identification of *phantasia* with other faculties of judgment, Aristotle means to deny that it is itself such a faculty (so e.g. Rees [111]). As Rodier saw ([42], II, pp. 412-13, 16) emendation at this point is unnecessary; and the associated interpretation is impossible. For Aristotle glosses 'faculties in accordance with which we judge' by the words 'and take things truly or falsely' (*alêtheuomen ê pseudometha*, 428a4). And his strategy throughout the section 428a5-b9 is not to argue that the dimension of truth and falsehood is inhabited by sense perception, knowledge, belief, etc., but not by *phantasia*. It is rather to maintain that, although *phantasia* is properly to be assessed for truth and falsehood no less than perception or belief, the assessment has or can have different results in the case of *phantasia* from those obtained in the other cases. This is the point of the sun example (428b2-9); and besides remarking that perceptions are always true, but some *phantasiai* false (428a11-12), Aristotle distinguishes *phantasia* from knowledge and understanding (*nous*) on the very same ground (428a16-18), and is prepared to concede an initial plausibility to the identification of *phantasia* and belief precisely because they cannot be differentiated in this way (428a18-19).

So the unity of Aristotle's conception of *phantasia* begins to look somewhat fragile. One might argue on his behalf that in different parts of *De An.* III 3 Aristotle endows *phantasia* with such very different features just because he

---

61. We need not suppose that the original association with thinking is abandoned. It is certainly significant that Aristotle relates *phantasia* to perception rather than to thinking in his definition at 429a1-2. But the significance lies in the evidence his treatment of *phantasia* affords of the consistency of his approach to psychology. The fact that Aristotle's definition is a *causal* definition suggests that he is characteristically concerned, in his discussion at 428b10 ff., with the question what it is in our psychological nature which makes us able to exercise *phantasia* in the way we do. And his answer 'prior perception' characteristically relates *phantasia* first and foremost to the hierarchy of faculties distinguished in Book II. It does not greatly illuminate the specific psychological character of *phantasia*. The definition is presumably supposed to be true equally of dreams and memory, where the prior perception must be a thing of the past, and of the 'seeing as' cases, phenomenologically quite distinct, in which the prior perception has to be contemporaneous (I take it that Aristotle insists on the priority here simply because it is a precondition of one's seeing *x* as *y* that one should see *x*). And the definition leaves it quite open what further conditions besides prior perception must be satisfied if the change that is *phantasia* is to occur. Do I have to activate *phantasmata* – and if so what governs my success? Or if *phantasmata* just happen to me, why those particular *phantasmata* at that precise moment? It is not even clear that the definition could not apply as well to Aristotle's conception of discursive thinking (*dianoeisthai*) as to his notion of *phantasia* (cf. III 8, 432a3-8; I 4, 408b1-29).

has different sorts of exercise of the imagination in view. Seeing a distant object as a man (cf. 428a12-15) *is* very like seeing, while imagining a set of places for mnemonic purposes (cf. 427b18-20) *is* very like thinking; and in the former case one does – albeit hesitantly – take something truly or falsely (viz. the distant object to be a man), but not in the latter case. It would perhaps be possible to place Aristotle's examples and his remarks about them on a complex, but consistent and unified, conceptual map of the imagination, in the style I have adopted in the two preceding sections of this paper. But profitable and charitable though the exercise might be, it is time to notice that Aristotle himself shows no sign of being aware of the tensions within his account of *phantasia*; nor, consequently, of the importance and difficulty of the philosophical task of saying just how thinking and sensing both contribute to the imagination. Moreover, some of the inconsistencies of Aristotle's account seem more than merely apparent. Doubtless the fact that in belief, unlike *phantasia*, one *necessarily* takes something truly or falsely (cf. 427b20-1)[62] does serve to differentiate *phantasia* and belief. Yet it does not follow (as he evidently thinks) that *phantasia* is not sometimes a sort of *hupolêpsis* closer to belief than to knowledge or practical understanding. As commentators have noticed, it is difficult to report or discuss such examples as the sun looking a foot across without introducing words like 'suppose', 'conjecture', etc., which connote precisely the sort of thinking involved in *hupolêpsis*; and Aristotle himself, in an unguarded moment, once uses *dokei* in presenting the example (*Insom.* 1, 458b29).[63]

Conclusion

My intention, however, has been to show reason to celebrate Aristotle's pioneering treatment of the imagination. The great virtue of his account is its recognition of the range of psychological phenomena which deserve to be associated in this familial concept. His attempt to generalise from them about the logical peculiarities of the imagination is not carried through with a clear and steady view of the whole topic. But it remains seminal for anyone who seeks a better understanding. For Aristotle reminds us of the variety of the phenomena we need to consider, and compels us to find ways

62. 'Takes something truly or falsely' is the sense *ê pseudesthai ê alêtheuein* must have if this observation is to supply a reason for differentiating belief and *phantasia*. It does not prove the difference Aristotle alleges, viz. that believing, unlike *phantasia*, is not in our power. Hamlyn (*ad loc.*) notes: 'The real point is that beliefs are determined at least by *our view of the facts*; this is not true of imagining something.' Cf. Scruton, *Art and Imagination*, pp. 94-7. This construction of the Greek is in agreement with Greek usage (cf. LSJ s.vv.); and it is supported by the fact that Aristotle at 428a4 glosses *krinomen*, 'judge', by *alêtheuomen ê pseudometha*.

63. But although Aristotle does appear to be committed to an inconsistency here, it is perhaps not a very serious one. For he could simply withdraw his claim that *phantasia* is quite distinct from *hupolêpsis*, while insisting that it is to be differentiated from the particular sort of *hupolêpsis* he has in mind at 427b17-24, viz. *doxa* (belief).

of connecting them; he puts in our hands, even if he himself does not exploit them very fully, many of the contrasts and comparisons which seem fundamental for the conceptual mapping of imagination; and his very inconsistencies suggest crucial problems in its comparative anatomy.[64]

64. In writing this essay I have incurred numerous debts of gratitude: to Prof. J.L. Ackrill, who proposed the topic to me; to the members of the Southern Association for Ancient Philosophy (and particularly Prof. D.W. Hamlyn), who heard and discussed an ancestor of the present paper at their meeting in Cambridge in 1973; and to Messrs. J. Barnes, M.F. Burnyeat and R.R.K. Sorabji, each of whom sent me valuable comments on a penultimate draft. I hope I have made profitable use of their generous help. The paper was read to the 1975 Symposium Aristotelicum; and it has been revised in the light of the discussion at the Symposium, and of comments made to me privately by its members, particularly (once more) Richard Sorabji and my chairman, Michael Woods.

8

William W. Fortenbaugh

Aristotle's Rhetoric *on Emotions*[1]

Should the account of emotion given by Aristotle in his *Rhetoric* be dismissed **40** as a popular treatment that avoids precision? I think not and in this paper want to argue that the *Rhetoric*'s treatment of emotion is important not only for rhetorical theory but also for ethical theory and philosophical psychology. Nevertheless there is a considerable body of scholarly opinion that looks upon this treatment of emotion as superficial.[2] The *Rhetoric*'s contribution, we are told, does not lie in the analysis of individual emotions **41** but rather in the fact that emotional appeal is promoted to a mode of persuasion coordinate with character and proof or apparent proof. Whereas previous authors of rhetorical treatises had treated emotional appeal as part of the prooemium and the epilogue, Aristotle conceived of emotional appeal as a tool that could be employed throughout an oration for the purpose of persuading the audience.[3] But when Aristotle came to discuss the individual emotions he did not break new ground. True to the method that he himself proclaimed appropriate to rhetoric,[4] he did not seek exactitude but contented himself with what was generally acceptable.

1. At the outset I want to acknowledge my debt to the National Endowment for the Humanities and to the Centre for Hellenic Studies. Their support enabled me to read and work upon this topic. I am especially grateful to the Director of the Centre for Hellenic Studies, Professor Bernard Knox, and to the Junior Fellows (1967-8) for discussing with me points made in this paper. I am also indebted to Professors Glenn R. Morrow and Charles H. Kahn who have made most helpful suggestions that I have endeavoured to incorporate.
2. C. Brandis, 'Ueber Aristoteles Rhetorik und die griechischen Ausleger derselben', *Philologus* 4 (1849), p.27, *Handbuch der Geschichte der griechisch-romischen Philosophie* (Berlin, 1860), III, i. 192; Cope [183], pp. 13-4; [182], II, p.8; E.L. Hunt 'Plato and Aristotle on rhetoric and rhetoricians' in *Studies in Rhetoric and Public Speaking in Honour of James Albert Winans* (New York, 1925), pp. 57-8; L. Cooper [186], p.xx; M. Dufour [190], Vol. 2, pp. 20-1; G. Kennedy [194], p.95, note 92. According to these writers, Aristotle is merely describing the external manifestations of emotions, and seeks only to present common opinion on the matter.
3. It is generally accepted that Aristotle's recognition of emotional appeal as a mode of persuasion coordinate with proof is new and important. See F. Solmsen [201], pp. 393-4; D.L. Clark, *Rhetoric in Graeco-Roman Education* (New York, 1957), pp.75, 80; Kennedy [194], p.94. The goal of this paper is not so much to emphasise the role Aristotle assigns to emotional appeal as to emphasise his analysis of individual emotions. It is the latter which needs to be re-evaluated.
4. For the view that Aristotle did not think exactitude appropriate to rhetoric and so did not strive for precise definitions and analyses when treating the subject-matter of deliberative, epideictic, and judicial oratory (I 4-14), see Brandis 'Ueber Ar.

William W. Fortenbaugh

There have been, of course, scholars who gave Aristotle's treatment of emotions a higher rating.[5] But these scholars are a minority whose opinions **42** have been without their proper influence. Accordingly, I want to focus upon and to re-evaluate Aristotle's treatment of the individual emotions. My approach will be in two parts. In the first part, I shall argue rather generally that the *Rhetoric*'s analysis of individual emotions did receive the close attention of Aristotle and so should not be passed off as popular and imprecise. In the second part, I shall argue that the *Rhetoric*'s account of emotion enjoys a threefold significance. First, by making cognition an essential part of emotional response, the *Rhetoric* offers an answer to Academic debate concerning the relationship of emotion to cognition. Secondly, in pointing out the involvement of cognition in emotion, the *Rhetoric* makes clear that emotions can be reasonable and that emotional appeal need not be a matter of charms and enchantments. And finally, this emphasis upon cognition helps to distinguish emotions from bodily drives and so helps to develop an adequate moral psychology.

1.

Let us begin with some concessions. It is true that the *Rhetoric* explicitly disclaims exactitude in analysis and definition (1359b2-8, 1360b7-8, 1366a32, b24, 1369b31-2) and that in one important case (pleasure, 1369b33-5), the *Rhetoric* offers a definition that is rejected by the *Nicomachean Ethics*. It is also true that when the *Rhetoric* comes to consider happiness, it offers a disjunctive definition and then adds that nearly everyone would agree that one or more members of the disjunction constitutes happiness (1360b14-18). These points may be admitted. But it would be unreasonable to conclude that the analyses and definitions given in the first two books of the *Rhetoric* are simply popular and in no way represent Aristotle's own **43** views.[6] Take the case of happiness. Here Aristotle does not offer a tidy definition. He satisfies himself with a definition that may be considered sufficient (1366b24, 1369b31) and appropriate to the occasion (1359b5, 1366a21, b24). But – and this is the important point – when he claims the assent of nearly everyone, Aristotle is primarily thinking of the members of

---

Rhetorik', pp. 27-9, *Handbuch* pp. 185-92; Cope [183], pp. 11-14; Hunt, *op. cit.*, pp. 51-2; E. Zeller, *Aristotle and the Earlier Peripatetics*, translated by Costelloe and Muirhead (New York, 1962), p.296; C.S. Baldwin, *Ancient Rhetoric and Poetic* (New York, 1924), pp. 15-16; Ross [16], p.272; A.-J. Festugière, *Aristote, le plaisir* (Paris, 1936), pp. lxii-lxiv; R. Gauthier and J. Jolif, *L'Ethique à Nicomaque* (Louvain, 1959), Vol. 2, p.781, note 14; I. Düring [15], pp. 139-40, 144, 148.

5. T. Gomperz, *Greek Thinkers*, translated by G. Berry (New York, 1912), Vol. 4, p.436; M. Heidegger, *Sein und Zeit* (Tübingen, 1963), p.183; F. Solmsen, *The Rhetoric and the Poetics of Aristotle*, Modern Library (New York, 1954), p, xvi, and [201], pp. 393-4. While P. Aubenque [131], pp. 300-17, emphasises (correctly) that the definitions advanced in the *Rhetoric* do not satisfy the standards of natural philosophy, he is quite clear that the definitions do give the form of individual emotions and deserve serious attention.

6. Cf. G. Lieberg, *Die Lehre von der Lust in der Ethiken des Aristoteles, Zetemata 19* (Munich, 1958), pp. 23-7, who argues that the definitions in Books I and II of the *Rhetoric* are offered as serious definitions and not simply popular opinions.

the Academy. He is not especially concerned with people in general. He offers a disjunction that is meant to cover the various views or at least the most important views under debate in the Academy. This is, of course, an old point.[7] But it must be emphasised, because it shows that in lecturing on rhetoric, Aristotle's thoughts are very much focused upon the Academy and the views being advanced by its members. This is not to say that Aristotle is totally unconcerned whether his disjunctive definition of happiness finds acceptance outside the Academy. But it is to say that Aristotle's primary audience is within the Academy and that his definitions and analyses may be expected to reflect interests and opinions current within the Academy.

Rather similar remarks can be made concerning the *Rhetoric*'s definition and analysis of pleasure as a movement of the soul and an intense and perceptible settling down into the natural state (1369b33-5). Aristotle's treatment of pleasure takes its impetus from the Academy. Only this time Aristotle does not offer a disjunctive definition that might satisfy all or most **44** members of the Academy.[8] Instead, he offers a particular view of pleasure that was made prominent within the Academy by Speusippus' polemic against Eudoxus and is familiar to us through Plato's *Philebus* and *Timaeus*. Still, Aristotle does not simply report the view of other members of the Academy. He seems to modify and supplement the view and so to make it his own.[9] I do not want to press this point. It cannot, I think, be established firmly that at the time of writing this portion of the *Rhetoric* Aristotle accepted without reservation the view of pleasure as a kind of motion. It is perhaps likely that he did. At least the view is found not only in the *Rhetoric* but also in another early work, Book VII of the *Physics* (246b20-247a19). However, this same view of pleasure is treated negatively in still another **45** early work, the *Topics* (121a27-39). In order to illustrate a particular method for rejecting alleged genera, Aristotle introduces the proposition

7. See J. Burnet, *The Ethics of Aristotle* (London, 1900), p.1, note 1, and 3, note 3; Festugière, *op. cit.*, p.lxiii.

8. According to Brandis, 'Ueber Ar. Rhetorik', p.27, Aristotle offers an account of pleasure and pain as movement not because he totally endorsed the Platonic notion, but because he was concerned only with an easily understandable explanation that avoided raising disputed points. I agree with Brandis in allowing the possibility that Aristotle set forth a view about which he had reservations. But I find it difficult to imagine this particular view avoiding controversy. Even if the dispute between Speusippus and Eudoxus was for the most part over and even if this view of pleasure had been advanced by Plato, it is unlikely that opinion within the Academy had formed a consensus in favour of this view. *Topics* 121a27-39 is, I think, a clear echo of continuing debate within the Academy. See also *A. Pr.* 25a9-12.

9. The *Rhetoric*'s definition of pleasure should be compared with the view set forth at *Philebus* 31D8-9, 42D5-6, 46C6 and *Timaeus* 64D1-2, 65A1. Lieberg, *op. cit.*, pp. 27-42, examines in detail the dependence of the *Rhetoric* upon the *Philebus* and shows how Aristotle adopted with some modification the physiological conception of pleasure as a return to one's natural state. According to Lieberg, Aristotle's interest in the Platonic precedent coupled with his attention to and modification of particular details (e.g. replacing the pronoun *hautês* or *hautón* (*Philebus* 31D8, 42D5) with his own term *huparchousan* (1369b34-5); developing or adding to the Platonic position so as to recognise a highest form of pleasure that occurs after the return to the natural state (1370a4-5)) makes evident that Aristotle is not simply trotting out a popular or current opinion but is concerned with establishing his own conception of pleasure.

that motion is the genus of pleasure and argues that because pleasure is neither locomotion nor alteration nor any other specific kind of motion, pleasure cannot be a motion. It is, of course, difficult to be certain of Aristotle's attitude toward any particular example in the *Topics*. He may think that this argument against pleasure as a kind of motion is a telling argument, or he may not.[10] Perhaps we may say that Aristotle introduced this particular argument against pleasure as a kind of motion because it was current in the Academy. Like other members of the Academy he was able to criticise the view of pleasure as motion, but he was also prepared on occasion to advance the view, perhaps because he found the view on the whole acceptable or at least better than any other view current in the Academy.

Concerning the analyses of happiness and pleasure more could be said. But perhaps enough has been said to suggest strongly that these and other analyses presented in the *Rhetoric* are serious efforts that should be seen within the context of Plato's Academy. If so, let us begin to focus upon the treatment of individual emotions in Book II, considering first an old objection to taking the treatment as a serious effort deserving close study. The objection is philological in nature: Aristotle introduces the definitions

46 of individual emotions with the word *estô* ('let (it) be' 1378a30, 1380a8, b36, 1382a21, 1383b12, 1385a17, b13), and this word is a sign that the definitions are of only a popular nature. Aristotle, it is argued, begins his definition of anger with the words 'let anger be' (1378a30) and thereby indicates the provisional nature of the offered definition.[11] But is this argument as strong as it is old? Certainly the use of *estô* in definitions is a characteristic of the *Rhetoric*[12] and on occasion it is possible that Aristotle uses this word to indicate the tentative nature of an offered definition. The disjunctive definition of happiness begins with *estô* (1360b14) and this may be a sign that the offered definition is meant to cover the several Academic views without making precise which view or combination of views captures the essence of happiness. But it should be observed that when Aristotle returns to a definition introduced by *estô* he may give no indication that the definition is less than his own.[13] Moreover, at least one definition introduced by *estô* cannot be described plausibly as a popular definition. This is Aristotle's definition of rhetoric: let rhetoric be a faculty of considering in each case the possible means of persuasion (1355b25-6). Here, Aristotle seems to be giving us his own definition of rhetoric. He neither follows the

10. Düring, 'Aristotle's use of examples in the *Topics*' in [37], takes this passage as a rejection by Aristotle of Plato's opinion that pleasure is a kind of motion. I respect Düring's judgment but cannot justify so positive a stand. On the general relationship between the *Topics* and *Rhetoric* see J. Brunschwig [208], Vol. 1, pp. xcvi-ciii.

11. The view that Aristotle used *estô* in the *Rhetoric* specifically to introduce imprecise and popular definitions goes back at least as far as L. Spengel, *Specimen Commentariorum in Aristotelis Libros de Arte Rhetorica* (Munich, 1839), pp. 10-17. Spengel was followed by Brandis, 'Ueber Ar. Rhetorik', p.28, note 42, and Cope [182], Vol. 1, pp. 73, 97, 188, Vol. 2, p.8. See also Dufour [190], Vol. 1, pp. 1, 39, 46, 47, 54, Vol. 2, pp. 20, 21, Festugière, *op. cit.*, p.lxiii, Aubenque [131], p.305, and Düring [15], p.140.

12. For *estô* in Book I, see 1355b25, 1360b14, 1362a21, 1363b7, 1368b6.

13. See 1363b13 and 1364b17 where Aristotle refers to the definition of goodness by saying simply 'we call' and 'has been defined'.

lead of Plato's *Phaedrus* nor adopts the view of rhetoric current among professional rhetoricians. Aristotle ignores Plato's insistence upon becoming a philosopher (*Phaedrus* 261A4) and being gifted in division (*Phaedrus* 263B7, 266B3-C9, 270B4, 271C10-D5, 273D8-E4). Moreover, Aristotle's emphasis upon the persuasive (1355b11, 15-16, 26, 32-3) seems discordant with Plato's emphasis upon truth in comparison with the persuasive and plausible (*Phaedrus* 259E-262C, 272D-273E) and with Plato's insistence that knowledge of truth is not a separable preliminary but a part of rhetoric (*Phaedrus* 260E6).[14] Aristotle, it seems, is not following the leader of the Academy. Yet neither is he following the view of professional **47** rhetoricians. For these men considered rhetoric to be the art of effecting persuasion. Gorgias called rhetoric the artificer of persuasion (Plato, *Gorgias* 453A2), and in this definition seems to have been followed by Isocrates (Quintilian, *Instit. Orat.* 2.15.4). For professional rhetoricians, success was essential to rhetoric; for Aristotle, it was not. Modifying the current view, he suggested viewing rhetoric as the faculty of observing and discovering the possible means of persuasion (1355b10-14, 25-6; cf. *Topics* 101b5-10).[15]

It may be, of course, that this definition of rhetoric is to some extent deficient or incomplete and that *estô* helps to point out this inexactitude. Perhaps the definition does need further qualification, for it contains no stated limitation upon the kinds of persuasion with which rhetoric concerns itself. There is a need to add a qualifying *in oratione*.[16] The rhetorician is concerned only with those means of persuasion that involve speech. Aristotle himself would acknowledge the need for this qualification. He had, after all, studied the *Gorgias* and so would be familiar with Gorgias' suggestion that the great benefit of rhetoric is the ability to persuade with speeches (*Gorgias* 452E1). But to acknowledge that the *Rhetoric*'s definition is in this way incomplete is not to say that it is popular or merely thrown out by way of example. On the contrary, it is simply to admit that this **48** definition, like most definitions and analyses in the *Rhetoric*, aims at being sufficient and appropriate to the occasion (1359b5, 1366a20-1, b24, 1369b31).

Sometimes Aristotle's interest in a definition may even lead him to seek an exactitude beyond that claimed for rhetoric. Consider his definition of goodness. This definition begins with an *estô* (1362a21) and lists various marks of goodness. In a certain sense the definition is popular. As in the

14. With *Phaedrus* 260E6, see R. Hackforth, *Plato's Phaedrus* (Cambridge, 1952), p.120, note 2. For a general discussion of Aristotle's divergence from Plato see Dufour [190], Vol. 1, pp. 11-14, Hunt, *op. cit.*, pp. 49-59.

15. On Aristotle's rejection of success as an essential feature of rhetoric see Quintilian, *Instit. Orat.* 2.15.13: 'Quidam recesserunt ab eventu, sicut Aristoteles dicit: rhetorice est vis inveniendi omnia in oratione persuasibilia'. See also Cope [183], pp. 28-33.

16. See Quintilian, *Instit. Orat.* 2.15.6-13 where Quintilian criticises those persons who define rhetoric by reference to persuasion without delimiting the kind of persuasion with which rhetoric is concerned. In what appears to be a carelessly written passage (2.15.13), Quintilian first adds a qualifying *in oratione* to Aristotle's definition of rhetoric and then seems to criticise Aristotle for failing to add this qualification. See Cope [183], p.34.

case of happiness, so here, everybody would endorse one or more of the enumerated marks of goodness. But while the several marks of goodness would be generally accepted, they would also be accepted by Aristotle. The definition includes nothing that is contradicted by the *Ethics*. Moreover, Aristotle extends the definition to cover not only things good in themselves but also things good as means. This is not a sign of indifference or carelessness on the part of Aristotle. The goods as means are all carefully grouped together (1362a27-9) and important terms are explained (1362a29-34). First he explains 'follows' by drawing a distinction between following simultaneously and following subsequently. Then he illustrates three different senses of 'productive'. A thing may be productive in the way that being healthy is productive of health, or in the way that food is productive of health, or in the way that taking exercise is productive of health. The example of being healthy producing health is of especial importance. For the example recurs in the *Nicomachean Ethics* (1144a4, 1174b25) and introduces Aristotle's own notion of a formal cause. Without overstating our case, we can say that Aristotle is interested in defining goodness. If he is presenting a definition that is generally acceptable either within the Academy or possibly outside the Academy as well, he is not doing so independently of his own views. An initial *estô* need not imply a popular definition unrelated to Aristotle's own philosophical commitments.

In respect of the treatment of individual emotions, we can be quite certain that the definitions offered are not just examples thrown out by way of illustration. Aristotle was well aware that emotion affects judgment **49** (1354b8-11, 1356a15-16, 1377b30-1378a5, 19-20). He recognised the importance of emotional appeal and treated persuasion 'through the hearers' (1356a14) as a special mode of persuasion coordinate with persuasion 'through demonstration' and persuasion 'through character'. For Aristotle a correct understanding of emotion was an essential part of the art of rhetoric. Each individual emotion must be analysed in three ways. The condition of men prone to an individual emotion, the objects of an individual emotion, and the grounds for an individual emotion must all be grasped. If the orator's understanding of individual emotions is deficient in any of these three areas, then he will be unable to arouse emotional response (1378a23-6). Aristotle was not going to be satisfied by more popular opinions, for he was well aware that a mastery of emotional appeal belongs only to the man that has investigated and come to understand what characterises and what causes individual emotions (1356a21-5).[17]

17. It should be emphasised that when Aristotle discussed the individual emotions he was providing his pupils not only with an interesting exercise in philosophical psychology but also with a mode of persuasion, with the knowledge necessary for successfully arousing and allaying emotion (1365b21-5, 1378a24-6). This close tie with a mode of persuasion seems to be lacking in the discussion of particular premisses that occupied so much of Book I. In this earlier discussion Aristotle is primarily providing materials for persuasion 'through demonstration'. He is not elucidating a mode of persuasion but rather supplying materials for enthymemes. (Of course, the discussion of virtue is also connected with persuasion 'through character' (1366a25-7, 1378a15-17).) These materials, it might be argued, may be popular opinions. For if an orator is to be persuasive he cannot use controversial premisses. His demonstrations must begin from generally accepted premisses (cf. 1357a12-13

Although the definitions of individual emotions are to be taken seriously,   **50**
this is not to say that they are precise in every detail. Such an assertion is too
easily refuted by the *De Anima*. For in this treatise, Aristotle criticises the
rhetorical or, as he styles it, the dialectical definition of anger.[18]
Nevertheless, it is important to notice that the *De Anima* does not reject the
Rhetoric's definition of anger. It simply (and predictably) suggests that this
definition of anger falls short of standards appropriate to physical
investigation. The definition is not erroneous, but it is incomplete. For while
it does give the form of anger, it makes no mention of matter or a bodily
correlate. On the other hand, anger cannot be defined adequately simply by
reference to a bodily correlate. Neither the dialectician who defines anger as
a desire for retaliation nor the materialistic student of nature who defines
anger as boiling of blood around the heart (*De An.* 403a30-b1) offers a
definition that satisfies the requirements of natural philosophy. A
competent student of nature will construct his definition from both of these
definitions (*De An.* 403b7-9). It is clear, therefore, that the definitions of
anger and other emotions given in the *Rhetoric* are not so much rejected by
the *De Anima* as supplemented. They are accepted and completed.   **51**

We have been arguing that the occurrence of *estô* in a definition is not in
itself grounds for dismissing a definition as something popular and
philosophically unimportant. We have acknowledged that the treatment of
individual emotions is incomplete but have argued that this deficiency can
be pinned down and does not constitute grounds for dismissing the *Rhetoric*'s
treatment of emotions as a popular account of little philosophical
significance. We can now approach the treatment of individual emotions
and inquire concerning their significance untroubled by the occurrence of
estô. But before moving on to the treatment of individual emotions, I would
suggest that *estô* is not used in the *Rhetoric* to mark the tentative nature of
definitions. Rather, it is used as part of, and possibly to emphasise, the
deductive method that Aristotle employs throughout large sections of Books
I and II of the *Rhetoric*. Within the Academy Plato had criticised severely
current rhetorical methods and had called for a new and philosophical
rhetoric. If rhetoric was to be taught in the Academy, it had to acquire at
least the appearance of scientific method. Toward this end, Aristotle
imposed a demonstrative method both upon his discussion of particular
premises in Book I and upon his discussion of emotions in Book II. He
organised his material deductively, laying down definitions and drawing

---

and Plato, *Phaedrus* 259E7-260A4, 272D2-273A1). This argument has some force as
long as it is directed at the discussion of particular premises in Book I. But it loses its
force when transferred to the discussion of emotions in Book II. For in discussing
emotions Aristotle is primarily concerned with a mode of persuasion. He is no longer
supplying 'filler' for the enthymemes of deliberative, epideictic, and judicial oratory.
Instead he is conveying an understanding of individual emotions that is fundamental
to mastering persuasion 'through the hearers'.

18. The dialectician's definition of anger as a desire for returning pain (*De An.*
403a30-1) is to be connected with the *Rhetoric*'s definition of anger as a desire for
revenge (1378a30). See Cope [183], p.13, Aubenque [131], pp. 304, 311, and D.W.
Hamlyn [44], p.80.

necessary conclusions.[19] But for Aristotle it was not simply a matter of
52 giving rhetorical instruction a scientific air. At this period in his career
Aristotle was very much interested in logical method. The introduction of
example and enthymeme into the art of rhetoric is a clear sign of this
interest. Aristotle had recently spent considerable time upon treatises
devoted to logical method and was probably still at work on these
treatises.[20] He was, therefore, prepared to bring a deductive method to
rhetorical instruction. It is not surprising to find in the *Rhetoric* a vocabulary
and method that recall the *Analytics*. In particular, it is not surprising to find
Aristotle using *estô* to lay down a definition or premiss from which he draws
necessary conclusions.[21] The vocabulary and method are common in the
Analytics.[22] Of course, in the *Analytics* the premisses introduced by *estô* are
illustrative and are not advanced as propositions of philosophical
importance. Indeed, letters may be used instead of formulated propositions
53 (e.g. *A. Pr.* 30a37-b2, *A. Pst.* 75a6-7, 9-11). But this does not mean that in
the *Rhetoric* definitions introduced by *estô* are merely illustrative and popular
in nature. For the cases are not identical. In the *Analytics* Aristotle is
primarily investigating logical method. In the *Rhetoric* Aristotle is *using*
logical method to investigate the materials with which a rhetorician must be

19. See, for example, the *Rhetoric*'s treatment of goodness. First Aristotle offers a
definition of goodness that begins with *estô* (1362a21) and enumerates several marks
of goodness. After pausing to clarify two terms Aristotle resumes with the phrase
'these things having been laid down' (1362a34) and proceeds to draw necessary
(*anankê* 1362a34, b3, 7, 10) inferences.

20. It seems fairly certain that Aristotle composed the relevant portions of the
Rhetoric either concurrently with or soon after the *Analytics*. See Düring [15], p.119
with note 7, Kennedy [194], p.85, F. Solmsen [29], p.223.

21. See above, note 19. For another example consider Aristotle's analysis of anger.
He begins with the words 'Let anger be (*estô*) a desire for revenge' (1378a30), and
after completing the definition of anger resumes with these words 'If anger is this,
then it is necessary (*anankê*) that ...' (1378a32-3). It may be noticed how Aristotle's
procedure agrees formally with that recommended by Plato in the *Phaedrus*. A *logos*
should begin with a definition (263D2-3) and subsequent portions should be
arranged according to a certain necessity (*anankê* 264B4, 7). But it would be false to
suggest that Aristotle's immediate inspiration is this portion of the *Phaedrus*. For here
Plato is concerned primarily with the organic unity of a *logos* (264C2-5) and possibly
with the method of division (265D3-266B1) that he calls dialectic (266C1, *Philebus*
17A4). In proceeding deductively Aristotle is not primarily influenced by the *Phaedrus*
but by his own *Analytics*. In his use of *estô* Aristotle seems to be drawing on the
vocabulary of the *Analytics* (see below, note 22) and in defining the individual
emotions he seems to be offering causal definitions that meet the standards of the
Posterior Analytics (see below, section 2) and that may have been worked out in his own
Diaireseis (see below, note 33).

22. *Estô* occurs in the *Analytics* both in connection with whole premisses and in
connection with single terms. The following list is only a sample: With premisses: *A.
Pr.* 25a14, 30a37, b9, 31a5, 10, 24; *A. Pst.* 75a6, 9, 81b30, 94b14, 98b26, 99a31; with
terms: *A. Pr.* 30b33; *A. Pst.* 78a31,40,b24, 84b9, 87b8, 93a29, 94a28, 98a9, b5, 12,
99b3. The plural *estôsan* also occurs: *A. Pr.* 27b12, 23. Professor Morrow has called my
attention to the fact that *estô* is also commonly used in Euclid's *Elements* to introduce
the first premiss of the 'given' in a demonstration. *Estô* is part of the vocabulary of
demonstration and as such had already been used by Aristotle not only in his *Analytics*
but also in his *Rhetoric*.

acquainted. In the investigation of logical method Aristotle will be satisfied with premisses that illustrate the method under consideration. In the investigation of emotions he will not be satisfied with illustrative premisses.

2.

In the preceding section we have argued that the *Rhetoric*'s account of emotions should not be dismissed automatically as popular and of little philosophical importance. In this section we shall ask what is the significance of this account both for the philosophy of mind and for the development of rhetorical and ethical theory. Let us start by looking at the *Rhetoric* itself. Here, at the beginning of Book II we find Aristotle introducing his treatment of emotion with the following statement: 'Emotions are that on account of which men so change as to differ in judgment and which are attended by pain and pleasure, for example anger, pity, fear, all other such and their opposites' (1378a19-22). This initial statement, we may suspect, is not offered as a final and precise definition of emotion. For it is too wide and can include physiological disturbances such as headaches and stomach-aches that are accompanied by pain and that do affect judgment. Qualification is needed.[23] In this respect Aristotle's immediately following remarks are important. It is necessary, he tells us, to analyse each emotion in three ways. In the case of anger, for example, we must distinguish how men prone to anger are disposed, at whom they are accustomed to be angry and on what grounds (1378a19-24). The mention of objects ('at whom', *tisin*) and grounds (*epi poiois*) is important; it strongly suggests that Aristotle does not dissociate cognition from emotion. For it is thoughts or beliefs that have objects and that explain and justify emotional responses. Unless Aristotle is confused, he does not conceive of emotions simply as inner (mental or bodily) feelings or sensations. For if he did conceive of emotions as simple sensations, he could not explain how emotions have objects and grounds. Stomach-aches, headaches, and other (bodily) sensations are not justified. They lack objects and grounds altogether. It is thoughts and beliefs that have objects and it is the

54

---

23. It may be instructive to compare this initial statement concerning emotion with the definition of rhetoric given in Book I (1355b25-6). Both need qualification. In both cases Aristotle passes over without mention a qualification that had been insisted upon by Plato. We have noted already (above, in section 1) Aristotle's failure to add a qualifying *in oratione* to his definition of rhetoric although he was familiar with Plato's *Gorgias* and the suggestion that rhetoric is the ability to persuade with speeches (452E1). The failure is hardly serious. Aristotle's audience within the Academy would understand an *in oratione*, if Aristotle failed to make the qualification explicit. The same is true of Aristotle's initial statement concerning emotion. It needs a qualification that had been made already by Plato and that would be supplied by Aristotle's audience. For in the *Philebus* (46-8) Plato had distinguished itches and tickles, hunger and thirst from emotions such as 'anger, fear, yearning, grief, emulation, envy and the like' (47E1-2). The former group he had referred to the body (more accurately, itches and tickles are referred to the body, while hungers and thirsts are referred to both the body and the soul (46B8-C4, 47C1-E3)) and the latter group to the soul. Aristotle's audience, like Aristotle himself, would be familiar with the *Philebus*' distinction and so prepared to add a qualifying 'psychic' to the initial statement concerning emotions.

142 *William W. Fortenbaugh*

occurrence of these cognitions in emotional response that explains why we can ask a man at whom he is angry and whether his anger is reasonable. Instead of viewing emotions simply as particular kinds of inner (mental) feelings or sensations that impel a man to behave in certain characteristic ways, Aristotle, we may suspect, includes cognition within his conception of emotion.

The accounts of individual emotions confirm this suspicion. Consider anger. Aristotle begins his treatment of this emotion with a definition: let **55** anger be a desire for revenge accompanied by pain on account of an apparent insult to oneself or one's own, the insult being unjustified (1378a30-2). The mention of apparent insult within the definition is important. The appearance of unjustified insult is for Aristotle an essential part of being angry. Whenever a man is angry, he thinks or believes or imagines that someone has done something and has done it unjustly (1378a30-b1, 1379b11-12). His anger always involves the thought of unjust treatment. If this cognition is absent, so is anger. For anger does not occur when men think that they suffer justly. As Aristotle explains, they do not think that they suffer unjustly; and anger was (said to be) this (1380b16-18). More precisely, anger was defined in part by reference to apparent insult, so that part of being angry is thinking oneself unjustly treated, and whenever this thought is not present, neither is anger.

Similar remarks can be made concerning Aristotle's analysis of other individual emotions. Fear, for example, necessarily involves the thought or belief of imminent danger. Fear is defined as a pain or disturbance resulting from the appearance of imminent evil (1382a21-2). The thought of impending danger is essential, so that a man cannot be afraid unless he thinks himself threatened. Aristotle makes this quite clear when he argues in the following manner: If fear is associated with the expectation of suffering something destructive, it is clear that no one is afraid who believes nothing can happen to him. No one is afraid of those things that he believes cannot happen to him, nor of those persons by whom and at those times when he thinks he cannot suffer harm (1382b29-32). The thought or imagination of imminent danger is part of the definition of fear, so that it is obvious and a matter of conceptual necessity (1382b33) that whenever men are afraid they think they can suffer harm.

For students of philosophical psychology, Aristotle's analysis of emotional response is in itself interesting. His emphasis upon cognition and its necessary involvement within emotional response may be said to **56** anticipate debate among contemporary philosophers.[24] Of equal interest and of more immediate importance to this paper is the way Aristotle's analysis relates to and indicates his answer to debate current within the Academy. For philosophical debate concerning the involvement of cognition

24. Aristotle's emphasis upon the necessary involvement of thought or belief in emotional response may be compared with the similar position of E. Bedford ('Emotions', *Proceedings of the Aristotelian Society* 57 (1956-7), pp. 281-304) and contrasted with the view of G. Pitcher ('Emotion', *Mind* 74 (1965), pp. 326-46). Pitcher offers a Wittgensteinian analysis according to which certain kinds of cognition are characteristic of but not essential to particular kinds of emotional response.

in emotional response is not new. On the contrary, the debate was lively within the Academy and is reflected in Plato's *Philebus* and Aristotle's *Topics*. In the *Philebus*, Socrates finds himself constrained to discuss the relationship of cognition to emotion and other kinds of pains and pleasures, when Protarchus balks at calling pleasure and pain true or false. Protarchus allows that opinion (*doxa*) may be true or false but refuses to admit that pleasure and pain, fear and expectation can be properly called true or false (36C6-D2). At first Socrates tries to win over Protarchus by pointing out similarities between opinion on the one hand and pleasure and pain on the other. Socrates' argument proceeds smoothly enough until he tries to establish that pleasures and pains, like opinions, can be mistaken. To establish this, Socrates argues that pleasures often occur together with (*meta* 37E10) false opinion. Socrates' choice of words is unfortunate. Protarchus construes 'with' as simple concurrence. He conceives of the opinion as something external to the pleasure[25] and so objects that in such a case the opinion would be false but no one would call the pleasure false (37E2-38A2). Refused an easy victory, Socrates undertakes a more exhaustive study of opinion and its relationship to pleasure and pain. He gives a rather graphic description of our thought processes and finally argues that just as opinions may lack a basis in reality, so pleasures and pains may be without grounds (*epi* 40D8). And what is true of pleasures and pains in general is, of course, true of painful emotions such as fear, anger and the like. They may be without foundation and so said to be false (40E2-4). Protarchus agrees and does not object when a little later Socrates says that true and false opinions 'fill up' pleasures and pains with their own affection (42A7-9).

The *Philebus* certainly makes clear that Plato saw an intimate relationship   **57** between emotion and cognition. But the *Philebus* does not make precise the relationship,[26] and we may guess that the relationship was still a matter of lively debate within the Academy.[27] We get some idea of this debate from

25. See R. Hackforth, *Plato's Examination of Pleasure* (Cambridge, 1958), pp. 69, 77. Protarchus' 'view is that the "mistakenness" is something lying outside the pleasure, a wrong opinion held concurrently with the feeling' (p.69). Perhaps it should be noted that Protarchus does not claim the view as his own. When Socrates congratulates him on his defence of pleasure, Protarchus modestly replies that he is merely saying what he hears (38A5). Perhaps we may add 'in the Academy'. Protarchus, we may conjecture, is reporting an argument current in the Academy. It is convenient to refer to this argument as Protarchus' view or, as I shall soon do, Protarchus' (mis-) understanding, but we should remember that Protarchus does not claim the view as his own.
26. 'With' (37E10) only gets Socrates into trouble. 'Follows' (38B9) needs qualification, while 'fills up' (42A9) is a metaphor that may avoid but does not solve the problem.
27. When Socrates finishes his account of envy and begs off giving a similar account of fear, love, and the other emotions, he wins Protarchus' consent by promising to continue the discussion tomorrow (50C10-E2). This promise may be a dramatic device to enable the dialogue to move on to new material, but it may be viewed also as a genuine reflection of discussion within the Academy. For emotions together with other kinds of pleasures and pains were a subject of current and lively debate among members of the Academy. When Plato makes Socrates promise to consider the subject again tomorrow, he would seem to be both reflecting and encouraging debate within the Academy.

144 *William W. Fortenbaugh*

the *Topics*. Cognition, it seems, was generally considered essential to emotional response. But in what way was cognition essential? There seems to have been a difference of opinion, Take, for example, anger. The *Topics* allows that the thought of outrage is essential to being angry (127b30-1). But in what way is it essential? Is it the genus of anger? Apparently not, for pain which is a more likely candidate is not the genus (127b26-32).[28] Can we say, then, that anger is pain with (*meta*) the thought of outrage (151a15-16)? Not without clarification. After the *Philebus* and Protarchus' (mis-) understanding of the preposition 'with', we cannot simply define anger as pain 'with' thought of outrage. We must go on and make precise how we are using 'with'. For 'with' can be construed in the following ways: 'and' (150a4), 'made up out of' (150a22), 'in the same receptacle' (150b35), 'in the same place' (150b36) and 'in the same time' (150b36). But in none of these senses, the *Topics* argues, is anger correctly defined as pain with the thought of outrage. What the definition really wants to show is that the pain of anger occurs on account of (*dia*) such a thought (151a16-17). The *Topics*, it seems, prefers a causal definition: anger is a desire for revenge on account of (*dia*) apparent insult (156a32-3), and in this preference agrees with the *Rhetoric* (1378a31) and reflects Aristotle's own contribution to the Academic debate.

58

To this Academic debate concerning the relationship between cognition and emotion, Aristotle brought his own logical skills. Agreeing with other members of the Academy that cognition and emotion are intimately connected and wishing to make clear the kind of connection that joins cognition to emotional response,[29] Aristotle opted for a connection that is

28. Brunschwig [208], Vol. 1, p.109, n.1, rejects *oligôrias* at 127b31 as a gloss on the grounds that the passage is concerned with determining the genus of anger, and while *hupolêpsis* (thought) is a genus, *hupolêpsis oligôrias* (thought of outrage) is not one. Whatever text we adopt, it remains true that this passage in conjunction with 151a15-16 and 156a32-3 reflects debate within the Academy concerning the relationship between emotion and cognition in general and anger and thought of outrage in particular.

29. It should be emphasised that Aristotle is clarifying or advancing the Academic discussion. He is not overthrowing previous work. This is particularly true in regard to the *Philebus*. This dialogue had not made precise the exact relationship between cognition and emotion but it had emphasised an intimate relationship. Certainly Aristotle had learned much from studying this dialogue. We have already noticed a close relationship between the accounts of pleasure in the *Philebus* and in the *Rhetoric* (above, section 1 and note 9) and have suggested that the *Rhetoric*'s initial statement on emotions assumes certain distinctions already made in the *Philebus* (above, note 23). We may add that there is close agreement between the accounts of envy given in the *Philebus* and *Rhetoric*. Both works agree in calling envy a pain (48B8, 50A7; 1386b18, 1387b23), in emphasising the grounds (*epi*) that explain an envious man's emotional response (48B11, 49D3,E9, 50A2,5; 1386b19, 1387b22-3, 1388a25), in pointing out that envious men are delighted at the misfortune of a neighbour or peer (48B11-12, 50A2-3; 1386b32-1387a3, 1388a24-7), in associating envy with bad character (49D6-7; 1386b33-1387a1), and in dissociating envy from the fearsome (49A7-C5; 1386b20-4). These similarities indicate the influence of the *Philebus* upon Aristotle's treatment of envy. This is not to say that Aristotle simply rewrote the account of envy given in the *Philebus*. But it is to say that even if Aristotle did not

both essential and causal. He analysed cognition as the efficient cause mentioned in the essential definition. In the *Posterior Analytics* Aristotle had insisted that questions of essence and questions of cause are one and the same (90a14-15, 31-2, 93a3-4, cf. *Meta.* 1041a28-9) and had illustrated this principle partly by reference to the eclipse of the moon. This stock example is especially clear and also relevant to our enquiry. For an eclipse has an efficient cause that is included in the essential definition. What is a lunar eclipse? asks Aristotle. It is a deprivation of light from the moon by the obstruction of the earth. What is the cause of a lunar eclipse, or why does the moon suffer eclipse? Because light fails owing to the obstruction of the   **59** earth (90a15-18). For Aristotle knowing the essence of an eclipse involves knowing the efficient cause (98b21-4). The obstruction of the earth is essential to the occurrence of a lunar eclipse and so is mentioned in its definition. The efficient cause of an eclipse that fails to mention the obstruction of earth is to that extent imperfect (*Meta.* 1044b13-15). In stating the essential nature of an eclipse we must give a definition that 'shows why' (*A. Pst.* 93b38), we must give 'an account of the cause' (*Meta.* 1044b15). We must define an eclipse as a deprivation of light on account of obstruction and so make plain that the obstruction of the earth is both essential to an eclipse and also the efficient cause of an eclipse.

The case of emotional response is similar. Cognition is both essential and the efficient cause and so is mentioned in a definition that 'shows why'. Just as Aristotle analyses an eclipse by considering the total situation including the efficient cause, so he analyses the entire emotional response including the thought or belief that moves a man to respond in a particular sort of way. He looks upon some sort of cognition as both essential to and also the efficient cause of emotional response. This comes out quite clearly in Aristotle's treatment of anger. The thought of outrage is essential to anger so that the absence of such a thought entails the absence of anger (1380b16-18). It is also the efficient cause of anger. Being wronged produces anger (1383b6-7). A man is moved to anger by a slight. For even a trifling slight such as a forgotten name can produce anger (1379b33-4). Outrage or more precisely the thought of outrage[30] is for Aristotle both essential to anger and also the efficient cause of anger. It is, therefore, included in the definition that 'shows why'. And it is just this kind of definition that Aristotle offers when he says, 'Let anger be (*estô*) a desire for revenge on account of (*dia*)   **60** apparent insult' (1378a30-1). It is simply not true that when Aristotle defines the individual emotion of anger he avoids *esti* and employs *estô*,

---

borrow directly from the *Philebus*, he did borrow indirectly through discussion in the Academy.

30. Anger may be caused by the mere appearance of outrage. Of course, when outrage actually occurs, it is natural to refer to the outrageous act as the efficient cause. We may compare *A. Pst.* 94a36-b8 where Aristotle introduces the Athenian attack upon Sardis as the efficient cause of the Persian Wars. Since the attack actually occurred, it is natural to pick out this attack as the efficient cause that moved the Persians to retaliate. Nevertheless, actual outrage is not essential to anger. Only the thought or imagination of outrage is essential, so that whenever a man is moved to anger he thinks or imagines himself insulted.

because the former term signifies the essence (*ti esti*) in the domain of truth while the latter introduces a definition that is merely sufficient and plausible in the domain of opinion.[31] Rather Aristotle gives us an essential definition that captures both the essence (*ti esti*) and the cause (*dia ti*). He is following the practise of the *Posterior Analytics* and giving definitions that 'show why'. His definition is not a popular throw-out. It is well formed and meets standards advanced in the *Posterior Analytics*.

We could go on and study each individual emotion, pointing out that some kind of cognition is both essential to and the efficient cause of each individual emotion. In the case of fear, for example, we might point out that Aristotle's definition is a causal definition. By including the appearance of imminent danger within the definition (1382a21-2), Aristotle forms a definition that 'shows why'.[32] And this 'account with the cause' permits him to argue that necessarily such things are fearsome as appear to possess destructive power (1382a27-30). Fearsome things (that is, those things that inspire or arouse the emotion of fear) are necessarily things that appear to be harmful, because fear is by definition a pain or disturbance due to the appearance of imminent danger. Perhaps, however, we have gone far enough to say with some confidence that the definitions and analyses of individual emotions given in the *Rhetoric* are not popular definitions and analyses to whose truth Aristotle was largely indifferent. On the contrary the treatment of individual emotions given in the *Rhetoric* is Aristotle's own

61 treatment. Moreover, it indicates Aristotle's own answer to the Academic debate concerning the relationship of cognition to emotional response. Cognition is not simply concurrent with (*meta*) emotional response. It is essential to and the cause of emotional response. This answer is characteristically Aristotelian and should be recognised as such. This is not to say that the account given in the *Rhetoric* is written specifically to answer the Academic debate. It is not. The *Rhetoric* investigates emotion because it must instruct the orator in persuasion 'through the hearers'. Still, the *Rhetoric*'s account presupposes and reflects Aristotle's own answer to the Academic debate. It makes clear his own view that may have been worked out and fully stated in the *Diaireseis*.[33] That work has not survived. But the

31. Cf. Dufour [190], Vol. 1, p.39: '*Esti* signifierait l'essence (*to ti esti*) dans l'ordre et le domaine de la vérité. *Estô* introduit une formule seulement suffisante et plausible dans l'ordre et le domaine de l'opinion.'
32. The fact that here (1382a21) Aristotle employs the preposition *ek* and not *dia* (as in the case of anger, 1378a31) is not significant. Even in the *Posterior Analytics* Aristotle does not control carefully his use of propositions. He uses *dia* to introduce the question of causation and to speak of definitions that 'show why' (90a15, 93b39). But in giving causal definitions Aristotle does not insist on using *dia*. In the case of the eclipse, Aristotle may use *hupo* to introduce the efficient cause (90a16, 93b7, *Meta.* 1044b14), or he may avoid a preposition by using a genitive absolute (90a18), or he may omit other elements in the definition and give the efficient cause in the nominative case (93b7, cf. *Rhet.* 1380b17-18 where Aristotle states that fear was (said to be) this, namely the thought of unjustified suffering).
33. It is, I think, likely that Aristotle first worked out his views on emotions in his *Diaireseis* and then incorporated these views into his treatment of individual emotions given in the *Rhetoric*. The account of emotions presented in the *Diaireseis* was probably not restricted to a formal division or simple list. It probably divided or analysed

Rhetoric has, providing us with a clear indication of how Aristotle explained the relationship between cognition and emotional response.

Aristotle's analysis of emotion and in particular of the essential involvement of cognition in emotional response is an important contribution to philosophical psychology. It is also important for rhetorical and ethical theory because it makes clear that emotions are not blind impulses. When a man responds emotionally, he is not the victim of some automatic reflex. On the contrary, he is acting according to his judgment. When a man becomes angry, he takes revenge because he thinks himself insulted. He is prepared to explain and justify his action by reference to an insult. He may, of course, be mistaken. He may think himself insulted when he has not been and when it should be clear to him that he has not been. In this case his anger is unreasonable and criticised as unjustified. But he may not be mistaken in thinking himself insulted. He may be correct in his belief and also have good reason for his belief. In this case the man's anger is reasonable. Upon request he can state his reason for being angry, point out that his anger is not based upon some momentary fantasy, and perhaps add that he is prepared to abandon his anger any time his beliefs are shown to be false or doubtful. His anger is reasonable in that it is justified by the particular situation and also is open to reason in that it can be altered by reasoned consideration.

Emotional responses can be intelligent and reasonable actions. This is important for rhetorical theory and may explain in part at least why Aristotle not only recognised persuasion 'through the hearers' as an effective means of persuasion but also dignified it by assigning it a position corordinate with persuasion 'through demonstration'. Persuasion 'through the hearers' is not to be confined to the prooemium and the epilogue, for emotions can be aroused and allayed by reasoned argumentation. When an orator demonstrates that danger is imminent, he is arousing fear in the audience. His reasoned arguments lead the audience to conclude that danger threatens. The hearers think their lives threatened, become frightened, and begin to think about their own safety. Fear makes them

62

(*diairein, Rhet.* 1378a22) each emotion in respect to the condition of the emotional man, the object of his emotion, and the grounds for his emotional response. On the *Diaireseis*, see H. v. Arnim, *Das Ethische in Aristoteles Topik, Sitzungsberichte der Osterreichischen Akademie der Wissenschaft in Wien*, 205.4 (1927), pp. 91-4, F. Dirlmeier, *Aristoteles, Eudemische Ethik* (Berlin, 1962), pp. 242, 259, 356-7; *Aristoteles, Magna Moralia* (Berlin, 1958), pp. 300-2. It should be added that it is at least debatable whether or not Aristotle wrote a *Diaireseis*. The fact that the catalogue preserved by Diogenes Laertius (5.23, number 42) mentions a *Diaireseis* in seventeen books cannot be taken as certain proof. See P. Moraux, [24], pp. 83-6. The *Eudemian Ethics* (1220b10-12, 1221b34-5, 1234a26) refers to *Diaireseis* concerning emotions, faculties, and dispositions. Since most scholars now accept the *Eudemian Ethics* as a work of Aristotle earlier than the *Nicomachean Ethics*, it may seem that these references in the *Eudemian Ethics* settle the issue. But it would be a mistake to claim that there remains no room for doubt. Those who follow Moraux and think that the *Diaireseis* mentioned by Diogenes Laertius are pseudo-Aristotelian compilations may well think that the mention of such collections by the *Eudemian Ethics* is a sign that this treatise is not genuine.

deliberate (1383a6-7). Such men are not the victims of some irrational force that compels them to act as they do. On the contrary, their action is both intelligible and intelligent. Their fear is based upon a reasoned consideration of the situation and so is reasonable. Moreover, it may be allayed in the same way that it was aroused. Further deliberation may convince the hearers that danger is not imminent and so lead them to abandon their fear and become confident. The same is true of anger. When an orator demonstrates that a particular man has acted in an outrageous and insulting manner, he excites anger in the audience. Further deliberation, however, may lead to an abandoning of this anger. If subsequent reasoning shows that a benefit and not an outrage has occurred, the audience will shift from anger to gratitude. The response will be intelligent and reasonable. The hearers are responding according to reasoned judgment and are not the victims of some external power. In particular, they have not abandoned their anger because of some charm or enchantment such as that advertised by Thrasymachus (*Phaedrus* 267C7-D1). Enchantments are outside the sphere of reason. They may cause or compel a man to behave in a particular way but such behaviour should not be confused with emotional response, reasonable or unreasonable.

    This is an important point. For it helps us to understand the importance of Aristotle's analysis of emotion. As long as emotion went unanalysed it was possible to look upon emotional appeal as a kind of persuasion distinct from and hostile to reasoned argumentation. In the absence of an examination of emotion that made clear the involvement of cognition in emotional response, it was possible to think of emotional appeal primarily as a kind of charm or enchantment that overcomes the hearer, that works upon him in the manner of a drug.[34] This comes out quite clearly in Gorgias' *Helen*. Here emotion is depicted as something that happens to an individual. It is like a disease (*nosêma*) in that its victims suffer a misfortune (*atuchêma*) and are outside the sphere of praise or blame (19). Emotional response is not so much an action as an unfortunate affliction that may be induced or caused in an individual. Emotional appeals are like drugs (*pharmaka* 14) that work upon the patient. They may be administered in a systematic or rational manner, but they do not depend upon judgment and the patient's reason.[35] Like a noxious potion they work upon the patient,

---

34. While both Thrasymachus and Gorgias spoke of charms and enchantments, neither seems to have investigated the nature of emotional responses like pity and fear. Such an investigation was left for Aristotle. See Solmsen [201], pp.392, 404; C. Segal, 'Gorgias and the psychology of the logos', *Harvard Studies in Classical Philology* 66 (1962), pp. 121, 133.

35. Segal, *op. cit.*, pp. 115-17, points out correctly that for Gorgias and Thrasymachus the ability to control emotion was a *technê*. Like a doctor the skilful orator proceeds systematically and may be said to operate in an artful manner. But it is the orator who acts in a rational manner. The audience is conceived of as a patient upon whom the orator works. Gorgias seems to emphasise this when he speaks of the soul suffering its own suffering (*paschein, pathêma* 9). This repetition of the idea of suffering in both verb and cognate accusative is emphatic and may recall the preceding mention of violent physical suffering (7). (See Segal, p.105). For Gorgias being overcome by emotion is analogous to being raped. Emotional response is not so much an action as something that happens to someone.

drugging and bewitching him (14). They have the power to charm (*thelgein* 10) their victim. He is overcome by wizardry (*goêteia* 10) and so cannot be held accountable for his behaviour. He may be said to suffer misfortune but he cannot be said to do wrong (15).

As long as this view of emotional response and emotional appeal went unchallenged it was natural to oppose the arguments of reason to the inspired incantations (*Helen* 10) of emotional appeal. We can understand why Gorgias made Palamedes tell the jury of Greek leaders that he would **64** not try to arouse their pity but rather would try to instruct (*didaskein*) them in the truth (*Palamedes* 33). Similarly we can understand why Plato made Socrates reject emotional appeal in favour of instruction (*Apology* 35B9-C2). Looked upon as an affliction divorced from reason, emotional response was naturally opposed to reasonable behaviour. It was Aristotle's contribution to offer a different picture of emotional response. Following the lead of Plato's *Philebus* and subjecting individual emotions to careful analysis, Aristotle developed a view of emotion that made clear the necessary involvement of cognition in emotional response and so made clear that emotional responses may be reasonable and unreasonable. Far from being hostile to reason, emotions are amenable to reason, so that an orator can arouse and allay emotion while presenting reasoned arguments. By demonstrating that no unjust outrage has occurred, the orator allays anger and by demonstrating that the defendant is an innocent victim, he excites pity. It is to Aristotle's credit that he pointed out the occurrence of judgment in emotional response and promoted persuasion 'through the hearers' to a position coordinate with persuasion 'through demonstration'.

It remains to speak briefly about the importance of Aristotle's analysis of emotion for ethical theory.[36] In picking out for analysis *pathê* that are distinguished by the involvement of cognition, Aristotle was marking off those *pathê* that are fundamental to his own bipartite or moral psychology and so of especial importance to his ethical theory. More precisely, in picking out and analysing those *pathê* that essentially involve some kind of thought or belief or imagination, Aristotle was picking out emotions and distinguishing them from bodily drives or directed dispositions such as hunger and thirst. Plato's tripartite psychology had not drawn this distinction clearly and so had not provided an adequate psychology for ethical theory. Hungers and thirsts are bodily drives, and in general do not depend upon a particular kind of cognition. When men are hungry, it is not normally because they think that something is the case. Rather they have an **65** empty stomach. Their hunger is explained not by reference to certain beliefs but by reference to physiological causes. In contrast emotions are explained by reference to thoughts and beliefs. They involve an assessment of the

36. Once again we must allow the possibility that Aristotle wrote a *Diaireseis* which included a study of emotion (see above, note 33), and which may have had a more immediate effect upon Aristotle's ethical theory than the account of emotions given in the *Rhetoric*. Still, the account given in the *Rhetoric* would reflect the study included in the *Diaireseis*. Moreover, in the *Rhetoric* Aristotle makes quite clear that rhetoric and ethics have common interests and that rhetoric is a kind of offshoot of ethics in so far as it studies character and emotion (1356a20-7, 1359b8-12). We are encouraged to look for relationships between the *Rhetoric* and Aristotle's ethical theory.

particular situation and so may be reasonable and unreasonable. Unlike bodily drives, emotional responses are normally open to criticism and are important for understanding moral virtue. As Aristotle saw, the morally virtuous man is one who is properly disposed toward emotional response (*EN* 1105b19-1106a13, cf. 1104b13-14, 1106b16-17).

Let me expand this point. It is, I think, true that the bipartite psychology employed by Aristotle in his ethical and political writings was developed in Plato's Academy.[37] Bipartition may be spoken of as 'a Platonic distinction'.[38] Still, we must guard against an over-simplified view of this development within the Academy. It is not enough to say that bipartition arose from tripartition by bringing together the spirited and appetitive parts of the soul[39] and to argue that this join was encouraged by the ambiguous position of the spirited part[40] and prepared for in the *Timaeus* by the connection of tripartition with the dichotomy of an immortal and mortal soul.[41] It is, of course, true that the ambiguous position of the spirited part between the reasoning and appetitive parts seems to have depended largely on the political structure of Plato's ideal state and that whenever such political considerations receded into the background, the spirited part could be thought of in terms of an emotion like anger and joined with the appetitive part to form the emotional side of man.[42] It is also true that the distinction between an immortal and mortal soul does encourage a bipartite view. Even though this dichotomy of an immortal and mortal soul is not conceptually identical with the dichotomy of moral psychology,[43] it does help to prepare for this dichotomy. Still, the move from tripartition to bipartition was not simply a matter of undoing the special status of the spirited part and collapsing the two lower faculties into a single psychic faculty. The move to bipartition also required an alteration or clarification of the status of the appetitive part. For this part is frequently (though not exclusively) connected with bodily drives that are not emotions. Yet it is emotions with which the appetitive part must be associated, if it is to join with the spirited part in making up the emotional side of man, which is for Aristotle at least the primary sphere of moral virtue.

This point may be developed by reference to the *Timaeus*. Here we find the appetitive part connected with hunger and other bodily needs (70D7-8) and quite indifferent to reason (71A3-5, D4). While the spirited part listens to reason, the appetitive part does not. It must be held down forcibly (70A5-6). It is like a wild beast feeding at a manger (70E4-6). The appetitive part is associated with hunger. But hunger is not an emotion such as anger and

66

37. See Rees [77], pp. 112-8.

38. F. Solmsen [53], p. 150.

39. Arnim, *op. cit.*, p.7; cf. Plutarch, *Moralia* 442B.

40. F.M. Cornford, 'Psychology and social structure in the *Republic* of Plato', *Classical Quarterly* 6 (1912), pp. 246-65; R. Hackforth, 'The modification of plan in Plato's *Republic*', *Classical Quarterly* 7 (1913), pp. 265-72; Rees, *op. cit.*, p.114.

41. Rees [77], p.113; H.J. Krämer, *Arete bei Platon und Aristoteles* (Heidelberg, 1959), pp. 146-7.

42. Even *Republic* 439E5 suggests such a join.

43. R. Heinze, *Xenocrates* (Leipzig, 1892), pp. 140-2; J. Burnet, *The Ethics of Aristotle* (London, 1900), p.63, note 1, criticised by Rees [77], p.113, note 30.

fear. For these emotions depend upon an assessment of the situation and are frequently, if not always, subject to rational control. In contrast hunger is a directed disposition or bodily drive that is normally not amenable to reason. Hunger is a drive that may be either held down or satisfied, but it is not open to reason in the way that emotions are. For hunger does not depend upon an appraisal of the situation but rather arises on account of physiological causes.

The appetitive part, it seems, is associated with bodily drives. This may be made clearer by considering sexual desire. For in the *Timaeus* sexual desire is treated in a manner similar to hunger. Both are depicted as animals (70E4, 91A2); both are presented as bodily conditions immune to reason. In the case of men, sexual desire is caused by marrow in the region of the genitals (91A4-B7). In the case of women sexual desire is touched off by protracted periods of barrenness (91B7-C7). In neither case does the desire depend upon an assessment of the situation. In both cases the desire is caused by bodily factors, so that relief comes not through reasoned argument but through intercourse and reproduction (91B7-D5). And if sexual desire does not depend upon an appraisal of the situation, neither does an excess of sexual desire. Sexual intemperance does not depend upon false assessments. It results from fluidity of marrow and porosity of bone. It deserves treatment and not censure (86C3-E3).

In the *Timaeus* hunger and thirst and sexual desire are not treated as emotions. They are depicted as bodily drives or directed dispositions that are not on a par with emotions such as anger and fear. There is merit in this analysis. The behaviour of a hungry man is quite different from the behaviour of an angry man. We respond to the former by meeting his need; we respond to the latter with reasoned argument. We give a hungry man food to calm his stomach and to alleviate painful sensations. We do not offer him reasoned arguments to alter his judgment. With appropriate qualifications something similar could be said about meeting the need of a man afflicted with sexual desire. My purpose, then, is not to criticise the account of hunger and sexual desire that is presented in the *Timaeus*. Rather I would emphasise that this account is an account of bodily drives and not of emotions. The *Timaeus* associates the appetitive part with bodily drives and not with emotions, and this association creates difficulties for simply joining together the appetitive and spirited part to form the emotional side of man. Despite the fact that the *Timaeus* introduces a dichotomy between an immortal and mortal soul and groups together the spirited and appetitive parts within the mortal soul, the *Timaeus* does not (without significant qualification) prepare the way for the dichotomy of bipartition. For bipartition is primarily a moral psychology. It is a psychology that is useful in ethical discussion because it enables one to distinguish between deliberate actions that are preceeded by reasoned deliberation and emotional responses that involve perception and assessment but are not preceded by reasoned deliberation.[44] Both kinds of action are intelligent. The agent is

67

---

44. The dichotomy is not absolute. Emotional response may follow upon and be controlled by reasoned argumentation. We have already noticed that the reasoned arguments of an orator may lead an audience to judge that danger is imminent and so to become frightened. Similarly an individual person may reflect upon his situation,

152   *William W. Fortenbaugh*

68   responsible and can give reasons that explain and justify his behaviour. In contrast the behaviour that results from a directed disposition is hardly action at all. The victim of acute hunger explains his behaviour not by citing reasons (how he sees the situation) but by citing bodily causes. He is driven and impelled. He is, as the *Timaeus* (86B1-87B9) points out, hardly a moral agent. His behaviour falls outside the dichotomy of bipartition; it is like involuntary disease, not like human action.[45]

A word of caution is called for. The *Timaeus'* treatment of the appetitive part may be considered special. For the *Timaeus* maintains a tripartite psychology even in sections of the dialogue that are marked by an obvious biological interest. The appetitive part is closely connected with bodily nourishment and even assigned to plants.[46] The concern of the *Timaeus* with bodily drives or directed dispositions such as hunger, thirst, and sexual desire may be thought to reflect the physiological interests of the dialogue. Directed dispositions may be assigned to the appetitive part and in a dialogue like the *Timaeus* such an assignation is not surprising. But it would be a mistake to think that such directed dispositions constitute the entirety of the appetitive part. For as the *Republic* makes clear, the appetitive part has many forms (580D11). It is connected with avarice (553C5, cf. 590B6) which does not depend upon a physiological cause but upon an evaluation (554A2, B2). Avaricious men are not driven to grasp at profit in the way that hungry men are driven to grasp at food. Their appetite is not caused by a physiological disorder but based upon an erroneous assessment. Yet their desires and actions are referred to the appetitive part. Indeed, in one passage the appetitive part is even labelled money-loving and gain-loving (581A6-7, cf. 553C5).

The appetitive part is not a simple faculty. It includes a thrifty element (560C7), a niggardly and avaricious aspect, that cannot be construed as a
69   directed disposition similar to hunger and thirst. Still, it is true to say that the desire for food and drink and the desire for sexual relations are for Plato central cases of appetition and of especial importance for understanding the appetitive part. In the *Republic*, Plato calls hunger and thirst most clear cases of appetite (437D3-4) and then proceeds to use thirst as an example in establishing the existence of the appetitive part, that faculty whereby the soul feels sexual passion, hungers, thirsts, and feels the flutter of other desires (439D6-8). And later when Plato wants to show how unreal are the pleasures of the appetitive part, he uses hunger and thirst as examples (585A8). Hunger and thirst and sexual drive are central to an understanding of the appetitive part. They are paradigm cases of appetition

---

conclude that his life is in danger, and become frightened. Still, emotional responses are frequently (perhaps all too frequently) not preceded by any kind of deliberation. A man simply assesses his situation in a certain way and acts appropriately. His action is not preceded by deliberation, but it is intelligent and is open to evaluation.

45. On involuntary disease as a misfortune, see Gorgias, *Helen* 19, discussed above, this section.

46. On the general problem of adapting tripartition to biological investigation see Solmsen [53], pp. 153-7, 160-1 and cf. M.J. O'Brien, *The Socratic Paradoxes and the Greek Mind* (Chapel Hill, 1967), pp. 170-1.

but they are not emotions. They are directed dispositions resulting from bodily causes.[47]

We can, I think, say that tripartition failed to draw a clear distinction between emotional responses and bodily drives. It did not pick out clearly those *pathê* that are marked by the involvement of cognition and are characterised by grounds and objects. This is not to say that Plato never saw the importance of this class of *pathê*. He did and in the *Philebus* focused his attention upon 'anger and fear and longing and grief and desire and emulation and envy and the like' (47E1-2). But it is to say that bipartition could not develop out of tripartition simply by joining together the appetitive and spirited parts of the soul. It was first necessary to distinguish emotional responses from bodily drives, to focus upon those *pathê* that necessarily involve cognition and so can be reasonable or unreasonable.[48] It was to Aristotle's credit that he followed the lead of Plato's *Philebus* and pressed forward with an exhaustive analysis that was important not only for **70** philosophical psychology and rhetorical theory but also for ethical theory. In analysing emotional response, Aristotle was turning his attention toward those *pathê* that are amenable to reason (*EN* 1102b30-1103a1) and are the domain of moral virtue (*EN* 1105b19-1106a13). He was developing a moral psychology that would serve him well in ethical and political investigations.

47. Cf. *Rep.* 439D1-8 and the comment of R.C. Cross and A.D. Woozley, *Plato's Republic, A Philosophical Commentary* (London, 1964), p.122.

48. This is not the only reason why bipartition could not arise by simply combining the spirited and appetitive parts. An additional reason is the fact that the spirited and appetitive parts together did not cover the entirety of man's emotional side. Shame is an important emotion and is assigned by the *Topics* (126a8) to the reasoning parts. This assignation is in agreement with *Republic* 571C9 and in possible disagreement with *Phaedrus* 253D6, 254A2, 256A6. (See Arnim, *op. cit.*, pp. 68-71, and O'Brien, *op. cit.*, pp. 167-9.) Whatever the proper assignation of shame it seems clear that tripartition was not well suited for picking out the emotional side of man. It was necessary to start over and group together emotions, including shame (*Rhet.* 1383b11-1385a15), that involve cognition and are marked by grounds and objects (*Rhet.* 1378a23-4).

9

Jacob Bernays

Aristotle on the Effect of Tragedy

1   Aristotle states his definition of the essence of tragedy at the beginning of
the sixth chapter of the *Poetics*:

> A tragedy ... is the imitation of an action that is serious and complete,
> having magnitude, expressed in seasoned language, each of the kinds
> appearing separately in its parts, in a dramatic and not a narrative
> form, accomplishing through pity and fear the catharsis of such
> affections. (1449b24-8)

In his *Hamburgische Dramaturgie* (no. 77) Lessing tried to explain this
definition, connecting it with Aristotle's remarks in the *Rhetoric* about 'pity
and fear', and attempting to defend it against French and German
misunderstandings. He did so with great success until he came to the word
perainousa ('accomplishing'). When he reaches these last six words, fraught
with difficulty as they are, he advances with less certainty; he has problems
first with *toioutôn* ('such'), which he seeks to alleviate in phrases which belie
his previous clear account of pity and fear:

> The word *toioutôn* refers to the pity and fear that have already been
> mentioned. Tragedy should arouse our pity and fear in order to
> purify these and such passions, but not all passions without
> discrimination. Aristotle says *toioutôn* and not *toutôn*: he says 'these
2 > and such' and not just 'these' in order to show that by 'pity' he means
> not just true pity but all philanthropic emotions, in the same way as
> fear includes not just the shrinking from an evil which is threatening
> but also every similar type of shrinking, even (as with sorrow and
> grief) from past and present evils. (ed. Fricke, pp. 328-9)

Further, *pathêmatôn* ('affections') means in Lessing's view precisely the
same as *pathôn* ('emotions'); and though earlier on he held in an even
balance the golden scales on which he weighs every word in the definition,
he fails to raise the question of why, if both words have the same sense,
Aristotle did not choose the word *pathôn* which he had already used of pity
and fear in the *Rhetoric*.

Finally, Lessing translates *katharsis* as 'purification': he will 'only say
briefly' what this 'purification' consists in. On this capital question,
however, everybody – even those 'who have grown up with the problem', to

whom Lessing appeals on a related topic (no. 83) – would have liked a thorough exposition – the more so because the closer definition of *katharsis* which Aristotle himself deemed indispensable and which in the *Politics* he says he is reserving for the *Poetics* in fact nowhere appears in the *Poetics* as we have them.

Lessing's explanation is this:

> Since, to be brief, this purification consists in nothing other than the metamorphosis of the passions into virtues, and since according to our philosopher every virtue stands between two extremes, it follows **3** that tragedy, if it is to change our pity into a virtue, must be capable of purifying us of both extremes of pity; and the same is true of fear. Tragic pity must purify the soul not only of the man who feels too much pity but also of the man who feels too little. Tragic fear must purify the soul not only of the man who fears no evil but also of the man who fears any evil, however remote or improbable. Thus where fear is concerned tragic fear must guide the man who feels too much and the man who feels too little; and where pity is concerned tragic pity must do the same. (no. 78, pp. 332-3)

We must admit that if such a metamorphosis of the passions into virtues is, in Aristotle's view, part of the *essential* nature of tragedy – and it is if he incorporates this sort of catharsis into his definition – then tragedy is for him *essentially* a moral event. Indeed, if we follow Lessing through all his remarks on excessive and deficient pity and fear, we might be tempted to call tragedy a moral house of correction which must have ready a remedy for every illegitimate display of pity and fear.

Naturally enough, nobody could be more inimical to such an **4** interpretation than Goethe who, as he changed with age, strove ever more consciously to eliminate teleology from his views on nature and art. In his *Nachlese zu Aristoteles Poetik* he says that 'music affects morality as little as any other art'; and turning to tragedy, on which he if anyone is qualified to speak, he continues: 'tragedy and tragic novels do nothing to soothe men's spirits but rather disturb their minds', and he adds that Aristotle, 'though he speaks most properly of the construction of a tragedy, could never have in mind the effect – and what is more the remote effect – that a tragedy might have on its audience' (*Gesamtausgabe*, Vol. 15 (ed. W. Rehm), pp. 897-900).

Goethe thus regarded it as essential to ban any moral aim from the definition of tragedy; and in his own attempt at interpreting Aristotle's words he let himself be guided by this conviction and tried to divert catharsis away from the audience and on to the tragic character by means of the following translation: 'Tragedy is the imitation of an important and completed event that, after a passage through pity and fear, concludes its business by balancing such passions'. Greek scholars will not need to be told that *di' eleou kai phobou perainousa ... katharsin* can never mean '*after* a passage through pity and fear *concluding with* catharsis', but only '*accomplishing* catharsis *through* pity and fear'. And Aristotelians, however uncertain they may be about the exact meaning of *katharsis*, know from Book **5** VIII of the *Politics* that this word always refers to a process in the emotions of those who see or listen to tragedy or music, and never to a balanced conclusion to the events portrayed therein.

However easy it proved to dismiss Goethe's translation as unfortunate, the countless later scholars who have discussed Aristotle's remarks have found it no easier to overcome the obstacles which warned Goethe away from Lessing's point of view. The most notable of these later scholars is Eduard Muller. After a diligent collection of the many straws scattered through Aristotle's other works, he arrived at the following conclusion: 'Who can any longer doubt that the purification of pity, fear, and the other passions consists in, or at least is very closely connected with, the transformation of the pain that engendered them into pleasure?' (*Theorie der Kunst bei den Alten*, Vol. 2, pp. 62, 377-88). But any attempt to define concepts by way of such disjunctive particles is always an awkward affair. Even if the part of Muller's sentence introduced by the word 'or' is correct, and we can accordingly say no more than that the transformation of pain into pleasure is *connected*, however closely, with catharsis, we are still justified in asking what catharsis *consists in*. Aristotle, we may safely say,
6   intended by catharsis some definite thing, and not just a 'this or that'; and if 'the tragic purification of the passions' has become one of those many cultural catchwords common on the lips of educated men and spurned by thoughtful men, Aristotle cannot really be held responsible for that.

For the clouds of inexactitude that hover round our phrase when the merchants of aesthetic jargon employ it, and the efforts to characterise catharsis as a transformation of passions into virtues or of pain into pleasure, can be ascribed to ignorance of Aristotle's own description of catharsis, which is after all an aesthetic term of his own invention. Those who overlooked this fact could hardly avoid translating *katharsis*, by way of the usual meaning of the verb *kathairô*, as 'purification'; and it then became inevitable to allow tragedy, as a purifying agent, to work on the passions as objects to be purified by operations more or less similar to those used everyday by housewives and by chemists as they separate the pure from the impure. If we are to leave this cul-de-sac and return to the highway, our investigations must concentrate on that passage in the *Politics*, which I have already alluded to and which commentators on the *Poetics* seldom quote; if the passage is not quite as thorough as we might wish, it is at least by no means as brief on the question of catharsis as is the definition in the *Poetics*.
7   Goethe seems to have heard only the vaguest rumours of the existence of this passage – no doubt from Herder, whose comments certainly arouse no expectation that it might be of use. Even Lessing, who once refers to it in passing (no. 78), oddly omits to follow up the reference – for anyone who has read the passage will find it still odder to suppose that Lessing knew the passage well and yet failed to realise its importance.

At this point in the *Politics*, VIII 7, Aristotle is attempting to show the place of the various musical harmonies in a well-ordered state.

> We accept the division of melodies proposed by certain philosophers into ethical melodies, melodies of action, and passionate or inspiring melodies, each having, as they say, a mode corresponding to it. But we maintain further that music should be studied, not for the sake of one, but of many benefits, that is to say, with a view to education, to

catharsis (the word catharsis we use at present without explanation, but when hereafter we speak of poetry we will treat the subject with more precision) – music may also serve for intellectual enjoyment, for relaxation, and for recreation after exertion. It is clear, therefore, that all the modes must be employed by us, but not all of them in the same manner. In education the most ethical modes are to be preferred, but in listening to the performances of others we may admit the modes of action and passion also. For emotions such as pity or fear, or again enthusiasm, exist very strongly in some souls, and have more or less influence over all. Some persons fall into a religious frenzy, whom we see as a result of the sacred melodies – when they have used the melodies that excite the soul to mystic frenzy – restored as though they had found healing and catharsis. Those who are influenced by pity or fear, and every emotional nature, must have a like experience, and others in so far as each is susceptible to such emotions, and all receive a sort of catharsis and are relieved with pleasure. The cathartic melodies likewise give an innocent pleasure to men. Such are the modes and melodies in which those who perform music at the theatre should be invited to compete. But since the spectators are of two kinds – the one free and educated, the other a vulgar crowd composed of mechanics, labourers and the like – there ought to be contests and exhibitions instituted for the relaxation of the second class too. And the music will correspond to their minds; for as their minds are perverted from the natural state, so there are perverted modes and highly strung and unnaturally coloured melodies. A man receives pleasure from what is natural to him, and therefore professional musicians may be allowed to practise this lower sort of music before a lower type of audience. (1341b32–1342a27)

This excerpt is best introduced by its final sentences that deal only indirectly with catharsis; for in these sentences we find incontrovertible proof of the distance which separates Aristotle from the thought of the last century, according to which the theatre is an offspring and a rival of the Church and an institution for moral improvement – proof that Aristotle is concerned to characterise the theatre as a place of amusement for the different classes of the general public. While Plato passionately proscribes the newfangled music which abandons ancient simplicity and is the source of every immorality (*Rep.* 424B; *Laws* 700, 797; cf. Cicero, *De Leg.* 2.15.38), Aristotle urges us to tolerate even the strangest forms of music. If there is a perverted public which can only enjoy pop music, then at the occasional festival where it seeks pleasure and refreshment we should provide it with inferior music and not try to bore and improve it with good music. And here, in connexion with the theatre, Aristotle issues the imperious command to eliminate from theatrical catharsis anything by means of which its moral element might overpower its capacity to give pleasure, by which moral improvement might become the principal aim of the drama and pleasure and amusement merely the essential means to that end, important only as the honey on the brim of the goblet that serves to lure on those who would have spurned the health-giving draught in its unsweetened state.

And why should we approach theatrical catharsis from a moral or from a

158   *Jacob Bernays*

hedonistic standpoint, rather than from the standpoint that Aristotle himself adopts in the *Politics*? That is neither moral nor purely hedonistic: it is a *pathological* standpoint.

   Aristotle's primary example of catharsis, which is drawn from the Greek experience of ecstasy, is pathological; and it is that which leads him to

11 consider the possibility of a similar cathartic treatment for all other emotions (1342a8-15). Men otherwise calm and placid were thrown into ecstasy by the Phrygian songs inherited from the mythical singer Olympus – that these rather than any other 'sacred melodies' are meant is made certain by another passage in Aristotle and by one in Plato; yet men possessed by ecstasy, *after* they have listened to or sung those intoxicating melodies, experience a sense of calm – rather as Catullus, in his *Attis*, might have done if he, the most poetical of Roman writers, had had as clear an understanding of the phenomenon of enthusiasm as the most sober-minded of Greek philosophers possessed. The poet would have had no need to chase the passionate youth around the forest after he had let him rave in Phrygian song, until he collapsed exhausted on his pillows, lost to the world until the following morning. On the contrary, as soon as his pent passion had poured forth in the mad delirium of the song, it would have been appeased and would have given way to a more thoughtful mood. In this way the poem would have lost, at most, the versification of a sunrise: it would certainly not have sacrificed any poetic virtue, and it would have gained inestimably in pathological truth, for it would have represented the catharsis of enthusiasm.

   If Aristotle's paradigm is taken from the realm of psychopathology, so too are the expressions by which he attempts to elucidate the notion of catharsis. Those whose ecstasy has been appeased, he says, are 'restored as

12 though they had found healing and catharsis' (1342a10). '*As though*' – not in sober fact; and thus *katharsis* here is no less metaphorical than *iatreia* ('healing'). Now we may ignore the very general sense of 'purification' for *katharsis*: this explains nothing just because of its generality; Aristotle can have had no occasion to add it *after* the much more concrete term *iatreia*; and it is so general that it would be absurd to precede it by the phrase 'as though' (*hôsper*), which marks out a metaphor. If, then, we take *katharsis* in a concrete sense, it must mean one of two things: *either* the absolving from guilt by way of certain priestly ceremonies – a lustration; *or* the removing or alleviating of sickness by some medical method of relief.

   Dionysius Lambinus hit upon the first meaning in his translation of the *Politics*: he renders *katharsis* by *lustratio seu expiatio*. If this sixteenth-century Frenchman remains the only notable perpetrator of this error, and if even now, when 'lustration through tragedy' has sprinkled its holy water over the mills of the Romantics, no one dares lay it at Aristotle's door, that is not entirely due to the few brief words with which Reiz dismisses it in his edition of the last two books of the *Politics*. (The last two books according to the traditional ordering: Reiz himself established the correct ordering.) The solid achievement of this founder of the Leipzig school of classical

13 scholarship has not received the recognition it deserves. And yet no one who gives the matter two minutes' reflection needs any help to realise how impossible it is that Aristotle, in a fashion totally foreign to his normal habits, should here have borrowed a philosophical term from the language

of popular religion – only to miss his real aim entirely. For he cannot have had in mind the ceremonies themselves – the incense and the ablutions – but at most the emotional changes in the object of these ministrations; and he must therefore have hoped to explain a perplexing emotional reaction – the calming of ecstasy by means of frenzied singing – by comparing it with another reaction no less perplexing, namely the feeling of release from guilt experienced by those who receive absolution. No one in his right mind could seriously credit Aristotle with so pointless and obvious a piece of verbal conjuring.

If, on the other hand, we understand *katharsis* in its only remaining sense, the medical one, our affairs prosper. *Katharsis* then becomes a special type of *iatreia* (which is why that term is used before it): ecstasy turns to calm through orgiastic songs as sickness turns to health through medical treatment – not through any treatment, but through one that employs cathartic means to fight off the illness. Thus the puzzling piece of *emotional* pathology is explained: we can make sense of it if we compare it with a pathological *bodily* reaction.

Shortly after this, at 1342a11, Aristotle, speaking of those who are **14** susceptible to a catharsis similar to the orgiastic type, singles out by name – in an unmistakable reference to tragedy – only the 'pitiful and fearful', and collects all the rest under the general title of *pathêtikoi* ('emotional'). And he is able to find no word more suitable to stand alongside *katharsis* than 'relief' (*kouphizesthai*: 1342a14). Obviously, this can have no connexion with ethics, since in this momentary relief there is not even a return to a normal condition; and it has, on the other hand, so little to do with pleasure that in order not to omit this indispensable notion Aristotle is obliged to add 'with pleasure' to the verb 'relieved'. Thus Aristotle's purpose in using the term 'relief' can only be to elucidate the emotional process by comparing it with an analogous bodily phenomenon.

Let no one primly wrinkle his nose and talk of a degradation of aesthetics to the rank of medicine. We are trying not to establish a final definition of tragedy, but to drive the words which Aristotle uses in *his* definition along the highway of methodical interpretation. If this road to the Muses' grove takes us past the temple of Asclepius, that is, in the eyes of Aristotelians, just one further piece of evidence that we are travelling in the right direction. The son of a royal doctor and himself a practising physician in his youth, Aristotle profited from the medical gifts he had inherited not only in **15** the rigorously scientific parts of his philosophy: his moral and psychological works, despite all the links that bind them to the *Metaphysics*, constantly reveal a lively concern for the physical side of things and a rejection not only of ascetisicm but also of any ethereal spirituality – a rejection common among doctors and working scientists but rare among philosophers, even in Greece, once they have ascended into the heaven of ideas. Indeed, even in purely logical and metaphysical matters Aristotle clearly preferred to draw his examples from the realm of medical experience: where, for example, he is claiming that an unconscious teleology marks both nature and true art – the artist does not ponder each step and therefore never stumbles, nature functions teleologically without becoming transcendent – no more suitable illustration occurs to him than the instinctive self-healing of the layman who, as though instructed by his illness itself, unthinkingly demands the right cure (cf. *Phys.* II 8, 199b31). If we accept the unequivocally medical analogy here, when we are dealing with the calm and healthy power of

16 nature, we have still less reason to reject an explanation of the term *katharsis* according to which strong emotional upheavals are compared to the symptoms of a physical illness, simply on the grounds that such an explanation has medical overtones. Apart from a fastidious disinclination to conjoin aesthetics and medicine, I do not expect any other objections from those readers who have followed my examination of the passage in the *Politics*; and before I apply my results to the doctrine of the *Poetics* I should like to state clearly the purely terminological conclusions of the investigations so far: *katharsis* is a term transferred from the physical to the emotional sphere, and used of the sort of treatment of an oppressed person which seeks not to alter or to subjugate the oppressive element but to arouse it and to draw it out, and thus to achieve some sort of relief for the oppressed.

Aristotle makes it perfectly clear that it is not the morbid matter but the unbalanced man who is the real object of catharsis: *those in ecstasy*, according to the *Politics* (1342a11), experience healing and catharsis; *the pitiful and the fearful* must be relieved by a feeling of pleasure (1342a15). Anyone who, after such unequivocal statements, could still think it possible that the definition in the *Poetics* should relate catharsis to quite a different object

17 must indeed nurture strange ideas of Aristotle's use of terms. Further, anyone prepared to countenance such an inexplicable violation of Aristotle's otherwise strict and determinate usage on the grounds that it is attractive but by no means compulsory to interpret the words *di' eleou kai phobou perainousa tên tôn toioutôn pathêmatôn katharsin* by reference to the exposition in the *Politics* must bring to mind the unhappy circumstances in which a modern reader finds himself when he tries to overcome the difficulties of this sentence – circumstances which Aristotle never envisaged and so of course could not alleviate. In the complete *Poetics* (i.e. in the 'treatise on poetry' in two books), he confined his definition of tragedy within the limits required by concision and brevity. As long as he attained conceptual completeness and correctness, he could find no reason on the ground of possible misunderstandings to expand his definition even by a few letters, for he had sufficiently guarded against any possibility of misunderstanding by the supplementary explanations that accompanied its individual terms. For the term *katharsis*, indeed, these explanations were, as the promissory reference in the *Politics* shows, as abundant as the significance of the question and the unfamiliarity of the term demanded. And the anthologist, whom we have both to thank and to blame for the extant *Poetics*, mercilessly cut these explanations out; he had no care for

18 philosophy, and he probably excised the passages for no other reason than they they *were* so comprehensive and so rich in purely philosophical thought. The state in which this leaves us can be illustrated from other parts of the definition. It begins with the claim that tragedy is 'the imitation of an action that is serious (*spoudaios*) ... expressed in seasoned (*hêdusmenôi*) language *chôris hekastôi tôn eidôn en tois moriois*'. What an intricate web of controversy would have been spun around these last words from *chôris* to *moriois* had they not been immediately followed by Aristotle's own interpretation, to the effect that different types of 'seasoning' are separately applied to the different parts of a tragedy, and that the language is enhanced in the choral passages by lyric chants, and in the dialogue simply by the metre: 'Here by "seasoned language" I mean that with rhythm and song superadded; and by "the kinds appearing separately" I mean that some parts are worked out with verse only, and others with song' (1449b29-31).

Even so Bernhardy completely misunderstood the application to tragic notion of the adjective 'serious' (*spoudaios*), simply because Aristotle's own explanation of this word does not immediately follow the definition but has already been provided a little earlier on. Bernhardy considers that *praxis spoudaia* is an action that has 'a moral nature and value, in contrast with the physical events of the epic' (*Grundriss der Griechischen Literatur*, Vol. 2 (Halle, 1845), p. 687). Aristotle himself, however, relies on his earlier account of the origins of each type of poetry. It is partly from this account that the **19** definition of tragedy is derived (1449b23); and indeed, from the second chapter of the *Poetics* onwards, Aristotle's exposition revolves around the opposition between the serious (*spoudaios*) and, first, the base (*phaulos*), then the ridiculous (*geloios*). What is serious is the subject of epic no less than of tragedy, which in the course of time absorbed the former (4, 1449a2); the base, on the other hand, is first the subject of 'iambic' satire, and then this in its turn develops into comedy, whose subject, the ridiculous, corresponds to the base. It is enough to consider the following passage: 'Just as Homer was in the serious style the poet of poets ... so too he was the first to outline for us the general form of comedy by producing <in the *Margites*> not a dramatic invective but a dramatic picture of the ridiculous' (4, 1448b34-9). We can no longer have any doubt about how Aristotle wished to characterise tragedy when he added the word *spoudaios*. He credited tragedy with *serious* material and comedy with the *ridiculous* not in order to avoid confusion with epic (which in his view is just as *spoudaios* and 'moral' as tragedy, and certainly not, in Bernhardy's anachronistic terms, 'physical'), but in order to draw a *material* distinction between tragedy and comedy **20** which are *formally* identical. In exactly the same fashion tragedy and epic, whose matter is identical, are formally distinguished in that part of the definition which states that tragedy tells its story 'in a dramatic and not a narrative form'.

In these cases misunderstanding cannot occur, or at least cannot prevail, because here even the modern reader does not depend solely on the definition, but may also profit from Aristotle's considerateness: each of his explanations tears one more veil from his draped definition, until it is finally revealed naked to the world – naked in every part except that containing *katharsis*. Here, thanks to the anthologist, we are deprived of any delicious denudement and faced with the definition in all its prim formality. We can only master it if, in place of Aristotle's own interpretation which has disappeared from the text of the *Poetics*, we use the substitute passage we have found in the *Politics* which, even if it does not exactly correspond to the definition, is for all that no less useful a guide to its central concept. Thus any explanations that are inconsistent with the terminological conclusions wrung from the *Politics* must, however grammatically correct they are and however easily they can be reconciled with modern aesthetic theories, be **21** dismissed out of hand: they are grammatical, and they are aesthetically up to date; but they cannot possibly be right, i.e. Aristotelian. Rather, an interpretation that is proved on the touchstone of the *Politics*, however surprising it may seem to a modern aesthetician, may confidently be accepted as the correct one, as long as it is linguistically admissible.

And in fact I cannot see that any serious objection can be brought against the following translation of the words *di' eleou kai phobou perainousa tên tôn toioutôn pathêmatôn katharsin*: 'By (arousing) pity and fear tragedy achieves an alleviating relief of such (pitiful and fearful) mental affections.' This translation allows itself no licence; in part, it satisfies the demands of an explanatory translation; in part it requires some interpretative justification. It satisfies the demands by choosing as a translation of *katharsis* not the ambiguous and unclear word 'purification' but a term which carries, like *katharsis* in the *Politics*, the overtones of a medical metaphor, and by borrowing from the same source the concept of 'alleviation' which Aristotle there couples with *katharsis*. The translation does, however, require justification at one point – not in connexion with the delicate grammatical relation which holds between *pathêmatôn* and the root of *katharsis*: we have dismissed any talk of the 'purification of the passions', and even the most conscientious grammarian could make no objection to our translation once *katharsis* is recognised as a medical metaphor, even if the same use of the genitive were not attested by examples in Aristotle, Hippocrates, and Thucydides. Rather, it is the translation of the word *pathêmatôn* as 'mental affections', with its implication of some standing, chronic condition, that requires justification. Of course, no one who is acquainted with the Greek language will want to deny that often, where it is not particularly important to make the distinction, the choice between *pathos* and *pathêma* lies at the whim of the writer, subject to a mere stroke of his pen. But however this may be, it is incumbent on a philosopher who is offering a definition to use all words, and especially abstract words, with the greatest possible strictness; and it is also incumbent on the reader of a definition to take its meaning in the strictest possible sense. Now a comparison of those passages in Aristotle where loose usage is improbable or impossible yields the following result: *pathos* is the condition of a *paschôn* and connotes the unexpected outbreak and overflowing of an emotion; *pathêma*, on the other hand, is the condition of a *pathêtikos* and connotes the emotion as inherent in the affected person, ready to break out at any time. Briefly, *pathos* is the emotion, *pathêma* the disposition or the affection. Aristotle's lost explanation will have indicated this strict sense in something like the following words: 'I mean by *pathêma* the condition of the *pathêtikos*.' At any rate he makes it abundantly clear in the *Politics* (1342a12) that it is the *pathêtikos*, the man with a permanent disposition and a deep-rooted inclination to a certain emotion – in the case of tragedy, the man piteous and fearful by disposition (*eleêmôn kai phobêtikos*), not the man who is feeling pity and fear – who is to find in catharsis the means to indulge his inclinations in a 'harmless' manner. But once we take *pathêmatôn* in this sense, the definition in the *Poetics* and the account in the *Politics* are mutually and perfectly illuminating on the question of the proper objects of *katharsis*. In the *Politics katharsis* is expressly applied to men (see above, p.160); the definition says that an alleviation or deflection of the affections or dispositions is brought about;

and who could possibly regard the object – I mean the real, not the grammatical object – of catharsis as anything other than the man who is given to these affections and subject to these inclinations?

The harmony between the Aristotle of the *Poetics* and the Aristotle of the *Politics* is not, however, the only advantage we may reap if we take *pathêmatôn* in its strict sense; we also find that, without endangering the rigour of the definition, it helps us with the word *toioutôn*, at which even Lessing's usually confident step faltered and which caused later commentators to stumble gracelessly. **24**

A logician like Lessing must have been well aware that an '*etcetera*', which is what he thought *toioutôn* had to mean, would explode not only this but every definition; for a definition ought to delimit the defined concept as narrowly as possible, while an *etcetera* throws everything open. A definition that contains an *etcetera* is as inadequate as a wall that contains gaps and holes. But Lessing thought that *toioutôn could* only mean *etcetera* here; and so he sought to correct, as far as he could, the mistake which he thought Aristotle had made, by reducing to the smallest possible number the swarm of passions which, in the train of 'pity and fear' press for 'purification' through tragedy. In the case of fear this worked, at least superficially; for fear is the 'shrinking from a threatening evil', and Lessing judged that 'fear, *etcetera*' included shrinking from a present and from a past evil, i.e. sorrow and grief. But when we come to 'pity', this temporal distinction will not hold water: the unfortunate earn pity on account of past, as well as present and future troubles; and the distinction in time alters only the degree and not the nature, nor indeed the name of the sensation (*Rhet.* II 8, 1386b1). **25** Lessing's reaction to this betrays more clearly than anything else the fact that the relevant section of the *Dramaturgie*, though long mulled in his head, was penned in haste: he states that 'pity and such' means 'pity and all philanthropic feelings' (see above, p.154).

When Lessing left the door so widely ajar, it is hardly surprising that his successors pulled down the walls; indeed one of the younger commentators on Aristotle's definition glosses the words *tôn toioutôn* thus: 'He says "and such" because pity and fear are accompanied by many other feelings that are closely related to them, e.g. the emotions of *love* and *hate*, which, however, when they are conjured up in a tragedy, either arise from pity or fear, or are closely related to them', etc. But if that were really so, what childish games Aristotle would be playing with himself and his readers! The point and purpose of this part of his definition can only be that of *determining* the tragic emotions. At first we think that he has reached this goal, and are impressed and grateful to Aristotle for the psychological expertise with which he has selected from all the feelings, emotions, and passions that teem in the human breast two complementary emotions as the truly tragic ones – **26** pity at the sorrow of others, and, inseparable from it, fear lest we feel sorrow ourselves. Then, with ever-increasing interest, we follow, in chapters 13-14, Aristotle's rigorous examination of all conceivable characters and situations, accepting them as tragic or rejecting them as untragic solely according to his own opinion as to whether or not they are capable of arousing precisely these emotions of pity and fear. Finally, we willingly surrender ourselves to that sentiment which, in our *Poetics*, unfortunately receives only summary expression: 'The tragic pleasure is that of pity and fear, and the poet has to produce it by a work of imitation' (14, 1453b12). And after all this, we are invited to say that nothing serious was ever meant by that promising determination of the emotions; for the definition contains, apart from pity and fear, an *etcetera* that expands it to include 'sorrow, grief, philanthropy, love, and hate'. Rather than allow ourselves to be mocked in this way, let us see if the *etcetera*, like other will-o'-the-wisps, does not vanish when we approach it.

For convenience, I quote the Greek words once again: *di' eleou kai phobou perainousa tên tôn toioutôn pathêmatôn katharsin*. Lessing remarks: 'But Aristotle says *toioutôn* and not *toutôn*, he says "these and such" ...' But Aristotle does **27** not say 'these and such'. If he wants to say that, he cannot do without the word 'and', any more than Lessing can: he must say *tauta kai toiauta* and he mostly uses the fuller expression, *tauta kai hosa alla toiauta*. Indeed, far from allowing the commentators so wide an arena as they are given by the words 'these and such', Aristotle does not even allow them as much space to play in as the single word 'such' would in English. For the Greek for 'catharsis of such passions' is *tên toioutôn pathêmatôn katharsin*; and today, if not in Lessing's time, every reasonably complete dictionary says that *toioutos* with the article can *only* refer to something that is mentioned in the sentence itself. Thus *ho toioutos* cannot be translated by 'such' in the sense 'of that kind': if the simple demonstrative 'this' will not suit, the only acceptable alternative is the word 'such' in its purely demonstrative sense (*talis*). Just as in English, in order to avoid the tedious repetition of a word, we may employ 'such' to refer back to a term without in the least expanding its **28** conceptual limits, so Greeks, and in particular Aristotle, liked using the pronoun *ho toioutos*.

The most cursory glance at any of Aristotle's major works reveals abundant examples of this usage; and the *Poetics* itself, however rudely shorn by the anthologist, offers among many others an example only one chapter away from our definition that would be quite sufficient proof by itself. Because it strikingly illustrates, from a different angle, the unwearying rigour of Aristotle's style, I should like to go into it briefly here. Aristotle is describing the simultaneous development in the epic period both of grave and noble poetry and of jocular and satirical verse. Men with poetic talent were attracted, he says, according to their own particular character, in the one direction or the other: 'For the graver among them would represent noble actions, and those of such personages; and the meaner sort the actions of the ignoble' (1448b25). Aristotle thought that the material for satire, which is essentially subjective, is exhaustively described by the phrase 'the actions of the ignoble'. For the epic, however, he sees two types of material. First there are objectively 'noble actions', whether indulged in by the divine Achilles or by the divine swineherd. But secondly, even the most solemn epic poet should not limit himself to the portrayal of noble actions and noble events, on pain of becoming sublimely tedious; rather, as Plato explains in a similar connexion (*Rep.* 396D), he must accompany his hero through every **29** stumble he may make 'through sickness, or love, or even drunkenness'. Thus Aristotle would have us regard intrinsically ignoble acts as ennobled for the epic if they emanate from a heroic character who is in other respects noble and worthy of the epic. Aristotle links these two types of material – noble acts and acts of noble characters – in the closest possible way by giving the serious epic *tas kalas praxeis kai tas tôn toioutôn* as its object. Here no one will deny that *tôn toioutôn* simply picks up the preceding adjective *kalas*, modifying its grammatical form but leaving its conceptual content totally unaffected. In just this way, the words *tôn toioutôn* in our definition continue the sentence by picking up (and subjecting to adjectival transformation) the two preceding nouns *eleos kai phobos*; and they do absolutely nothing else. *Tôn toioutôn pathêmatôn* simply means *eleêtikôn kai phobêtikôn pathêmatôn*.

Now that we can strike the putative *etcetera* from the list of controversial questions raised by our definition, the only problem seems to be why Aristotle, since he means simply pity and fear, does not choose the simple demonstrative, and write *toutôn tôn pathêmatôn*. This problem is, however, already solved for anyone who has been convinced by the interpretation of *pathêma* put forward above (p.162). For the words *eleos* and *phobos* will lead a **30** Greek to think first only of the *pathos*, the occurrent emotion of pity and fear, and not of the *pathêma*, the lasting affection. However, Aristotle must be concerned with the latter if what he calls catharsis is to take place; and since the Greek language had not formed special nouns for the affections, as opposed to the emotions, of pity and fear, his only alternative was to resort the circumlocutions, using *pathêma* and the relevant adjectives. Aristotle could not conceive of 'the catharsis of the affections of pity and fear' in any other Greek words than *eleêtikôn kai phobêtikôn pathêmatôn katharsin*; and he *expressed* this notion in our sentence, which already contains the words *eleos kai phobos*, by employing an ordinary Greek abbreviatory device and penning the phrase *tôn toioutôn pathêmatôn katharsin*.

Is this interpretation, in which all the details balance and support one another, deceptive, or have we really solved the problem, beset as our path was by the briars of the anthologist? Is our use of the signpost leading to the *Politics*, and our observation both of Aristotelian and of universal Greek usage, sufficient to establish an interpretation of the definition that is so indisputable and so universally illuminating that we may assess its consequences without more ado? It would betray too passionate a belief in the power of logic and method over the world in general and over the learned world in particular if we imagined that a solution to a problem that **31** has produced so many discussions and has exhibited so many ramifications could win general acceptance so long as the grounds on which it is based remain purely logical and methodical. Anyone who is interested enough in the subject to have followed this discussion will probably also have been interested enough to form his own views on the question. In cases like this, there are few scholars who do not already belong to one party or the other; and those whose opinion is already formed are not often convinced by an argument, however well-constructed, that relies solely on evidence that is already well known. It is more likely that conviction will be achieved by the unexpected discovery of new pieces of evidence that fatten up the files. And indeed there is no reason to doubt that such new evidence might appear. Just because the anthologist excised Aristotle's explanation of catharsis from *our Poetics*, there is no reason to think that it is irretrievably lost in all its parts. In the course of time, the archives of Greek literature have fallen into disarray, and it is sometimes wiser to look for things *not* in their proper place, but rather to poke around hopefully in the corners. We should not shun the peculiarly archival air that normally gathers in such dark corners, and we must sometimes inhale a quantity of dust before we can lay hands **32** on the document for which we are searching.

10

Norman Gulley

Aristotle on the Purposes of Literature

3   In beginning this inaugural lecture I am aware that the notion of inauguration carries the notion of what is propitious. To inaugurate, in its literal Latin sense, is to take omens from the flight of birds. It has a transferred sense of consecrating a place or installing a person in office. In this sense the implication is that the ceremonial omens are favourable. Here are two modern dictionary definitions of it:[1] (i) to begin or initiate under favourable circumstances, with a good deed or omen, or with propitious exercises; (ii) to commence or enter upon, especially something beneficial.

This suggests that, in an inaugural lecture, I should say something about the beneficial nature of what I am entering upon and indicate in what respects the omens are favourable for me. It suggests also, perhaps, since my profession is to provide students with a classical education, that I should indicate the benefits of a classical education.

But this would be too extensive a programme for the occasion. What I propose to do is to give you a sample of Greek thought. It is a piece of analysis by a Greek philosopher. The philosopher is Aristotle. The analysis is highly original. Its influence on European literary theory has been considerable. Perhaps these are good enough reasons for looking at it today. But I have a further reason for selecting this piece of analysis. Its conclusions have their place in Aristotle's views about what constitutes a truly beneficial education. In this respect they can serve to illustrate what I consider to be a distinctive feature of an education in the classics. If I say something, however briefly, about this when I have dealt with the analysis, I will be meeting in some part the strictly inaugural requirements of my lecture.

The piece of Aristotelian analysis I want to discuss is part of his analysis of what he calls the *poiêtikê technê*, the poetic art. The Greek phrase has a generic sense which gives it much wider application than the English 'poetic art'. It means the art of producing or constructing something. It embraces
4   products such as beds and pots and temples and tables as well as literary products. Before Aristotle, there was a specific use of it to refer to literary composition in verse, and a similarly specific use of the noun *poiêtês* for the verse composer, specific uses which have largely prevailed in English since we took over the Greek words. Aristotle is not happy about this specific sense. Granting that there is a literary species of *poiêtikê technê*, why should metrical form be a distinctive quality of it? For it was clear to Aristotle that the specifically literary art he wished to analyse included instances not

---

1. *Webster's New International Dictionary*, 2nd edn., s.v.

written in verse, for example a Socratic dialogue, and excluded others which *were* written in verse, for example Empedocles' scientific work *On Nature* (*Poet*. 1447b9-20).[2] Nor was Aristotle happy about the use of a generic term – *poiêtikê* – for a literary species. But he accepts the difficulty of finding a suitable specific term. As he points out, no one up to his time had found one (1447b9). He himself does not offer one.

We have had the same difficulty in English. Perhaps it will serve as an advance indication of the kind of literary field Aristotle wants to define if we look briefly at two English candidates for a title for this field. The first is 'literature' in the narrow modern sense which makes the more generic term do duty for the more specific. In this sense 'literature' is used chiefly, in Webster's dictionary phrase,[3] 'of writings distinguished by artistic form or emotional appeal', as opposed to those which are technical or erudite or informational or utilitarian. We sometimes add the adjective 'imaginative' when we use 'literature' in this sense. It is the sense we have principally in mind when we speak of a student of English or French or German 'literature'. We think of such students as readers of novelists and dramatists and poets rather than of historians and philosophers and scientists. This narrow use of 'literature' indicates fairly well, I think, the subject of Aristotle's analysis.

The other candidate is 'fiction' in its literary use. This is an altogether neater and more specific term. In its basic literary significance as a Latin term it comes very close to what Aristotle wants to analyse as an art. Unfortunately, modern English uses of the word make it unsatisfactory in several respects. Its most popular use excludes its application to all dramatic and most poetic literature (I use 'poetic' here in the usual English sense). Its scholarly use is much wider but still, I think, too narrow as an indication of the full range of Aristotle's *poiêtikê technê*. Scholars readily classify *Hamlet* as fiction. Most of them fight shy of the term when it comes to the *Sonnets*. And I am not sure that Aristotle would have wanted to rule out the *Sonnets*. However, despite the lack of a precise specific term, whether in Greek or English, to indicate the range of Aristotle's subject, perhaps these preliminary remarks will serve as a rough indication of it.

Let me now turn to Aristotle's analysis. He begins in his brisk, systematic way by classifying the *poiêtikê technê* as a form of imitation (*mîmêsis*; 1447a16). He specifies its medium as language. He adds that this is both a prose and a verse medium. It is not verse, he says, which distinctively marks off the literary artist from other writers. It is the imitative nature of his art (1447b15, 1451b28-29). And having made this obviously basic distinction, Aristotle rather blandly leaves us to infer, partly from examples he gives of *non*-imitative literature, what he means here by imitation.

Here are his examples (1447b16-20, 1451a38-b5). A work on medicine or natural science is non-imitative. A work on history is non-imitative. And Aristotle emphasises that putting such works into verse does not make them imitative works. So we can see that the literary artist's field of operation is non-factual and non-theoretical. At least it is not his job to give information

2. Subsequent references to Aristotle's text are to the *Poetics*, unless otherwise stated.
3. *Op. cit.*, s.v. Surprisingly omitted from the third edition.

about matters of fact or to provide a scientific explanation of what is already
established in its structure. The distinction, then, between non-imitative
and imitative literature (I use 'literature' here in the broad sense) is a
distinction between literature which uses language descriptively to refer to
what is already there to be described or explained, and literature which is
the product of a *poiêtikê technê*. And in Aristotle's analysis the literary
significance of the phrase *poiêtikê technê*, the art of making or constructing or
creating something, entails that what the artist directly expresses in
language is, in the broadest sense of the word, fictional. The artist makes it
up. So that there is a close connection between using language to imitate
something and using it to present what is fictional. It would appear that it is
only through fictions that you use language to imitate something.

6   Now when Aristotle uses 'imitation' as a term to describe what the artist
is attempting to do he is using a term which was used readily by the Greeks
in reference to literary works. Down to Aristotle's time the Greeks were
accustomed not so much to the private reading of literature as to literary
performances, whether dramatic performances or the public recitations of a
rhapsode. Both the actor and the rhapsode were readily thought of as
imitators (see Plato, *Rep.* 392cff.). As we ourselves might say when watching
a dramatic performance: That isn't *really* Macbeth strutting about up there.
It's Willie Morgan dressed up. He is dressed up to look *like* Macbeth,
indeed he is attempting to behave *like* Macbeth, to represent him. It is this
Willie Morgan level of imitation which made the idea of imitation in
reference to literature familiar to the Greeks. But this level does not interest
Aristotle. As he points out (1462a11-13; see also 1450b19-20), the dramatic
poet can achieve his aim whether you watch his story enacted by Willie
Morgan and company or you read it. What interests Aristotle is the
usefulness of the notion of imitation, or representation as we would more
naturally call it, once the Willie Morgan level is removed.

You cannot apply the Willie Morgan analogy at another level in any
simple and straightforward way. You cannot say that as Willie Morgan
represents Macbeth, so Macbeth represents someone else. But you can say
that what Macbeth does and says, and the various events put into his life by
the artist, represent something other than what is directly presented by the
artist, that is, what is directly described through the conventional references
of his language. As Aristotle has indicated, this direct kind of description is
proper to an entirely different kind of literature. But the imitative literary
artist, in presenting his fictions, is giving significance to those fictions by
making them represent something else. So what are his fictions intended to
represent?

Aristotle's initial answer to this is a broad specification of the field of
operation for representations. He says that the field is human behaviour
(1448a1, 27-8). This is a sound enough answer. Certainly it is sound as a
generalisation from the Greeks' past practice in the art of literature. But it is
clear that Aristotle had further grounds for specifying this field as proper for
7   the work of the literary artist. Most importantly, he recognised that it is a
field with a high degree of variability in its events (*EN* 1094b14-19).
Patterns of behaviour differ from individual to individual. And no one
individual is likely to follow a perfectly regular and consistent pattern.
There is *no* set pattern. Nor are there agreed rules for commending or

condemning this pattern rather than that. A wide range of moral attitudes is possible. This makes the field of human behaviour the richest possible field for literary invention. It satisfies the important condition that wide freedom in *inventing* patterns of events inside it remains compatible with plausibility.

There is one more specification which Aristotle makes about the field – that it is the *moral* aspects of human behaviour which the literary artist is especially concerned with (1448a1-5). We must not take this in too narrow a sense. Aristotle's point is that the aspects of human behaviour which are fundamental for the artist's purposes are those which are capable of engaging our moral sympathy or antipathy in any way. It is essential for the artist to prompt reactions of approval or disapproval, whether with regard to what a character says or does or with regard to what happens to him. If Hamlet passes the salt, this directly serves the artist's purposes only in respect of any moral significance it has, for example if Hamlet passes the salt as salt, knowing it to be poison, to someone he intends to kill, or if he passes it as a pre-arranged signal for removing the king's head. Similarly, when Tolstoy describes Anna Karenina's abrupt death at the railway station, his intention is not to illustrate that people who throw themselves under railway trains lose their lives. As Aristotle would have said, that sort of truth belongs to non-imitative literature, perhaps a treatise on physiology. What Tolstoy and Aristotle consider to be relevant to the artist's purposes are those aspects of her death which engage our moral sympathies, for example our sense of the bad luck or the unfair treatment which brought her to suicide. It is an engagement of our emotions which is essential in what is represented, not the provision of information.

This specification of the representational field gives a broad indication of what is represented in literary art. We can be more specific if we take into account what Aristotle says about the artist's concern with the universal. He says (1451b5-10) that the literary artist tries to express what is universal **8** rather than what is particular; he presents particular events and particular people; but he intends them to represent the kind of things which certain kinds of people say and do. It is in this respect, Aristotle says, that the literary artist's construction is 'more philosophical' than history.

This Aristotelian notion of the universalising aim of literature is now a very familiar one. Here are some simple examples. In his Preface to *Chuzzlewit* Dickens says that at the time of its composition Mrs Sarah Gamp was a fair representation of the hired attendant on the poor in sickness, and that Mrs Betsey Prig was a fair specimen of a hospital nurse. Moreover, the events making up the fictional lives of these two characters are intended by Dickens to represent certain general moral truths about the behaviour of people of this kind, for example that it is socially undesirable that the treatment of sick people should be left to this kind of person. Similarly, Jonas Chuzzlewit is representative of a bad type of character resulting from a bad type of education. And note that Dickens says that the recoil of Jonas' vices on the old man who educated him 'is not a mere piece of poetical justice, but the extreme exposition of a direct truth'.

This last statement makes explicit that what Jonas' fictional fortunes represent can be formulated as a general moral truth. Dickens is inviting us to agree that, while in his fictional world the truth or falsity of what takes place is irrelevant, yet the fictional image can *represent* what is generally true and in that way point obliquely to what it does not express directly.

In most respects Dickens' remarks indicate well enough what Aristotle means when he says that the literary artist expresses what is universal, and that his work is more philosophical than the historian's. Aristotle is saying that the literary artist's fictions are designed to prompt generalisations. They are designed to prompt us to see that what Agamemnon, for example, is doing in this particular situation is the sort of thing which that sort of man is likely to do in that sort of situation. By this means they are designed to prompt generalisations about recurring patterns of events in human life − 'pride goes before a fall' and 'he who hesitates is lost' are two very trite examples. This is the sort of thing a Greek chorus tends to talk about in order to prompt the audience to make the right inferences from what is presented to what is represented.

But in one important respect it would be misleading to take Dickens' remarks as a guide to Aristotle's meaning. Dickens claims that his fictions represent what is true. Aristotle makes no such claims for the literary artist. He claims that his work is more philosophical than the historian's. But this does not imply, nor is it intended to imply, that the literary artist has some special insight into the nature of things or that he aims in his work to represent the truth. Aristotle himself explains that it is in respect of its tendency to express what is universal rather than what is particular that he describes the literary artist's work as 'more philosophical' than the historian's. His explanation sufficiently specifies the meaning of 'more philosophical' here. To be 'more philosophical' is to have a greater propensity towards *sophia* ('wisdom') than the other man. And at the beginning of his *Metaphysics* (*Meta.* 981a25-b20) Aristotle illustrates what it means to say that one man is 'wiser' than another. He illustrates from a number of examples that one person is properly called 'wiser' than another in so far as he has a better grasp of general principles. A doctor is reckoned 'wiser' in the field of medicine than the man who just knows that he has stomach-ache. A master-builder is reckoned 'wiser' than the man who humps the stones. Similarly, a literary artist is reckoned 'wiser' than the man who records particular facts. For it is part of his job to make generalisations within his operational field of human life and behaviour.

I have given a good deal of emphasis to this point. For it is important not to read into Aristotle's mention of 'philosophical' any grandiose conception of the literary artist as a speculative thinker. Conceptions of that kind have been the source of much of the misguided idealisation of Aristotle's views on literature since the Renaissance. The kind of idealisation I have in mind is illustrated by Wordsworth, in his Preface to the second edition of the *Lyrical Ballads*. He presents Aristotle's view as the view 'that Poetry is the most philosophic of all writing'.[4] He goes on: 'It is so: its object is truth, not individual and local, but general, and operative; ... carried alive into the heart by passion'. Aristotle would have approved of the terms 'general' and 'operative'. He would have approved of Wordsworth's link between these terms and specifically emotional effects. But he would have dissociated himself from the views that 'Poetry is the most philosophical of all writing' and that 'its object is truth'. Admittedly Wordsworth offers the first view as

4. *Wordsworth's Poetical Works*, ed. de Selincourt (Oxford, 1944), Vol. 2, pp. 394-5.

one which has been 'told' to him. But he really should have checked it.

One thing which is abundantly clear about Aristotle's literary universals is that it is not their truth-value which is a criterion for their validity. It is their evocative function, their value in arousing attitudes of fear and pity, surprise and admiration, amusement and indignation. When Aristotle gives his fine analysis of what is the best tragedy he is giving an analysis of the most effective means of achieving certain emotional effects. In the case of tragedy the emotions to be aroused are pity and fear (1449b27). And the artist's aim is not simply to arouse them but also to *regulate* them. Aristotle recognises that what the artist represents has not merely what I have called an evocative capacity in affecting the emotions. It has also a regulative capacity. It is this latter capacity which Aristotle's notion of *katharsis* (1449b28) or *purgation* of emotion is concerned with. Whatever else we might think of this notion as a piece of psychology, it does at least include the valuable insight that imaginative literature can regulate the quality and the intensity of particular emotions so as to achieve what are considered desirable results. It is here, according to Aristotle, that we should look for the purposes of literature. Aristotle is right. All literary art is propagandist in its aims. Accepting this, Aristotle considers it important that its emotional effects should be good effects.

In furthering this purpose the literary universals act as essential middlemen. For the artist is appealing, through his fictions, to what Aristotle calls *philanthrôpia* (1452b38, 1453a2, 1456a21), fellow-feeling, the kind of community of emotions and interests which Conrad, in his own discussion of the purposes of fiction, calls 'solidarity'.[5] Hence it is by generalising his appeal, by so constructing his fictions that they can represent the general rather than the particular, that the artist gains the emotional effects he wants. As regards the truth-value of what is represented, Aristotle's view is that it is not the artist's proper aim to try to represent what is true in his field of operation, that is, the field of moral behaviour. In this field it is the job of the *moral philosopher* to enquire into the problem of what general propositions can be established as true. And it is the aim of the moral philosopher, not the literary artist, to present the truth as he sees it, if he chooses to put his inquiries into writing. The guideline for the artist, in Aristotle's view, is not what *is*, but what *can be* (1451a36 ff.). And according to the genre he is working in he has to judge what can *plausibly* be represented, that is, he must avoid anything improbable or irrational which is likely to thwart his aim of engaging his readers' sympathies. In this field of moral behaviour, as indeed in any other, Aristotle would have thought it a curiously oblique and superfluously elaborate method, with no advantages of either clarity or precision, to employ imitative literature to achieve a presentation-of-truth aim.

There are many varied reasons for the tendency in much European criticism since the Renaissance to idealise Aristotle's views on the aims of the literary artist. One reason is that his views were often overlaid by the didactic Roman ideals of Horace's *Ars Poetica*. Another, which I have already noted, is that Aristotle's remarks about the literary artist's 'more philosophical' approach readily lent themselves to metaphysical dressing-

11

---

5. In his Preface to *The Nigger of the Narcissus*.

up. It became very easy to put forward as a basically Aristotelian view the
didactic notion that the poet's job was to communicate to others his vision
of the truth. The literary attitudes of Johnson, in his *Preface to Shakespeare*,
provide a simple illustration of this.[6] Aristotelian notions are reflected in
many parts of this Preface, as they are in the Wordsworth Preface.
Shakespeare's characters, says Johnson, 'are commonly species'. 'They act
and speak by the influence of those general passions and principles by
which all minds are agitated.' But note that Johnson asserts as a general
principle, in Horatian vein, that the end of poetry is to instruct by pleasing.
He does not, of course, mean instruction in any and every field. He means
moral instruction, through the representation of moral truths which the
artist implicitly invites his readers to accept. Indeed he raps Shakespeare's
knuckles very sharply for giving more attention to pleasing than to
instructing, and for 'sacrificing virtue to convenience' as he puts it. What he
means by this is that Shakespeare's plays represent general views about the
relation between virtue and happiness which he, Johnson, considers to be
false. The poet should limit himself, he says, to what he calls 'just
representations of human nature'. This will rule out 'irregular combinations
of fanciful invention'. The mind can only repose, Johnson says, on 'the
stability of truth'.

This last remark is a particularly interesting example of the kind of
metaphysical idealism grafted on to Aristotle's views on literature by
English critics. Notice how readily an individual critic's moral convictions
can be equated with the stability of truth and used to determine what are
just representations and what combinations of the artist's invention are
regular. There is no immediately obvious implausibility in this. And what
goes for the critic goes for the author. In the infinitely varied field of moral
behaviour and moral attitudes the author has as much freedom in claiming
truth for the general views which he intends his fictions to represent as he
has in constructing his fictions. And in each respect much freedom is
compatible with plausibility. Thus the equation of what is represented with
what is true is easy to make. It is not only easy. It is extremely tempting to
make it in the case of fictional literature. It is a token of the value of the
fictions. We respect the truth. And it is understandable that the frequent
criticism that fictional literature presents what is false should be taken as a
criticism that it is lacking in value. Hence the temptation to maintain that,
while what is directly presented cannot claim to be true, yet what is
represented can claim to be true. Indeed it is sometimes claimed as one of the
strengths of a representational theory that it effectively by-passes the
criticism that the first-level symbolism of fiction is false and trivial. It does
so by claiming truth for its second-level symbolism.

I think it is one of the great merits of Aristotle's theory that he avoids this
temptation. He was very well aware of the kind of criticism I have
mentioned. In the *Poetics* he deals explicitly with a number of such criticisms
(1460b6 ff.). And it is worth looking briefly at his answer to them. It will
serve to make a little more precise his views on this important question of

6. Quotations from the Yale edition of Johnson's *Works*, Vol 7 (New Haven, 1968),
pp. 59 ff.

the truth-aims of the literary artist. The main criticism Aristotle had to   **13**
meet was that literature was lacking in serious purpose and value because it
was a tissue of false statements, of absurdities and impossibilities. This sort
of criticism can take two forms. It can be argued that the fictional
statements made by the literary artist are necessarily false. Or it can be
argued that his statements are in fact false; they can be shown to be false by
reference to what is in fact the case. Let us look at the first form. If I say that
Mr Micawber was recklessly improvident, or that Mr Squeers was
unpopular with his pupils, or that Mrs Gamp was ungrammatical in
speech, I am saying what is true only in the trivial sense of stating correctly
what Dickens portrays as being the case. It is nonsense to ask whether the
statements are true in any sense which implies that Mr Micawber or Mr
Squeers or Mrs Gamp at some time existed, and were, respectively,
improvident, unpopular, and ungrammatical. And since it is nonsense to
ask this, it might be argued that Dickens is not writing about anyone, either
in these cases or in the case of his other fictional characters, and that
whatever he states to be the case with regard to them is necessarily false. His
imaginative fictions might on this ground be criticised as at best profitless
and at worst calculated to misguide and deceive.

The other form of criticism – that the literary artist's statements are in
fact false – was used in a variety of ways by Plato in the *Republic* (377B ff.,
598D ff.). Here are some of Aristotle's own examples of this kind of
criticism, taken from the *Poetics* (1460b18 ff.). It might be argued, he says,
that the literary artist is guilty of technical inaccuracies in his work, for
example in medical detail, or that he makes false theological assumptions,
or that he is grossly idealistic in depicting the moral behaviour of his
characters, or that he describes what is impossible or irrational, for example
the behaviour of the Greeks and Trojans in standing idly by while Achilles
pursues Hector, or, as we might add ourselves, Alice drinking out of the
bottle and shooting up in size.

Neither Aristotle nor any other Greek, as far as I know, distinguished
these two forms of criticism. But I think it likely that the frequent criticism
in Greece, dating from as early as the eighth century B.C. (cf Hesiod,
Theogonia 27-8), that poets were liars sometimes confused the two forms of
criticism in its attitudes and allowed one to intensify the other. Aristotle   **14**
realised the importance of meeting this criticism. His distinction between
imitative and non-imitative literature enables him to do this. Non-imitative
literature, as we have seen, uses its language descriptively, with reference to
what is already there to be described or explained. It is the statements of
this kind of literature to which truth or falsity apply as the proper standards
of correctness. If the criticism that the statements of fiction are necessarily
false had been made explicit in Greece, Aristotle's answer to it would rightly
have been that it is not their function to be true or false; the criteria of truth
and falsity do not apply to them.

This kind of answer comes out clearly when Aristotle is dealing with the
second form of criticism – that the statements of fiction are in fact false.
What is to be noted about this form of criticism is that, unlike the first; it
can be applied not only to what is directly presented by the literary artist
but also to what he implicitly *represents* through his fictions. Aristotle's
answer to it applies to both these levels. His answer (1460b14 ff.) is that it is

what is *artistically* correct which matters, not any other kind of correctness, not, for example, the kind of correctness we call truth. And an artist's fictions are artistically correct if their construction is such as to achieve certain emotional effects. The appropriate emotional effects will differ from one literary genre to another. But in *no* genre will the truth of what is represented be a criterion for success in evoking the emotions. The literary artist's working criterion is not truth, but plausibility.

Aristotle is shrewdly perceptive in what he says about the varying limits, from one literary genre to another, of what is artistically plausible. In tragedy you soon lose the sympathy of your audience if you introduce events which fly in the face of natural laws or if the behaviour of your characters transgresses all psychological probability. Tragedy is too close to the facts of life for that. In epic the area of plausibility is a good deal wider (1460a11ff.). Homer, says Aristotle, tells the best tall stories. He knows how to give an air of conviction to the impossible. And this, as Aristotle says in his familiar dictum, is better than failing to give conviction of what *is* possible (1460a26-27, 1461b11-12). The golden rule is to observe the limits of plausibility appropriate to the genre in which you are working. And you must be consistent in this. Oedipus cannot be transplanted to the Mad Hatter's tea **15**   party nor Mrs Gamp to *The Cherry Orchard*. Nor would we forgive Miss Austen if Mr Darcy suddenly committed hara-kiri in the hall at Petersfield.

All that Aristotle says on this score of what is artistically correct is well said. Much of it concerns the proper application of this criterion at the level of what is directly presented by the literary artist. But what makes it especially important for the literary artist to have a good eye for what he can *plausibly* present is the fact that the particularities of his fiction represent what is universal, and succeed in their aim only if these representations too have the requisite plausibility. Plausibility in detail at level one governs plausibility at level two. Such general views about human behaviour and the human situation as are *represented* by the artist need make no claim to be true. But they must have sufficient plausibility to gain the emotional effects the artist is seeking.

Perhaps you remember the man Brown in Conrad's *Lord Jim*, the 'latter-day buccaneer' as Conrad calls him, who 'sails in his rotten schooner into Jim's history, a blind accomplice of the Dark Powers'. Brown's part in Jim's history illustrates what Conrad, in a letter to Bertrand Russell, called his 'deep-seated sense of fatality governing this man-inhabited world'.[7] And there are other things which Conrad wants to represent through Jim's fictional experiences, general views about the psychology of cowardice and self-esteem and self-discipline. Conrad tells us, in his preface to *The Nigger of the Narcissus*, what purposes he thinks the literary artist serves by his representations. Much of what he says is remarkably Aristotelian in spirit, especially his distinctions between the artist and the thinker or scientist, and his thesis that the essential appeal of fiction as an art is to temperament and not, as he puts it, 'to that part of our being which is dependent on wisdom'. Yet in the end Conrad cannot resist making the claim that the artist, like the thinker or scientist, seeks the truth, and that what the artist

7. Quoted by Russell in his essay on Conrad in *Portraits from Memory* (London, 1956).

reveals through his fictions is 'all the truth of life'. Thus Conrad provides yet
another illustration of the metaphysical idealisation of the Aristotelian view
of literary art. An interesting reflection of the influence of this idealising
tradition is found in Webster's dictionary definition of 'imitation' (*op. cit.*,
s.v.) in its aesthetic sense. It is, says Webster, 'a simulation of life or reality **16**
in art; imaginative embodiment of the ideal form of reality'. Webster adds
that this is 'a use following Aristotle'. But notice the metaphysical
transformation of Aristotle's notion of imitation.

I have spent a long time discussing Aristotle's view of the relation
between what the literary artist represents and what is true. Yet it is a point
of special importance in any consideration of literary values. In upholding
the values of imaginative literature post-Renaissance European criticism
has always tended to use the 'insight-into-the-truth' card as its trump-card.
Aristotle's views on the values of literature are also decisively influenced by
his acceptance of the value of this card. For the reason why Aristotle gives a
comparatively *low* value-rating to literature is that he considers the 'insight-
into-the-truth' card to be a card which the literary artist can never
legitimately play.

You may ask why the lack of any such card in your hand entails that you
have a comparatively poor hand. The answer lies in the end to which the
playing of the card is directed. This determines the comparative value of
your cards. And in the large game of human life the value of imaginative
literature has to be measured against other activities or studies in relation to
the end of life. That is how Aristotle measured it. Naturally and
straightforwardly Aristotle, like any other Greek thinker, makes his value
judgments in relation to some conception of human excellence – *aretê* – in a
broad moral sense. Equally naturally he looks at human excellence
functionally and starts from the notion of man as a rational animal (*EN*
1097b25 ff.) And perhaps it is equally natural again, since Aristotle is a
philosopher, that he finished with a conception of human excellence in
terms of what he considers to be the highest intellectual activities (*ibid.*,
1177a12 ff). This is not the occasion for considering the metaphysical and
other grounds on which Aristotle bases his grading of intellectual activities.
But his conclusion is that the wisdom which is the distinctive mark of
human excellence is found through the pursuit of truth in high realms of
theory – in physics, in mathematics, in metaphysics, and in theology (*Meta.*
982a5 ff., 1026a6-32). Literature cannot measure up to these. In Aristotle's
view the proper methods and aims of literature are such that neither the
practice nor the study of it calls for the exercise of high intellectual activity. **17**
It does not have the pursuit of truth as its aim. Even if it did have such an
aim it does not operate in a field in which any properly scientific method is
applicable. Nor is it a field which can provide objects of study with a high
metaphysical grading. As Aristotle puts it, man may be the best of the
animals but he is not metaphysically the best of objects (*EN* 1141a33-b2).

Now all this does not mean that for Aristotle imaginative literature is
without value. He values it for its capacity to refine and extend our emotional
sensibilities. And he values its capacity to *regulate* those sensibilities. Indeed,
since literary works are artificial things, producible in an enormous range of
patterns, Aristotle sees that their regulative function can be socially and
politically important. In his *Politics* (1340a ff.) he recognises, more generally

than in the *Poetics*, that imitations or representations, whether in music or literature, can be used in a system of education to regulate emotion and hence character to an approved pattern. In this way they can further human excellence, at the practical level of character training. And this constitutes, for Aristotle, the final purpose of imaginative literature.

We may disagree, of course, with Aristotle's hierarchy of values, a hierarchy which puts literature and music in the kitchen, logic and mathematics in the dining-room, and philosophy and theology in the drawing-room. We may think there are good grounds for adjusting these value-ratings. But any changes which may be made in the comparative value-ratings do not invalidate in any way Aristotle's ideal of the educated man as one who does not spend his time exclusively in the kitchen or the dining-room or the drawing-room but spends time in them all and recognises the relative value of each of them for the furtherance of the good life.

This is an ambitious ideal of education. Yet it must not be thought that it is in any way exceptional in the world of classical civilisation. It can fairly be said to be the standard type of ideal in Greek and Roman thought. There are, naturally enough, movements up and down in the value-rating of this or that subject of study. In respect of particular value-ratings the contrast between Greek and Roman ideals is in fact a fairly sharp one. Yet the Greek educational ideal of the truly wise man remains unchanged in Rome in **18** certain fundamental respects. It is still an ideal of human excellence in a broad moral sense. It has the same comprehensiveness in the range of studies thought to be necessary for realising the ideal and the same resistance to specialisation. And each field of study is evaluated in relation to the common moral end which it serves.

I hope I will not be thought guilty of special pleading if I say that this classical ideal of education finds its clearest and indeed most appropriate exemplification in classical studies. The student of classics studies a civilisation. He studies its languages and literature, its religion and philosophy, its history and art. I consider this to be valuable and beneficial for much the same reasons as Aristotle when he put forward his own educational ideals. I think too that there is an increasing recognition nowadays that what best educates a university student for life and leisure – and perhaps too for business – is to work in this kind of broad and varied and demanding field of study. This recognition is reflected in the curricula of some of the universities, especially the newer universities, as well as in the discussions of professional educationists. It is a trend which Aristotle and I wholeheartedly support.

BIBLIOGRAPHY

1. TEXTS

The classic edition of the Greek text of Aristotle was prepared by Immanuel Bekker for the Berlin Academy, and published in 1831; references to Aristotle's works are standardly given by page, column and line of this edition. As a text, however, it has been largely superseded; most of Aristotle's works can be found in the OCT, Teubner, Budé and Loeb series.

The standard English version of Aristotle is the 'Oxford Translation':

[1] J.A. Smith and W.D. Ross (eds.), *The Works of Aristotle translated into English* (Oxford, 1910-52).

There is an extremely useful abridgment of this in

[2] R. McKeon (ed.), *The Basic Works of Aristotle* (New York, 1941). The volumes in

[3] J.L. Ackrill (ed.), *The Clarendon Aristotle* (Oxford, 1961-) contain translations and commentaries tailored to the needs of the Greekless philosophical reader. The commentaries by W.D. Ross are invaluable, not least on account of the comprehensive and accurate English analyses of the texts w ch they contain:

[4] W.D. Ross (ed.), *Aristotle's Metaphysics* (Oxford, 1924).

[5] *id.*, *Aristotle's Physics* (Oxford, 1936).

[6] *id.*, *Aristotle's Prior and Posterior Analytics* (Oxford, 1949).

[7] *id.*, *Aristotle's Parva Naturalia* (Oxford, 1955).

[8] *id.*, *Aristotle's De Anima* (Oxford, 1961).

Many of the ancient Greek commentaries were published by the Prussian Academy in the series

[9] *Commentaria in Aristotelem Graeca* (Berlin, 1882-1909).

Several of Aquinas' Latin commentaries are now available in English. An indispensable aid to the study of Aristotle is

[10] H. Bonitz, *Index Aristotelicus* (Berlin, 1870);

there is an English concordance, based on the Oxford translation:

[11] T.W. Organ, *An Index to Aristotle in English Translation* (Princeton, 1949).

A comprehensive bibliography of writings on Aristotle up to 1896 can be found in

[12] M. Schwab, *Bibliographie d'Aristote* (Paris, 1896),

and a selective one in

[13] M.D. Philippe, *Aristoteles*, Bibliographische Einführungen in das Studium der Philosophie, 8 (Berne, 1948).

Our bibliography can be supplemented by

[14]. *Isis Cumulative Bibliography 1913-65.*

Many of the books mentioned in this list contain their own bibliographies; Düring's *Aristoteles* [15] has a particularly good one. The Archivum Aristotelicum of Berlin is eventually to produce a comprehensive continuation of Schwab.

2. GENERAL

There is a magisterial guide to all aspects of Aristotle's life and thought:

[15] I. Düring, *Aristoteles* (Heidelberg, 1966).

Of several shorter studies in English that give a general account of Aristotle's thought, the following are especially good:

[16] W.D. Ross, *Aristotle* (London, 1923).

[17] D.J. Allan, *The Philosophy of Aristotle* (Oxford, 1952).

[18] J.H. Randall, *Aristotle* (New York, 1960).

[19] M. Grene, *A Portrait of Aristotle* (Chicago, 1963).

[20] G.E.R. Lloyd, *Aristotle* (Cambridge, 1968).

It is still worth consulting

[21] G. Grote, *Aristotle* (3rd edition, London, 1883).

The surviving evidence about the life of Aristotle is collected in

[22] I. Düring, *Aristotle in the Ancient Biographical Tradition*, Studia Graeca et Latina Gothoburgensia 5 (Göteborg, 1957).

See also Volume I of

[23] A.H. Chroust, *Aristotle* (London, 1973).

All questions about Aristotle's writings are exhaustively discussed in

[24] P. Moraux, *Les Listes anciennes des ouvrages d'Aristote* (Louvain, 1951).

There is an amusing reconstruction of Aristotle's lecture-room in

[25] H. Jackson, 'Aristotle's lecture-room and lectures', *Journal of Philology* 35 (1920), pp. 191-200.

On the history of Aristotelianism, see

[26] P. Moraux, *Der Aristotelismus bei den Griechen*, Peripatoi 5 (Berlin, 1973), and on the history of the Lyceum

[27] J.P. Lynch, *Aristotle's School* (Berkeley and Los Angeles, 1972).

A major part of the scholarly work done on Aristotle during the last fifty years has taken its start from the hypothesis of

[28] W.W. Jaeger, *Aristotle* (English translation by R. Robinson; 2nd edition, Oxford, 1948; first German edition, Berlin, 1923).

Two of the most ambitious contributions to this line of scholarship are

[29] F. Solmsen, *Die Entwicklung der aristotelischen Logik und Rhetorik*, Neue Philologische Untersuchungen 4 (Berlin, 1929)

and

[30] F.J. Nuyens, *L'Evolution de la psychologie d' Aristote* (Louvain, 1948; originally published in Flemish, 1939).

Solmsen's views are conveniently expounded in

[31] J.L. Stocks, 'The composition of Aristotle's logical works', *Classical Quarterly* 27 (1933), pp. 114-24,

and Nuyens' in the introduction to Ross' edition of the *Parva Naturalia.*

The scholarly squabbles which these works have excited can be enjoyed at second-hand in

[32] A.H. Chroust, 'The first thirty years of modern Aristotelian scholarship', *Classica et Mediaevalia* 24 (1963/4), pp. 27-57.

Two papers by Ross and Owen (chapters 1 and 2 of our Volume 1) offer two views of the present state of play in this field:

[33] W.D. Ross, 'The development of Aristotle's thought', *Proceedings of the British Academy* 43 (1957), pp. 63-78.

[34] G.E.L. Owen, 'The Platonism of Aristotle', *Proceedings of the British Academy* 50 (1965), pp. 125-50.

Since 1957 triennial Symposia Aristotelica have been held in Europe; their published proceedings provide excellent examples of modern Aristotelian scholarship. See:

[35] I. Düring and G.E.L. Owen (eds.), *Aristotle and Plato in the mid-Fourth Century*, Studia Graeca et Latina Gothoburgensia 11 (Göteborg, 1960).

[36] S. Mansion (ed.), *Aristote et les problèmes de méthode* (Louvain, 1961).

[37] G.E.L. Owen (ed.), *Aristotle on Dialectic* (Oxford, 1968).

[38] I. Düring (ed.), *Naturforschung bei Aristoteles und Theophrast* (Heidelberg, 1969).

[39] P. Moraux (ed.), *Untersuchungen zur Eudemischen Ethik*, Peripatoi I (Berlin, 1970).

[40] P. Aubenque (ed.), *Etudes sur le Métaphysique d'Aristote* (forthcoming).

[41] G.E.R. Lloyd and G.E.L. Owen (eds.), *Aristotle on Mind and the Senses* (Cambridge, 1978).

3. PSYCHOLOGY

On the *De Anima* the two leading commentaries are

[42] G. Rodier, *Aristote: Traité de l'âme* (Paris, 1900, with French translation).

[43] R.D. Hicks, *Aristotle: De Anima* (Cambridge, 1907, with English translation).

There are less extensive commentaries by W.D. Ross [8], and also

[44] D.W. Hamlyn, *Aristotle's De Anima Books II and III* (Oxford, 1968, with translation), in [3].

[45] W. Theiler, *Aristoteles über die Seele* (Berlin, 1959, with German translation).

The commentary of St Thomas Aquinas was translated into English by K. Foster and S. Humphries as

[46] *Aristotle's De Anima in the version of William of Moerbeke and the commentary of St Thomas Aquinas* (London, 1951).

The *Parva Naturalia* is a collection of short treatises: *De Sensu, De Memoria et Reminiscentia, De Somno et Vigilia, De Insomniis, De Divinatione per Somnum, De Longitudine et Brevitate Vitae, De Juventute et Senectute de Vita et Morte, De Respiratione*.

The most informative modern commentary for the whole collection is probably that in Latin in

[47] P. Siwek, *Aristotelis Parva Naturalia graece et latine* (Rome, 1963, with Latin translation).

Also valuable are W.D. Ross [7], and the footnotes to

[48] J.I. Beare's translation (1908) of the first five treatises in Vol. 3 of [1].

For the *De Sensu* and *De Memoria* there is

[49] G.R.T. Ross, *De Sensu et De Memoria* (Cambridge, 1906, with English translation).

There is a commentary on the *De Memoria*:

[50] R. Sorabji, *Aristotle on Memory* (London, 1972, with English translation).

For two treatises, there is an extended preface in

[51] H.J.D. Lulofs, *De Insomniis et De Divinatione per Somnum* (Leyden, 1947).

These psychological works are closely connected with the physical treatises which precede them in the traditional order, *GC* and *Meteor.*, and with the biological works which follow, *PA*, *GA* and *MA*. A different approach to psychology is found in the treatises concerned with human action, *EE*, *EN*, *Pol.*, *Poet.* and *Rhet.*, whose second book is concerned with character and emotions. Different again is the metaphysical discussion of the soul in *Meta.* VII and VIII, of action in IX 5, and of intellect in XII 9. Finally, an epistemological approach appears in *A. Pst.*, which is concerned with scientific knowledge.

Early views on psychology are included in the fragments of *Eudemus*, *Protrepticus*, *De Philosophia*.

Aristotle's work on psychology is the subject of [41].

Aristotle compiled a history of earlier views on the soul in *De An.* I, on which see

[52] S. Mansion, 'Le rôle de l'exposé et de la critique des philosophies antérieurs chez Aristote', in [36], pp. 35-56.

Two helpful papers especially devoted to the antecedents of Aristotle's psychology are

[53] F. Solmsen, 'Antecedents of Aristotle's psychology and scale of beings', *American Journal of Philology* 76 (1955), pp. 148-64,

and the section entitled 'Nature and Soul' in

[54] F. Solmsen, *Aristotle's System of the Physical World* (Ithaca, 1960).

See also the invaluable older works of

[55] J.I. Beare, *Greek Theories of Elementary Cognition* (Oxford, 1906), and

[56] G.M. Stratton, *Theophrastus and the Greek Physiological Psychology before Aristotle* (London, 1917).

More speculative attempts in the tradition of *Geistesgeschichte* to identify early Greek concepts of man and the soul are to be found in [113] and in

[57] R.B. Onians, *The Origins of European Thought* (Cambridge, 1951), and

[58[B. Snell, *The Discovery of Mind* (Oxford, 1953).

Following Jaeger's discussion in [28] of the development of Aristotle's psychology, F. Nuyens produced a major work in Dutch in 1939, translated into French as [30] in which he distinguished three stages in Aristotle's thought about the soul. This account was endorsed in its main outlines by W.D. Ross (see our Vol. 1, chapter 1, and the introductions to [7] and [8]), and by many scholars. But it was already questioned in part by D.A. Rees, e.g. in

[59] D.A. Rees, 'Theories of the soul in the early Aristotle' in [35], pp. 191-200.

A major onslaught started with

[60] I. Block, 'The order of Aristotle's psychological writings', *American Journal of Philology* 82 (1961), pp. 50-77.

Block still made use of a genetic method of interpretation, while reversing some of Nuyens' dating. But the use of this method, as regards the main psychological works, is itself called into question by Kahn, in our volume, and by

[61] W.F.R. Hardie, 'Aristotle's treatment of the relation between the soul and the body', *Philosophical Quarterly* 14 (1964), 53-72, and in Chapter 5 of

[62] W.F.R. Hardie, *Aristotle's Ethical Theory* (Oxford, 1968).

Two contributions in support of Block are:

[63] H.J. Easterling, 'A note on *De Anima* 413a8-9', *Phronesis* 11 (1966), pp. 159-62,

and

[64] A. Preus, '*On Dreams* 2, 459b24-460a33, and Aristotle's *opsis*', *Phronesis* 13 (1968), pp. 175-82.

The subject has recently been reviewed by

[65] C. Lefevre, *Sur L'évolution d'Aristote en psychologie* (Louvain, 1972).

Aristotle's view of the relation of body to soul is discussed in our volume by Kahn, Sorabji (first paper), Barnes and Ackrill. A distinctive interpretation was offered by

[66] F. Brentano, *The Psychology of Aristotle* (Berkeley, 1977, translated by R. George from the German of 1867 [cited by our authors]),

and in

[67] *id., Psychology from an Empirical Standpoint* (London, 1973, translated by A.C. Rancurello, D.B. Terrell, and L.L. McAlister from the German of 1874), who attributed to Aristotle his own intentionalist account of mental phenomena.

For a materialist interpretation, see

[68] T. Slakey, 'Aristotle on sense perception', *The Philosophical Review* 70 (1961), pp. 470-84.

Varying positions closer to Descartes' have been suggested by Solmsen [103] by Hicks [43], p. 563 and by G.R.T. Ross [49], pp. 5-7, while W.D. Ross [16], ch. 5, held that Aristotle oscillated between a materialist and a Cartesian position. The contrast between Aristotle and Descartes drawn by Kahn and Sorabji has been taken further by

[69] G.B. Matthews, 'Consciousness and life', *Philosophy* 52 (1977), pp. 13-26,

but questioned by

[70] W.F.R. Hardie, 'Concepts of consciousness in Aristotle', *Mind* 85 (1976), pp. 388-411.

The whole subject of the relation between body and soul in Aristotle has been discussed also by

[71] P. Siwek, *La Psychophysique humaine d'après Aristote* (Paris, 1930)

and by W.F.R. Hardie [61]. Ackrill, in our volume, attacks the interpretation according to which the human soul, for Aristotle, is the person rather than some attribute of the person. See for this view

[71A] D. Wiggins, *Identity and spatio-temporal continuity* (Oxford, 1967), IV. 2.

Special problems are created by Aristotle's early views, which, according to Jaeger and Nuyens, but not Owen, made the soul separable from the body ([28], [30], [34]), and by his treatment of the active intellect, which some regard as giving humans a kind of life after the death of the body (see below). The question whether Aristotle believes that each person's soul is a distinct form is discussed by

[72] R. Albritton, 'Forms of particular substances in Aristotle's metaphysics', *Journal of Philosophy* 54, (1957), pp. 699-708.

On Aristotle's attitude to theories according to which the soul is the 'harmony of the body' see chapter 3 of Jaeger [28], and

[73] H.B. Gottschalk, 'Soul as harmonia', *Phronesis* 16, (1971), pp. 179-98.

See now also for a general treatment of the relation of body and soul

[74] E. Hartman, *Substance, Body and Soul* (Princeton, 1978).

Aristotle distinguished various capacities of the soul: the power to take in nourishment is the most widespread, belonging even to plants. Animals have in addition sense perception and desire, while men add to these intellect, which they share with the disembodied divinities. The relation to each other of these various capacities or types of soul is discussed by F. Solmsen [53], by S. Mansion in [41], by

[75] S. Mansion, 'Deux définitions différentes de la vie chez Aristote', *Revue Philosophique de Louvain* 71 (1973), pp. 425-50.

and by

[76] A.C. Lloyd, 'Genus, species and ordered series in Aristotle', *Phronesis* 7 (1962), pp. 69-70.

A quite different way of dividing the soul, into a part that reasons and a part that listens to reason, is exploited in the ethical works, and this is discussed by Fortenbaugh and Rees in [130], [59] and in Chapter 8. See also

[77] D.A. Rees, 'Bipartition of the soul in the early Academy, *Journal of Hellenic Studies* 77 (1957), pp. 112-18.

Of the various capacities of the soul, Aristotle devotes most attention to sense perception. In the present volume, the subject is treated by Kahn and by Sorabji (second paper). The bare facts of Aristotle's theory are assembled by Beare [55]. There is an instructive series of writings by Hamlyn: besides his [44], see

[78] D.W. Hamlyn, 'Aristotle's account of aesthesis in the *De Anima*', *Classical Quarterly* n.s. 9 (1959), pp. 6-16.

[79] D.W. Hamlyn, *Sensation and Perception* (London, 1961).

[80] D.W. Hamlyn, 'Seeing things as they are', Inaugural Lecture at Birkbeck College, London, 1965.

The infallibility of the senses is discussed by Hamlyn, and by

[81] I. Block, 'Truth and error in Aristotle's theory of sense perception', *Philosophical Quarterly* 11 (1961), pp. 1-9.

[82] A.J.P. Kenny, 'The argument from illusion in Aristotle's *Metaphysics*',

Mind 76 (1967), pp. 184-97.

[83] M. Scholar, 'Aristotle's *Metaphysics* 1010b1-3', *Mind* 80 (1971), pp. 266-8.

For the theory that perceiving involves the reception of form without matter, see, besides Barnes in chapter 2 and Sorabji in chapter 3,

[84] G. Van Riet, 'La théorie thomiste de la sensation externe', *Revue Philosophique de Louvain* 51 (1953), pp. 374-408.

[85] C.J.F. Williams and R.J. Hirst, 'Form and sensation', *Proceedings of the Aristotelian Society*, suppl. vol. 39 (1965), pp. 139-72.

There are further treatments of sense perception in A. Preus [64], T. Slakey [68], A. Graeser [41], and

[86] F. Solmsen, 'Aesthesis in Aristotelian and Epicurean thought', *Mededelingen der Koninklijke Nederlandse Akademie van Wetenschappen Afd. Letterkunde* N.R. 24.8 (1961), pp. 241-62.

[87] I. Block, 'Aristotle and the physical object', *Philosophy and Phenomenological Research* 21 (1969), pp. 93-101.

[88] I. Block, 'On the commonness of the common sensibles', *Australasian Journal of Philosophy* 43 (1965), pp. 189-95.

[89] A. Stigen, 'On the alleged primacy of sight in Aristotle', *Symbolae Osloenses* 37 (1961), pp.15-44

[90] S. Cashdollar, 'Aristotle's account of incidental perception', *Phronesis* 18 (1973), pp. 156-75.

The idea of a common sense or a central sense faculty is discussed in Chapter 1, in [88], and in

[91] I. Block, 'Three German commentators on the individual senses and the common sense in Aristotle', *Phronesis* 9 (1964), pp. 58-63.

[92] D.W. Hamlyn, '*Koinê aesthêsis*', *The Monist* 52 (1968), pp. 195-200.

[93] A.C. Lloyd, 'Nosce teipsum and conscientia', *Archiv für Geschichte der Philosophie* 46 (1964), pp. 188-200.

[94] M. de Corte, 'Notes exégétiques sur la théorie aristotélicienne du Sensus Communis', *New Scholasticism* 6 (1932), pp. 187-214.

[94A] L.A. Kosman, 'Perceiving that we perceive', *Philosophical Review* 84 (1975), pp. 499-519.

For the theory that sense perception is a mean or mid-point, much of the large literature is surveyed by

[95] T. Tracy, *Physiological Theory and the Doctrine of the Mean in Plato and Aristotle* (The Hague, 1969).

His bibliography can usefully be supplemented by:

[96] W.F.R. Hardie, 'Aristotle's doctrine that virtue is a mean', *Proceedings of the Aristotelian Society* 65 (1964-5), pp. 53-72.

It is the concluding pages of this which bear on Aristotle's theory of sense perception and these have not been included in our reprint of the article in Volume 2. There is further controversy on the correct interpretation of the doctrine between Slakey [68] and Sorabji (chapter 3).

For the physiology of sense perception, see besides Beare [48] and [55], and Nussbaum [136]

[97] J. Neuhauser, *Aristoteles Lehre von dem sinnlichen Erkenntnissvermögen und seinen Organen* (Leipzig, 1878),

the notes to
[98] W. Ogle, *Aristotle on the Parts of Animals* (London, 1882; see especially *PA* II 10-17 on the sense organs),
    the notes to two Loeb editions,
[99] A.L. Peck, *Aristotle, Parts of Animals* (Cambridge, Mass, 1961), and
[100] A.L. Peck, *Aristotle, Generation of Animals* (Cambridge, Mass., 1953; especially pp. 589-93);
also
[101] *ibid.*, 'The connate pneuma: an essential factor in Aristotle's solutions to the problems of reproduction and sensation', in *Science, Medicine and History*, Essays in honour of Charles Singer, ed. E.A. Underwood (Oxford, 1953), Vol. 1, pp. 111-21.
[102] F. Solmsen, 'Tissues and the soul', *The Philosophical Review* 59 (1950), pp. 435-68,
[103] F. Solmsen, 'Greek philosophy and the discovery of the nerves', *Museum Helveticum* 18 (1961), pp. 150-97.
and the contributions of J. Wiesner, G. Verbeke, G.E.R. Lloyd to [41].

In Aristotle's view, to understand the senses, one must know their objects: colour, sound, odour, flavour, etc. For his theory that other shades are mathematical ratios of black and white, see
[104] P. Kucharski, 'Sur la théorie des couleurs et des saveurs dans le De Sensu aristotélicien', *Revue des Etudes Grecques* 67 (1954), pp. 355-90,
and
[105] R. Sorabji, 'Aristotle, mathematics and colour', *Classical Quarterly* 22 (1972), pp. 293-308.
Interest in dark-light colour theories was renewed when Goethe championed them against Newton. Newton did, however, experimentally verify some of the colour effects obtained by combining black with white and dark with light. Aristotle's difficulties over the motion and direction of light, of sight, or of the effects of colour, are brought out by
[106] S. Sambursky, 'Philoponus' interpretation of Aristotle's theory of light', *Osiris* 13 (1958), pp. 114-26.
For other deviations from Aristotle's theory among his successors, see
[107] H.B. Gottschalk, 'The *De Coloribus* and its author', *Hermes* 92 (1964), pp. 59-85.
Aristotle's theory of sound is contrasted with the theories of his successors in
[108] H.B. Gottschalk, 'The *De Audibilibus* and Peripatetic acoustics', *Hermes* 96 (1968), pp. 435-60.

Various mental states are regarded by Aristotle as functions of the faculty of sense perception. One is imagination, for which see Schofield in this volume and
[109] J. Freudenthal, *Uber den Begriff des Wortes phantasia bei Aristoteles* (Göttingen, 1863).
[110] K. Lycos, 'Aristotle and Plato on appearing', *Mind* 73 (1964), pp. 496-514.
[111] D.A. Rees, 'Aristotle's treatment of *phantasia*', in *Essays in Ancient Greek Philosophy*, ed. J. Anton and G. Kustas (Albany, New York, 1971), pp. 491-505.

[112] J. Engmann, 'Imagination and Truth in Aristotle', *Journal of the History of Philosophy* 14 (1976), pp. 259-65

For memory, see Sorabji [50], who has chapters on remembering, memorising and recollecting, and M. Grene [19], who has a chapter on the *De Memoria*. For dreaming see Lulofs [51], and the interesting background material in chapter 4 of

[113] E.R. Dodds, *The Greeks and the Irrational* (Berkeley and Los Angeles, 1963).

Aristotle's brief reference to the active intellect in *De An*. III 5 has provoked more discussion than any other aspect of his account of the intellect. The active intellect was identified with God by the ancient commentator, Alexander of Aphrodisias. St. Thomas Aquinas regarded it as part of the human being, a part which could continue to exist when the body perished. For a brief account of the many interpretations, see Hicks [43], pp. lxiv-lxix, who also collects (in Greek) the fragments of Theophrastus' criticism of Aristotle's theory (pp. 589-96). Theophrastus' criticism is also discussed in

[114] E. Barbotin, *La Théorie aristotélicienne de l'intellect d'après Théophraste*, thèse (Paris, 1954).

For a fuller survey of interpretations, see:

[115] O. Hamelin, *La Théorie de l'intellect d'après Aristote et ses commentateurs* (Paris, 1953).

Two deflationary writers are:

[116 P. Moraux, 'A propos du *nous thurathen* chez Aristote', in *Autour d'Aristote*, Recueil d'Etudes Offerts à Mgr. A. Mansion (Louvain, 1955), pp. 255-95,

and Hamlyn [44], [79].

See further F. Brentano [66], and

[117] F. Brentano, *Aristoteles' Lehre vom Ursprung des menschlichen Geistes* (Leipzig, 1911).

[118] A. Mansion, 'L'immortalité de l'âme et de l'intellect d'après Aristotle', *Revue Philosophique de Louvain* 51 (1953), pp. 444-72.

[119] J. Rist, 'Notes on Aristotle *De Anima* 3.5', *Classical Philology* 61 (1966), pp. 8-20.

and chapter 16 of Hardie [62].

The idea that God is the object of his own thought is connected by Norman in chapter 6 with the idea that the act of thinking is identical with its object. On this, see further the essay on Aristotle by Anscombe in

[120] G.E.M. Anscombe and P.T. Geach, *Three Philosophers* (Oxford, 1961) and

[121] J. Owens, 'A note on Aristotle, *De An*. III 4, 429b9', *Phoenix* 30 (1976), pp. 109-18.

On non-discursive thought, see:

[122] K. Oehler, *Die Lehre vom noetischen und dianoetischen Denken bei Platon und Aristoteles*, Zetemata 29 (Munich, 1962), pp. 151-69, and

[123] A.C. Lloyd, 'Non-discursive thought – an enigma of Greek philosophy', *Proceedings of the Aristotelian Society* 70 (1969-70), pp. 261-74.

The account of thinking in *De An*. III 4-8 is supplemented in *Mem.*, on which see Sorabji [50], pp. 6-8. On the idea of indivisible objects of thought, see E. Berti in [41], and P. Aubenque in [40]. Analogies with touching and seeing are discussed by

[124] S.H. Rosen, 'Thought and touch: a note on Aristotle's *De Anima*', *Phronesis* 6 (1961), pp. 127-37.

One kind of abstractive process, thinking of geometrical figures in abstraction from physical matter, is examined by

[125] K.J.J. Hintikka, 'Aristotelian infinity', *Philosophical Review* 75 (1966), pp. 197-218.
[126] I. Mueller, 'Aristotle on geometrical objects', *Archiv für Geschichte der Philosophie* 52 (1970), pp. 156-71 (both reprinted in our Vol. 3).

This is to be distinguished from the abstractive process involved in the formation of general concepts or propositions (*A. Pst.* II 19: *Meta.* I 1). The intellectual abilities analysed in *EN* VI are helpfully sorted out by

[127] L.H.G. Greenwood, *Aristotle: Nicomachean Ethics Book VI* (Cambridge 1909).

For those involved in science, see

[128] J.H. Lesher, 'The meaning of *nous* in the *Posterior Analytics*', *Phronesis* 18 (1973), pp. 44-68.
[129] L.A. Kosman, 'Understanding, explanation and insight in the *Posterior Analytics*', in *Exegesis and Argument* (ed. E.N. Lee, A.P.D. Mourelatos and R.M. Rorty), *Phronesis* Suppl. 1, 1973.

On the kind of contemplation involved in the happy life described in *EN* X, see our Vol. 2.

On the emotions there is a valuable series of articles by Fortenbaugh which includes the one we have reprinted as chapter 8. He has put his views together in:

[130] W.W. Fortenbaugh, *Aristotle on Emotion* (London, 1975).

Also valuable is the discussion of *Poet.* 14 in G.F. Else [139], and see

[131] P. Aubenque, 'La définition aristotélicienne de la colère', *Revue Philosophique* 147 (1957), pp. 300-17.

A good account of voluntary motion is given by W.F.R. Hardie [62]. See also D.J. Furley and J.B. Skemp in [41], and

[132] S.G. Etheridge, 'Aristotle's practical syllogism and necessity', *Philologus* 112 (1968), pp. 20-42.
[133] G.E.M. Anscombe, 'Thought and action in Aristotle', in *New Essays on Plato and Aristotle*, ed. R. Bambrough (London, 1965), reprinted in our Vol. 2.
[134] D.J. Allan, 'The practical syllogism', in *Autour d'Aristote*, Recueil d'Etudes offert à Mgr. A. Mansion (Louvain, 1955), pp. 325-40.
[135] D.J. Furley, *Two Studies in the Greek Atomists* (Princeton, 1967), 2nd Study (the relevant portions are reprinted in our Vol. 2). There is a major new edition and discussion of *MA*:
[136] M. Nussbaum, *Aristotle's De Motu Animalium* (Princeton, 1978).

For further references see Vol. 2.

Nutrition is a function of the soul, as well as sense perception, thought and desire. For Aristotle's lost treatise, see

[137] P. Louiš, 'Le traité d'Aristote sur la nutrition', *Revue de Philologie* 3rd series 26 (1952), pp. 29-35.

See the notes to Ogle [98], esp. p.202, to Peck [99] and [100], esp. pp. lxiii-lxvii of [100], and to

[138] H. Joachim, *Aristotle on Coming-to-be and Passing-away* (Oxford, 1922).

4. POETICS

The *Poetics*, as we have it, is incomplete. Some fragments of an earlier work, *On Poets*, survive.

There is a stimulating, but controversial, commentary by

[139] G.F. Else, *Aristotle's Poetics: The Argument* (Cambridge, Mass., 1957).

The standard English commentary is probably still that of

[140] S.H. Butcher, *Aristotle's Theory of Poetry and Fine Art* (London, 1895; 4th ed., London, 1932).

There are also good commentaries by

[141] I. Bywater, *Aristotle on the Art of Poetry* (Oxford, 1909).

[142] A. Gudeman, *Aristoteles Poetik* (Berlin and Leipzig, 1934).

[143] D. de Montmollin, *La Poétique d'Aristote* (Neuchatel, 1951).

[144] D.W. Lucas, *Aristotle Poetics* (Oxford, 1968).

See further the amplified rendering by

[145] L. Cooper, *Aristotle on the Art of Poetry* (1913; revised ed. Ithaca, 1947).

A major philological study, published as three articles in 1865, 1866, 1867, has been collected into one book as

[146] J. Vahlen, *Beiträge zu Aristoteles Poetik*, ed. H. Schöne (Leipzig, 1914, repr. 1965).

A concise account of the great influence of the *Poetics* in the Renaissance is supplied by

[147] L. Cooper, *The Poetics of Aristotle, Its Meaning and Influence* (New York, 1927).

The same author considers what Aristotle might have said in the lost discussion of comedy:

[148] L. Cooper, *An Aristotelian Theory of Comedy* (New York, 1922).

There is a useful set of lectures by

[149] H. House, *Aristotle's Poetics* (London, 1956).

Aristotle defines tragedy as a kind of imitation. Imitation and the nature of poetry are discussed by Gulley in chapter 10, and by

[150] R. Ingarden, 'A marginal commentary on Aristotle's *Poetics*', *Journal of Aesthetics and Art Criticism* 20 (1961-2), pp. 163-73, 273-85.

Dorothy Sayers humorously finds in Aristotle's recipe the perfect anticipation of the modern detective story:

[151] D. Sayers, *Unpopular Opinions* (New York, 1947).

Aristotle claims that through pity and fear, tragedy accomplishes the *katharsis* of such emotions. Is it the audience which experiences *katharsis*, and is *katharsis* similar to a religious purification, or to a medical purging? Bernays' article, favouring the medical view, here translated as our chapter 9, has almost swept the field.

Anticipations, going back to the Renaissance, have been traced by

[152] I. Bywater, 'Milton and the Aristotelian definition of tragedy', *Journal of Philology*, 64 (1901), pp. 267-75,

and in his commentary [141] pp. 152-3.

Within the Bernays tradition, see

[153] A.W. Benn, 'Aristotle's theory of tragic emotion', *Mind* 23 (1914), pp. 84-90.

[154] W.J. Verdenius, '*katharsis tôn pathêmatôn*', in *Autour d'Aristote*, Recueil d'Etudes Offert à Mgr. A. Mansion (Louvain, 1955), pp. 367-73.

[155] R. Stark, *Aristotelesstudien*, Zetemata 8 (Munich, 1954; 2nd ed. 1972).

[156] F. Dirlmeier, '*katharsis pathêmatôn*', *Hermes* 75 (1949), pp. 81-92.

[157] W. Schadewaldt, 'Furcht und Mitleid?', *Hermes* 83 (1955), pp. 129-71.

[158] H. Flashar, 'Die medizinischen Grundlagen der Lehre von der Wirkung der Dichtung in der griechischen Poetik', *Hermes* 84 (1956), pp. 12-48.

[159] M. Pohlenz, 'Furcht und Mitleid? Ein Nachwort', *Hermes* 84 (1956), pp. 49-74.

However, the medical analogy, and the idea that catharsis occurs in the spectators has been challenged by G.F. Else [139], commenting on *Poet.* 6 and 14. And yet another heterodox view has been offered by

[160] L. Golden, 'Catharsis', *Transactions and Proceedings of the American Philological Association* 93, (1962), pp. 51-60.

[161] L. Golden, 'Mimesis and catharsis', *Classical Philology* 64 (1969), pp. 145-53.

The theory of *katharsis* may be seen as a reply to Plato, who criticised Poetry for playing on the emotions (*Republic* 602-7), and asked what good Poetry could do. For this aspect of *katharsis*, see Gulley, chapter 10, Else [139] on *Poet.* 14, and Fortenbaugh [130].

On the conventional interpretation, the tragic hero's downfall must be due to *hamartia*, in order that our pity may be aroused, and so purged. But can *hamartia* be a simple error, or must it be something more culpable? Perhaps the most eloquent exposition of the culpability view is by

[162] P.W. Harsh, '*hamartia* again', *Transactions and Proceedings of the American Philological Association* 76 (1945), pp. 47-58.

The prevailing view is that there is an error not necessarily culpable. This is well argued by Else [139] on *Poet.* 13, by

[163] J.T. Sheppard, *The Oedipus Tyrannus of Sophocles* (Cambridge, 1920), pp. xxiv-xl.

[164] E.R. Dodds, 'On misunderstanding the *Oedipus Rex*', *Greece and Rome* 13 (1966), pp. 37-49, reprinted in E.R. Dodds, *The Ancient Concept of Progress*, (Oxford, 1973), pp. 64-77.

See also a paper which connects *hamartia* with the old idea that those whom the gods wish to destroy they first drive mad:

[165] R.D. Dawe, 'Some reflections on Ate and Hamartia', *Harvard Studies in Classical Philology* 72 (1967), pp. 89-123.

The view that the tragic hero's character must contain a culpable flaw is rejected in the following studies of *hamartia*:

[166] P. van Braam, 'Aristotle's use of *hamartia*', *Classical Quarterly* 6 (1912), pp. 266-72.

[167] O. Hey, '*Hamartia*: zur Bedeutungsgeschichte des Wortes', *Philologus* 83 (1928), pp. 137-63.

[168] I.M. Glanville, 'Tragic error', *Classical Quarterly* 43 (1949), pp. 447-56.

[169] M. Ostwald, 'Aristotle on *hamartia* and Sophocles' *Oedipus Tyrannus*', in *Festschrift Ernst Kapp* (Hamburg, 1958).

The tragic hero's character is further discussed by

[170] A.W.H. Adkins, 'Aristotle and the best kind of tragedy', *Classical Quarterly* 16 (1966), pp. 78-102.

[171] S.M. Pitcher, 'Aristotle's good and just heroes', *Philological Quarterly* 24 (1945), pp. 1-11, 190-1.

The controversy is comprehensively surveyed by

[172] J.M. Bremer, *Hamartia* (Amsterdam, 1969).

A good article, which brings one up to date on the progress of the controversy since Bremer, is

[173] T.C.W. Stinton, '*Hamartia* in Aristotle and Greek tragedy', *Classical Quarterly* n.s. 25 (1975) pp. 221-54.

The plot requires an unexpected reversal (*peripeteia*). Is it the hero who fails to expect it, while the audience remains in the know? So Vahlen [146], and

[174] F.L. Lucas, 'The reverse of Aristotle', *Classical Review* 37 (1923), pp. 98-104.

Or is there a shift in the situation, which the audience is not invited to foresee? So

[175] P. Turner, 'The reverse of Vahlen', *Classical Quarterly* 9 (1959), pp. 207-15.

Else [139] connects the peripeteia with the hero's mistake (*hamartia*), and subsequent recognition.

Character, plot, and their relative importance or unimportance are discussed by Humphrey House [149], chapter 5.

[176] J. Jones, *Aristotle and Greek Tragedy* (London, 1962), chapter 1.

[177] C. Lord, 'Tragedy without Character: *Poetics* 6, 1450a24', *Journal of Aesthetics and Art Criticism* 28 (1969-70), pp. 55-62.

See also:

[178] W.J. Verdenius, 'The meaning of *êthos* and *êthikos* in Aristotle's Poetics', *Mnemosyne* (3rd series) 12 (1945), pp. 241-57.

Links with Aristotle's ethics are brought out by many of the articles on *harmartia*. See Else [139], van Braam [166], Glanville [168], Stinton [173]. See also

[179] G.K. Gresseth, 'The system of Aristotle's *Poetics*', *Transactions and Proceedings of the American Philological Association* 89 (1958), pp. 312-35.

Poetry is distinguished from history by being more universal. This idea is discussed by Gulley in chapter 10, by House [149], chapter 4, and by

[180] G. de Ste Croix, 'Aristotle on history and poetry, *Poet.* 9, 1451a36-b11', in *The Ancient Historian and his Materials*, ed. B.M. Levick (Farnborough, 1975).

5. RHETORIC

There is a commentary by
[181] L. Spengel, *Aristotelis ars Rhetorica* (Leipzig, 1867),
and a posthumous one, in 3 volumes, by
[182] E.M. Cope, edited by J.E. Sandys, *The Rhetoric of Aristotle with a Commentary* (Cambridge, 1877).
An introduction to this is provided by an earlier work
[183] E.M. Cope, *Introduction to Aristotle's Rhetoric* (London, 1867).
The Teubner edition has an ample preface:
[184] A. Roemer, *Aristotelis Ars Rhetorica* (Leipzig, 1923).
There is a useful introduction to the Modern Library version of
[185] F. Solmsen, *The Rhetoric and Poetics of Aristotle* (New York, 1954).
See also the translation, amplified for the benefit of students of composition and public speaking, by
[186] L. Cooper, *The Rhetoric of Aristotle* (New York, 1932).
There is an abridgment, written by the philosopher Thomas Hobbes, entitled
[187] *A Briefe of the Art of Rhetorique* (date uncertain).
This can be found in any edition of his collected works.

Of general works on the *Rhetoric*, a major one is that of F. Solmsen [29]. A different view is given by
[188] W.M.A. Grimaldi, *Studies in the Philosophy of Aristotle's Rhetoric*. Hermes Einzelschriften (Wiesbaden, 1972).
Some of the older studies are reprinted in
[189] R. Stark (ed.), *Rhetorika* (Hildesheim, 1968).

Besides the Rhetoric, Aristotle wrote several other rhetorical works, but all that survives is some fragments of the *Gryllos*, included in Vol. 12 of the Oxford Translation [1]. The *Rhetorica ad Alexandrum* is not by Aristotle.

It has been much disputed whether the *Rhetoric* is a relatively unified work, or a patchwork written over a long period. The patchwork view is taken, among the scholars mentioned above, by Roemer [184] and Solmsen [29], while relative unity is favoured by Grimaldi [188] and Cope [182], [183]. For an excellent statement of the latter view, see Düring [15], pp. 118-25. If it is relatively unified, there is still disagreement as to whether it should be assigned predominantly to the early period of Aristotle's teaching in the Academy (eloquently argued by Düring, *loc. cit.*), or to the latest period, as is suggested for example in the introduction to the Budé edition of
[190] M. Dufour, *Aristote Rhétorique*, 3 vols. (Paris, 1932-73).
The controversy is summarised by
[191] P.D. Brandes, 'The composition and preservation of Aristotle's Rhetoric', *Speech Monographs* 35 (1968), 482-91.

Another dispute has been over whether Aristotle's definitions in the *Rhetoric* are merely popular, or serious analyses on his part. This is well handled by Fortenbaugh in chapter 8. See also the reading below on the relation of rhetoric to dialectic.

On the connexion between Aristotle's *Rhetoric* and the 'exoteric' writings, see:

[192] W. Wieland, 'Aristoteles als Rhetoriker und die exoterischen Schriften', *Hermes* 86 (1958), pp. 323-46.

For the historical antecendents of Aristotle's *Rhetoric*, see
[193] W. Kroll, 'Rhetorik' in the Pauly-Wissowa *Realencyclopädie* Supp. 7. (1940), cols. 1039-1138.
[194] G. Kennedy, *The Art of Persuasion in Greece* (London, 1963).
[195] V. Buchheit, *Untersuchungen zur Theorie des Genos Epideiktikon von Gorgias bis Aristoteles* (Munich, 1960), which has a useful bibliography.
The texts are collected and annotated in
[196] L. Radermacher, *Artium Scriptores, Sitzungsberichte der Osterreichischen Akademie der Wissenschaft in Wien*, 227.3 (1951).
Aristotle's relation to Plato is discussed by Fortenbaugh in chapter 8. For Aristotle's influence on the subsequent history of the subject, see
[197] F. Solmsen, 'The Aristotelian tradition in ancient rhetoric', *American Journal of Philology* 62 (1941), pp. 35-50, 169-90.

Aristotle's conception of rhetoric is discussed by
[198] T.M. Crem, 'The definition of rhetoric according to Aristotle', *Laval Théologique et Philosophique* 12 (1956), pp. 233-50, and by
[199] K. Barwick, 'Die Gliederung der rhetorischen *technê* und die horazische Epistula ad Pisones', *Hermes* 57 (1922), pp. 16-18.
[200] W. Rhys Roberts, 'Notes on Aristotle's *Rhetoric*', *American Journal of Philology*, 45 (1924), pp. 351-361.
The role Aristotle gives within rhetoric to the appeal to emotions is treated by
[201] F. Solmsen, 'Aristotle and Cicero on the orator's playing upon the feelings', *Classical Philology* 33 (1938), pp. 390-404.
For the role of mnemonics in rhetoric, see
[202] F. Yates, *The Art of Memory* (London, 1966).

The relation of Aristotle's *Rhetoric* to his logic is studied by Solmsen [29], Grimaldi [188], and
[203] E.H. Madden, 'The enthymeme, crossroads of logic, rhetoric and metaphysics', *The Philosophical Review* 61 (1952), pp. 368-76.
[204] E.H. Madden, 'Aristotle's treatment of probability and signs', *Philosophy of Science* 24 (1957), pp. 167-72.
[205] S. Raphael, 'Rhetoric, dialectic and syllogistic argument: Aristotle's position in *Rhetoric* I-II', *Phronesis* 19 (1974), pp. 153-67.
On Aristotle's *Rhetoric* as the origin of propositional logic, see:
[206] G. Plebe, 'Retorica aristotelica e logica stoica', *Filosofia* 10 (1959), pp. 391-418.
The notion of a *topic*, and its role in the *Rhetoric*, is explained by
[207] W.A. De Pater, 'La fonction du lieu et de l'instrument dans les

Topiques', in [37], esp. pp. 168-75.

The relation of the *Rhetoric* to the *Topics* is discussed by

[208] J. Brunschwig, *Aristote Topiques*, Budé edition, Vol. 1 (Paris, 1967), pp. xcvi-ciii, and its relation to dialectic by Ryan [211], and by

[209] C. Thurot, *Etudes sur Aristote (Politique, Dialectique, Rhetorique)* (Paris, 1860), sect. 4, pp. 154-81.

For the relation of Aristotle's *Rhetoric* to his ethics, see, besides Fortenbaugh in chapter 8,

[210] L.W. Rosenfield, 'The doctrine of the mean in Aristotle's *Rhetoric*', *Theoria* 31 (1965), pp. 191-8.

[211] E.E. Ryan, 'Aristotle's *Rhetoric* and *Ethics* and the ethos of society', *Greek, Roman and Byzantine Studies* 13 (1972), pp. 291-308.

The definitions of pity and fear in *Rhet.* II are referred to in some of the writings listed under *Poetics*. The treatment of equity in *Rhet.* I 13 is seen as a forerunner of Roman distinctions by

[212] R. Maschke, *Die Willenslehre im griechischen Recht* (Berlin, 1926).

For a fuller bibliography on this, see our Vol. 2.

INDEX OF ARISTOTELIAN PASSAGES

1356a21-5	138
1357a12-13	138 n17
4-14	133 n4
4 1359b2-8	134
1359b5	134, 137
1359b8-12	149 n36
5 1360b7-8	134
1360b14-18	134
1360b14	136 and n12
6 1362a21	136 n12, 137, 140 n19
1362a27-9	138
1362a29-34	138
1362a34	140 n19
1362b3, 7, 10	140 n19
7 1363b7	136 n12
1363b13	136 n13
1364b17	136 n13
8 1365b21-5	138 n17
1366a20-1	137
1366a21	134
9 1366a25-7	138 n17
1366a32	134
1366b9	59 n47
1366b24	134, 137
10 1368b6	136 n12
1369b31-2	134
1369b31	134, 137
11 1369b34-5	135 n9
1370a4-5	135 n9
1370a28	123
II	134 n6, 136, 139 and n17
1 1377b30-1378a5	138
1378a15-17	138 n17
1378a19-24	141
1378a19-22	141
1378a19-20	138
1378a20	47 n13
1378a22	147 n33
1378a23-6	138
1378a23-4	153 n48
1378a24-6	138 n17
2-11	37 n8, 47 n12
2 1378a30-b1	142
1378a30-2	142
1378a30-1	145
1378a30	37 n8, 136, 139 n18, 140 n21

1378a31	144, 146 n32
1378a32-3	140 n21
1378b9	39
1379b11-12	142
1379b33-4	145
3 1380a8	136
1380b16-18	142, 145
1380b17-18	146 n32
4 1380b35	58
1380b36	136
1382a8	58
5 1382a21-2	142, 146
1382a21	136, 146 n32
1382a27-30	146
1382b29-32, 33	142
1383a6-7	148
1383b6-7	145
6 1383b11-1385a15	153 n48
1383b12	136
1383b13	136
7 1385a16	58 n45
1385a17	136
8 1386b1	163
9 1386b18, 19	144 n29
1386b20-4	144 n29
1386b32-1387a3	144 n29
1386b33-1387a1	144 n29
10 1387b22-3	144 n29
1387b23	144 n29
1388a24-7	144 n29
1388a25	144 n29
13 1389b32	37

Poetica

1 1447a16	167
1447b9-20	167
1447b9	167
1447b15	167
1447b16-20	167
2 1448a1-5	169
1448a1	168
3 1448a27-8	168
4 1448b25	164
1448b34-9	161
1449a2	161
6 1449b23	161
1449b24-8	154
1449b27, 28	171

GENERAL INDEX

ability (*dunamis*), A's analysis of, 56-7; *see* capacity, faculty, power
Academy, its discussion of psychology, 103, Ch.8 *passim*
Ackrill, J.L., 63, 132 n64
action (*praxis*), and desire, 56-61, 64; and *phantasia*, 123 and n51; subject of literature, Ch.10 *passim*
activity, actualisation (*energeia*, *entelecheia*), of perception, 27-8, 37, 39, 42, 45-6; of object of sense, 52; of imagination, 105 n11, 111, 113, 130 n61; of intellect, 29-31, 39-40, Ch.6 *passim*; and definition of soul, 27, 37, 43, Ch.4 *passim*
affection (*pathēma*, *pathos*), 35-6, 38, 46, 47-8, 105 n11, 117, 154, 162-5
aisthanesthai (perceive), 23-4, 28 n82, 46-7
aisthēma (percept), 122 and n49
aisthēsis (perception, sensation), 3, 23-5, 38 n10, 53, 118 nn40, 41
aisthētērion (sense organ), 14
aisthētikē (sensory), *mesotēs* 24 n66; *phantasia*, 118 n41; *psuchē* 20, 26
aisthētikon (faculty of sensation or perception), 6, 8 n23, 14, 20, 27 n79
aisthēton (object of perception), 8, 9 n24
akrasia (weakness of will), 56-7, 110
Alcmaeon, 19 n54
alētheuein (take truly), 130, 131 n62
Alexander of Aphrodisias, 12 n32, 26 n74, 29 n86, 100; *see* pseudo-Alexander
Allan, D.J., 108 n18, 127 n57
alloiōsis, *alloiousthai* (alteration, alter), 37-8
alteration, in perception, 37-8, 46, 48-9, 54-5; *see* affection, process
Analytics, terminology and method, 140; the theory of definition in *A.Pst.*, 78, 145-6
anankē (necessity), 140 nn19, 21
Anaxagoras, 44 n6, 53 n31

anger, A's analysis of, 36-7, 47, 54-5, 56, 60, 62, 63, Ch.8 *passim*; subject of, 43 n2, 50
animals, souls of, 2, 3-5, 66, 73-4; consciousness of, 25-6, 30; internal sense of, 15; physiological systems of, 20-2; modes of perception, 77-8; movement, 58, 61-2, 108-10; imagination, 109 n20, 115 and n35, 118 n41, 126 and n55
Apology, on death, 23 n65; on emotion in oratory, 149
aporia, A's technique of, 16 n46, 18 n51; about perception and awareness, 9-13, 24-5 (cf. 28-30); about self-thinking, 29
appear, *see phainesthai*
apsuchos (soulless, lifeless), 3, 33
Aquinas, St. Thomas, 9 n24
archē (principle, source), of sensation, 14, 21, 26, 35; *see* central faculty/organ of sensation
Armstrong, D.M., 59 n49, 60
Arnim, H. von, 146 n33, 150 n39, 153 n48
Aubenque, P., 134 n5, 136 n11, 139 n18
Austin, J.L., 105, 117
autos (self), 94
awareness, 4-5, 10-13, 18, 22-31, 46 n10, 47-50, 56, 62 n57, 64; *see* consciousness, reflexive
axe, 65-7, 71-2

Baldwin, C.S., 133 n4
Balme, D.M., 102 n4
Barnes, J., 42, 45-7, 49 n22, 50, 52, 56 n39, 59 n49, 132 n64
Beare, J.I., 7 n22, 9 n24, 12 n32, 17 n48, 29 n48, 49 n22, 103 n2, 104 n5, 116 n37
Bedford, E., 142 n24
Bekker, I., 28 n82
belief (*doxa*), in Plato's *Republic*, 78; and